Notes on Bergson and Descartes

VERITAS
Series Introduction

"... the truth will set you free" (John 8:32)

In much contemporary discourse, Pilate's question has been taken to mark the absolute boundary of human thought. Beyond this boundary, it is often suggested, is an intellectual hinterland into which we must not venture. This terrain is an agnosticism of thought: because truth cannot be possessed, it must not be spoken. Thus, it is argued that the defenders of "truth" in our day are often traffickers in ideology, merchants of counterfeits, or anti-liberal. They are, because it is somewhat taken for granted that Nietzsche's word is final: truth is the domain of tyranny.

Is this indeed the case, or might another vision of truth offer itself? The ancient Greeks named the love of wisdom as *philia*, or friendship. The one who would become wise, they argued, would be a "friend of truth." For both philosophy and theology might be conceived as schools in the friendship of truth, as a kind of relation. For like friendship, truth is as much discovered as it is made. If truth is then so elusive, if its domain is *terra incognita*, perhaps this is because it arrives to us—unannounced—as gift, as a person, and not some thing.

The aim of the Veritas book series is to publish incisive and original current scholarly work that inhabits "the between" and "the beyond" of theology and philosophy. These volumes will all share a common aspiration to transcend the institutional divorce in which these two disciplines often find themselves, and to engage questions of pressing concern to both philosophers and theologians in such a way as to reinvigorate both disciplines with a kind of interdisciplinary desire, often so absent in contemporary academe. In a word, these volumes represent collective efforts in the befriending of truth, doing so beyond the simulacra of pretend tolerance, the violent, yet insipid reasoning of liberalism that asks with Pilate, "What is truth?"—expecting a consensus of non-commitment; one that encourages the commodification of the mind, now sedated by the civil service of career, ministered by the frightened patrons of position.

The series will therefore consist of two "wings": (1) original monographs; and (2) essay collections on a range of topics in theology and philosophy. The latter will principally be the products of the annual conferences of the Centre of Theology and Philosophy (www.theologyphilosophycentre.co.uk).

Conor Cunningham and Eric Austin Lee, *Series editors*

Not available from Cascade

Deane-Peter Baker	*Tayloring Reformed Epistemology: The Challenge to Christian Belief.* Volume 1
P. Candler & C. Cunningham (eds.)	*Belief and Metaphysics.* Volume 2
Marcus Pound	*Theology, Psychoanalysis, and Trauma.* Volume 4
Espen Dahl	*Phenomenology and the Holy.* Volume 5
C. Cunningham et al. (eds.)	*Grandeur of Reason: Religion, Tradition, and Universalism.* Volume 6
A. Pabst & A. Paddison (eds.)	*The Pope and Jesus of Nazareth: Christ, Scripture, and the Church.* Volume 7
J. P. Moreland	*Recalcitrant Imago Dei: Human Persons and the Failure of Naturalism.* Volume 8

Cascade

[Nathan Kerr	*Christ, History, and Apocalyptic: The Politics of Christian Mission.* Volume 3]¹
Anthony D. Baker	*Diagonal Advance: Perfection in Christian Theology.* Volume 9
D. C. Schindler	*The Perfection of Freedom: Schiller, Schelling, and Hegel between the Ancients and the Moderns.* Volume 10
Rustin Brian	*Covering Up Luther: How Barth's Christology Challenged the* Deus Absconditus *that Haunts Modernity.* Volume 11
Timothy Stanley	*Protestant Metaphysics After Karl Barth and Martin Heidegger.* Volume 12
Christopher Ben Simpson	*The Truth Is the Way: Kierkegaard's* Theologia Viatorum. Volume 13
Richard H. Bell	*Wagner's Parsifal: An Appreciation in the Light of His Theological Journey.* Volume 14
Antonio Lopez	*Gift and the Unity of Being.* Volume 15
Toyohiko Kagawa	*Cosmic Purpose.* Translated and introduced by Thomas John Hastings. Volume 16
Nigel Zimmerman	*Facing the Other: John Paul II, Levinas, and the Body.* Volume 17
Conor Sweeney	*Sacramental Presence after Heidegger: Onto-theology, Sacraments, and the Mother's Smile.* Volume 18
John Behr et al. (eds.)	*The Role of Death in Life: A Multidisciplinary Examination of the Relation between Life and Death.* Volume 19
Eric Austin Lee et al. (eds.)	*The Resounding Soul: Reflection on the Metaphysics and Vivacity of the Human Person.* Volume 20

1. Note: Nathan Kerr, *Christ, History, and Apocalyptic*, although volume 3 of the original SCM Veritas series, is available from Cascade as part of the Theopolitical Visions series.

Orion Edgar	*Things Seen and Unseen: The Logic of Incarnation in Merleau-Ponty's Metaphysics of Flesh.* Volume 21
Duncan B. Reyburn	*Seeing Things as They Are: G. K. Chesterton and the Drama of Meaning.* Volume 22
Lyndon Shakespeare	*Being the Body of Christ in the Age of Management.* Volume 23
Michael V. Di Fuccia	*Owen Barfield: Philosophy, Poetry, and Theology.* Volume 24
John McNerney	*Wealth of Persons: Economics with a Human Face.* Volume 25
Norm Klassen	*The Fellowship of the Beatific Vision: Chaucer on Overcoming Tyranny and Becoming Ourselves.* Volume 26
Donald Wallenfang	*Human and Divine Being: A Study of the Theological Anthropology of Edith Stein.* Volume 27
Sotiris Mitralexis	*Ever-Moving Repose: A Contemporary Reading of Maximus the Confessor's Theory of Time.* Volume 24
Sotiris Mitralexis et al. (eds.)	*Maximus the Confessor as a European Philosopher.* Volume 28
Kevin Corrigan	*Love, Friendship, Beauty, and the Good: Plato, Aristotle, and the Later Tradition.* Volume 29
Andrew Brower Latz	*The Social Philosophy of Gillian Rose.* Volume 30
D. C. Schindler	*Love and the Postmodern Predicament: Rediscovering the Real in Beauty, Goodness, and Truth.* Volume 31
Stephen Kampowski	*Embracing Our Finitude: Exercises in a Christian Anthropology between Dependence and Gratitude.* Volume 32
William Desmond	*The Gift of Beauty and the Passion of Being: On the Threshold between the Aesthetic and the Religious.* Volume 33
Charles Péguy	*Notes on Bergson and Descartes.* Volume 34
David Alcalde	*Cosmology without God: The Problematic Theology Inherent in Modern Cosmology.* Volume 35

NOTES ON
BERGSON & DESCARTES

Philosophy, Christianity,
and Modernity in Contestation

Charles Péguy

Translation, Introduction, and Notes by
Bruce K. Ward

Foreword by
John Milbank

CASCADE *Books* • Eugene, Oregon

NOTES ON BERGSON AND DESCARTES
Philosophy, Christianity, and Modernity in Contestation

Veritas 34

Copyright © 2019 Editions GALLIMARD, Paris, 1935. All rights reserved. Except for brief quotations in critical publications or reviews, no part of this book may be reproduced in any manner without prior written permission from the publisher. Write: Permissions, Wipf and Stock Publishers, 199 W. 8th Ave., Suite 3, Eugene, OR 97401.

Cascade Books
An Imprint of Wipf and Stock Publishers
199 W. 8th Ave., Suite 3
Eugene, OR 97401

www.wipfandstock.com

PAPERBACK ISBN: 978-1-5326-5073-4
HARDCOVER ISBN: 978-1-5326-5074-1
EBOOK ISBN: 978-1-5326-5075-8

Cataloguing-in-Publication data:

Names: Péguy, Charles, 1873–1914, author. | Ward, Bruce K., translator. | Milbank, John, foreword writer.

Title: Notes on Bergson and Descartes : philosophy, Christianity, and modernity in contestation / Charles Péguy, with a foreword by John Milbank.

Description: Eugene, OR: Cascade Books, 2019 | Series: Veritas 34 | Includes bibliographical references.

Identifiers: ISBN 978-1-5326-5073-4 (paperback) | ISBN 978-1-5326-5074-1 (hardcover) | ISBN 978-1-5326-5075-8 (ebook)

Subjects: LCSH: Bergson, Henri, 1859–1941 | Descartes, René, 1596–1650 | History—Philosophy | Time—Philosophy

Classification: B2430.B43 P42 2019 (print) | B2430.B43 (ebook)

Manufactured in the U.S.A.   AUGUST 21, 2019

Originally published in French as *Note sur M. Bergson et la philosophie bergsonienne; Note conjointe sur M. Descartes et la philosophie cartésienne.* Paris: Éditions Gallimard, 1935. Translated with permission.

To Ian and Graeme Ward

Contents

Foreword by John Milbank ix

Acknowledgments xxxv

1 Introduction 1

2 Note on Bergson and the Bergsonian Philosophy 26

3 Conjoined Note on Descartes and the Cartesian Philosophy 56

Appendix: "The Secret of the Man of Forty" 235
—Annette Aronowicz

Bibliography 259

Index of Names 263

Foreword:
Charles Péguy and the Betrayal of Time

Péguy and Bergson

IN THIS VOLUME, BRUCE Ward has brought to an English-speaking public for the first time Charles Péguy's two characteristically undulating and intricate final essays which are concerned with the philosophy of Henri Bergson, but which also serve to summarize the French poet's entire thoughts about philosophy, Christianity, literature, history, and politics. His faithful translations ably convey the unique tenor of Péguy's incantatory style, in which endless reiteration is juxtaposed with frequent apparent digression, and which is inseparable from the novel content that he wished to convey.

At the core of this content is the view that Bergsonian philosophy represents a revolutionary moment in the history of French and so of Western culture—since for Péguy the two virtually coincided, in both directions. As such, it is for him on a par with the thinking of Plato, who proposed the eternity of truth, and of Descartes, who intended to dispose with human disorder. Bergson now proposes, according to Péguy, to put our thinking back in touch with finite reality, which is the living out of time. If we follow him in this respect, then we can render our participation in eternal truth more genuine and immediate, and we can achieve an *ordre* that is less extrinsic than Cartesian or Racinian *ordonnance*, but is instead intrinsically at one with the experienced order of life itself.[1]

Péguy also calls attention to those features of Cartesian thought that are more Augustinian and rendered still more so by the tradition of French spiritualism (after François Fénelon and Pierre Maine de Biran)

---

1. See Péguy, "Victor-Marie, comte Hugo," especially 220–308.

in which Bergson stood: beginning reflection with the experience of God, affirming creation as continuous; seeking for an intuitive rather than rule-governed logical sequence; advertence to empirical evidence beyond the reach of reasoning; firm commitment to the rational project one has set for oneself. But he sees all these features as more consistently adhered to by Bergson.

The latter, like Victor Hugo, for Péguy in effect offers a specifically French romanticism that remains also a classicism.[2] An approach and a style for which clarity is not the enemy of depth, and radiant insight does not end problematic perplexity, but rather opens it more manifestly to view. And a philosophy that above all, in the Cartesian tradition, adheres to the reality at once of matter and yet also of spirit. English reductive empiricist associationism and German idealism are thereby equally refused. Likewise English utilitarianism and Germanic Kantian formalism. Likewise again, both German idealist acosmism and Germanic vitalist pantheism. A duality of spirit and matter is instead insisted upon and yet also, after Bergson, qualified, since finite spirit is now seen as emerging within time and the material processes of motion.

Péguy invokes at the heart of these texts the Bergsonian concept of duration (*durée*). As he insists, Bergson was not advocating an irrationalism, but was rationally pointing out (in the ultimate wake of David Hume via the mediation of Biran) that our most fundamental mental processes are experiences of felt intuition whereby non-quantitative multiplicities merge, intertwine, and mutually develop within us.[3] These processes at

---

2. Péguy appears explicitly to reject romanticism, but by this he means an unhealthy obsession with the melancholic, the diseased, the sadistic, and the death-haunted—all of which he associated (of course, to a large degree unfairly and inaccurately) with specifically German romanticism. But the complexity in this categorisation is revealed when it turns out that he regards the more *classicist* Racine as nonetheless more proto-romantic, on account of his albeit tidily-presented dark obsessions, which render human beings more arbitrarily and tragically fated by the Jansenist God than by the gods of the Greeks, than the much more lingeringly Baroque and "Romanesque" (as the French say) Corneille (see further below). In terms of Péguy's own commitment to such a Romanesque, with its biases to the tragicomic and an almost fairy-tale ethical idealism, one can validly speak of an alternative, for him "French" romanticism, after the acknowledged example of Hugo. Yet ironically, in view of Péguy's supreme cultural indifference to anything modern outside of France, so much of this seems highly akin to central currents in English literary tradition in terms of crucial concerns with innocence, childhood, romance, creative imagination, magical reconciliations, and so forth.

3. See Bergson, *Time and Free Will*, *Matter and Memory*, and *An Introduction to Metaphysics*.

once compose our subjectivity and yet from the outset (in contrast to the assumptions of phenomenology) lead us outside it, because they overflow any attempted determinate unification of awareness and are at one with the unfolding process of natural motion and of time within us. For this reason, our access to the external world is not simply by observation and representation, but through an immediate indwelling of its processes, which permits a sympathetic resonance with all other finite beings. Motion is not primarily mechanical, since (as again Hume pointed out) the notion of one body having an efficient influence on another, entirely separate and discrete, body is not rationally comprehensible and indeed paradoxically involves an *unexplained* action at a distance. It is instead a process of vital, creative, and spontaneous development between dynamic realities that are as much conjoined as divided.

This continuous intermingling composes the sequence of time. In its primary reality it is at once irreversible, because unilaterally developmental, and yet also inseparable, in all finite beings, from trace-memories of the past and anticipatory projections of the future, whether unconscious or conscious. This is because, as Péguy underlines, past, present, and future are not just relatively different points according to position on a single scale, as they would appear to be in a spatial representation, but are rather inherently different in their ontological quality. Thus, the past as past is not a past present moment, as if that moment were still somehow lingering in a ghostly fashion, but is rather absolutely past as spiritual memory (of which, for Bergson, neural traces are only the vehicle) even though there is no present moment at all without this memory trace and its continuously habitual influence. Similarly, the future is not just a future anterior (though it is crucially also that), a present moment to come or one that will eventually "have been over," but is also the real horizon of eschatological promise, of hope, and of the always incomplete. It is just this note of expectation that ensures that the present moment is not merely one of habitual memory, both unconscious and conscious, but also something inherently unfinished and still existentially lived with "suppleness," rather than being the *tout fait*, the always already over and incarcerated.

For Bergson, in the long-term wake of Augustine, space is secondary to time. Space consists of all the more hardened, rigidified, habituated deposits of motion and temporal flow, which give rise to both quantity and the sheer exteriority of things "outside us." This by no means, however, confines us within some sort of solipsism and mere secondariness of empathy, because Bergson also considered that material things themselves consist in a dynamic series of pulsating and vibrating images, and that knowledge arises when these images become representatively conscious within us in a necessarily partial fashion. He thereby articulated a version of a theory of knowledge by identity that is not without some kinship to the scholastic epistemology of *species*. But at the same time, spatial stiffening in Bergson does hold a certain not just subordinate but also defective ontological status, which eventually encourages him to contrast the fixity of nature and of more "natural" human societies with the dynamism and absolutely free creativity of spirit.

After Bergson, who affirmed the accuracy of the poet's construal of his thought, Péguy emphasizes above all the importance of remaining in the present moment. Instead of doing so, we constantly treat the present as if it were already the past—as if it was entirely determined, entirely foreclosed, entirely predictable and unoriginal.

In this way, Péguy sustains the Bergsonian link between presence and freedom. Instead of thinking of causality and liberty as problematic opposites, the French philosopher articulated a mode of vitalism whereby a kind of free spontaneity goes all the way down to the depth of material nature. In consequence, the elaboration through habit of complex dynamic emotional processes within our minds is always composing a specific kind of individuated and characterized liberty. It follows that, for both the philosopher and the poet, to be genuinely free is to be creative, to do something entirely new. Yet this notion is the very opposite of supposing freedom to be something unprecedented: to the contrary, just because the creative is a matter of unique style, it is also a matter of long gestation and formation. In this way, Bergson refuses the picture whereby human freedom is confronted by a series of external pressures or external options. Instead, it only arises as an ever more consciously shaped process of unique habituation which then allows us to act with "originality" in a specific arising circumstance.

It is this notion of freedom as creativity that Péguy above all wishes to uphold: human beings actively and not just passively participate in divine creation in a "literal" sense.[4] The open-endedness of the future properly acts as a salve against the ever-present danger of the hardening of habit into identical repetition. The genius is the person most able to guard against this danger and yet no one is really free of it. Thus, the

---

4. Péguy, "Dialogue de l'histoire et de l'âme charnelle," especially 629.

creativity of the child always exceeds even that of the genius and the earliest ages of humankind remain the most creative ones. In any developed culture, the originality of the child will manifest itself often as disobedience, but beyond even the creativity of revolt lies the creativity of foundation—of the more radically phylogenic infancy that once gave rise to cities, though also that which, in excess of the mere negativity of revolution, newly gave rise to the French Republic in modern times.[5]

Modernity is for Péguy above all the process of suppression of free, creative presence. It denies the present in the name of both the past and the future—although the past and present falsely thought of as impossible pure presences left behind and still to come. Thus, it seeks immediately to stockpile the present as the past, in order all the better to plan and calculate the future, which, by definition on this model of endless postponement, is never really going to arrive. For previous societies, to live in the present was to live for the day with no thought for the morrow (as the Gospels teach) and to live in hope under heaven of eternal life. Modernity, by contrast, is a process of systematic continual sacrifice to an absolute utopian future that can never come to pass, for ontological rather than political reasons.

In this fashion, we can newly see that the suppression of antique contemplation is *also* the suppression of real labor, of real action, and so of a *real* modernity, if one can put it that way. However, Péguy's grasp of the implications of Bergsonian duration is not one-sided. He does not merely see that it is a diagnosis of our suppression of the present. He also sees that it a diagnosis of our betrayal of other dimensions of time. Thus, to the occlusion of presence we can also add the suppression of irreversibility and the suppression of positive habit as non-identical repetition.

In the second case of the suppression of irreversibility, Péguy says that modern people characteristically think that they can always begin all over again and start from an absolute beginning.[6] But to the contrary, if our freedom is only developed memory and habit, this is impossible. We are always pre-situated and circumscribed by our cultural histories, by our personal biographies, and also by the process of ageing, which tends to rigidify our habits and so to limit the range of our real possibilities, as illustrated by the disillusioning eventual fates of none other than Susannah, Figaro, and even Cherubino, "those professionals of youth" (as

5. Ibid., 629–32.
6. Ibid., 718–20.

Péguy puts it), in the final play of Beaumarchais' *Figaro* trilogy, *La Mère Coupable*.[7]

We have realistically to act in the light of all this, yet modernity pretends otherwise. This, one could interpolate, is the reverse face of that utilitarian calculation, which squeezes out the present in favor of the planning of the future by an accumulated past. For modern people also fantasize that they can, especially as individuals, "freely" remove themselves from this process altogether—sometimes, indeed, through mere fantasy. In this way they are the dualistic victims of the false ontological model of liberty as mere extrinsic response to "pressure" and to "option" which Bergson so well diagnosed and denounced.

In the third case of suppression of positive habit, we encounter one of the most central and interesting tensions in Péguy's outlook.[8] We have already seen that he tends to insist on the unique opening creative power of the first in a series—on founders of new cities, including Christ, on the antique, on childhood, on the initial rather than the later works created by genius. One could legitimately say that this is rather like the generative power of absolute Unity in Neoplatonism, or the fontal and inexhaustible power of God the Father, especially in Eastern Christian Trinitarian theology.

Yet at the same time, Péguy equally insists that there is no pure isolated original moment prior to repetition. Thus for him, a significant historical event becomes so retrospectively, by ritual repetition, as with Bastille Day—of which Péguy famously said that the first such commemoration was the storming of the Bastille itself.[9] This is not a denial of real historicity, but, after Bergson, a more accurate understanding of that in which historicity truly consists. For if a past event is not really there any more, then its absolutely *real* present persistence is in memory, which is always selective and creative. One can protest here about memory's distortive capacity and that is certainly true, but one must not forget that the event as once lived was never of itself *tout fait*; its very event character was not as yet fully decided. In this perspective the question of historical accuracy does not evaporate, but it is shown that a "true depiction of a past event" is inseparable from the question of loyalty to that event, and of commitment or otherwise to its tonality and valency. It is just for this

---

7. Ibid., 594–618; Péguy, "Clio," especially 1060–68, 1074–79.
8. See Milbank, "There's always one day which isn't the same as the day before."
9. Péguy, "Clio," 1083.

reason that Péguy, in Pascalian fashion, sees the model of New Testament fulfillment of prophecy (a surprisingly consummate maximum loyalty to its tonality) as more objectively characteristic of real historical process than the usual models of causal determinism by which historians are lured and which ignore the saturated, creatively arising and so uncaused dimension of any truly significant—and so "really historical"—event.

Within this perspective, Péguy considers that Christ, while being, as the divine person who unites divine with human nature, all-inspiring, was also, as a human individual, simply the first person in the series of saints, uniquely characterized like every human individual and not as such "the best" at everything—the best writer or artist or cook, or athlete or politician, for example. In this sense then, even the divine humanity is more clarified and revealed through later non-identical repetitions of sainthood, under the guidance of the Holy Spirit within the church. One might also say that this recognition of the need for "a supplement at the origin" (to use Derridean terminology) corresponds to the view of Trinitarian doctrine that the Father is entirely and "reversely" constituted as origin by his generation of the Son.

Nevertheless, what is fascinating in terms of later debates is that Péguy neither opts purely for the "romanticism" and "modernism" of the pure expressive origin, nor for the "postmodernism" of the paradoxical need for repetition at the outset. Rather, he seems to hold both in tension and this is symbolized (again with a Derridean echo) by the balance he sustains between orality and writing. On the one hand, he consistently associated the primacy of the present moment with the superiority of the voice, above all with French oral Catholic peasant culture, whereas both Judaism and Protestantism are said to be religions of the book and so to risk the hardening of habit. On the other hand, he also insisted that the hero and saint would be without effect in memory and tradition save for the role of the recorder: of the Gospel writers, of the playwright celebrating the deeds of the martyr, and of the more accidental record that is the legal report of the trial of Joan of Arc.

It is for this reason that his stylistic response to Bergson exceeds that of the modernists: he is not interested, as with Marcel Proust or Virginia Woolf, in merely reporting the supposed "givens" of subjective consciousness and memory (which is in effect to reduce Bergsonianism to phenomenology), nor in expressing pure symbolic replicas of duration that are then paradoxically timeless, as in the case of sheerly abstract art. Instead, he seeks actively to *perform* duration, in such a way that his additions to memory through commemoration, which inevitably recast it, nonetheless, just for that reason, remain engaged in a realist and "re-presentational" (and not just postmodern "playful") fashion with a past that is shared and historical, as well as private and autobiographical.

This tension involved in Péguy's style and philosophy between pure origin and necessary addition at the outset is nonetheless in a way unresolved and thereby invites a gloss. One can argue that it is coherent, because merely to insist on "writing," on an "original repetition," on emanation as exhausting the One, or on the Son as the entire expression of the Father, is to invite the riposte that thereby the supplement, or the endless sequence of supplementations (which may, as for postmodernism, be continuously subversive) have after all become themselves the absolutely fixed origin. Thus, to sustain the "postmodern" point against absolute foundations, one must after all insist on a certain mysterious foundational excess: after all upon "orality," on an origin before repetition, on the transcendality of "the One," rather than it being just the first in a numerical series. And even on the fontal transcendence of the Father, which one can reconcile with his being exhaustively, even as origin, the generation of the Son, through the thesis that the Holy Spirit as the substantively relational "interpretation" of the Son is the only way in which this mysterious original excess can be at once manifested and also "reversely" (by a doubling of reversal) constituted. If childhood is for Péguy primary, then so is that *vieillissement* (aging) that begins already, he says, at age thirty, and yet is able to recover, universalize, and infinitize the innocence that in a sense childhood merely intimates. Obviously this is for him the supreme significance of the age at which Christ undertook his ministry after his reception of the Spirit.[10]

In more finite and participated terms, this "spirituality" is manifested in Péguy's own reading and writing practices, in the way in which he constantly moves forward and backwards in a spiraling motion, as Bruce Ward says in his Introduction. His stylistic use of micro-repetition witnesses to the need constantly to be in the re-affirming present, where the original inspiration can never be regarded as safely established once and for all, but must be endlessly re-established against the lure of complacent decay through re-insistence and slight variation according to changing context. This is the "oral" and "present" component. At the same time, repetition witnesses to the reality that the present is always a

---

10. Péguy, "Dialogue de l'histoire et de l'âme charnelle," *passim*.

ritual, non-identical repetition of past, habitual significance, only established through continuity. This is the "written" and "past" component. But beyond either, Péguy's stylistic conjoining of both origin and issuing series in terms of both future hope and specific reinterpretation as active political engagement in the present moment and era provides the third and "future" component of spiritual "finality."[11]

Péguy's Modification of Bergson

Is it the case that in all these ways Péguy merely puts a more specifically Catholic gloss upon Bergson? That is surely not so, because one can also validly detect philosophical modifications in his unique recension. Above all, Péguy inserts on his own account the thematics of grace and of the event.

For Bergson, as we have seen, the invoking of memory in duration amounts to a positive aspect to the working of habit, which alone permits freedom to arise. Nor does Bergson think of spatial habituations, which are images (as already mentioned) as being in a merely negative relationship to temporal process. The "stoppages" are also necessary links and shapings of dynamic entities, which, Bergson later insisted in conversation with the Thomist A. D. Sertillanges, remain themselves "substances."[12] Yet at the same time, he does regard spatial fixity as possessing a necessarily negative and retarding aspect. This is especially apparent in *Creative Evolution*, about which Péguy has more reserves, as Ward stresses. In that text, nature gives rise to two opposite impulses: one to an ordered stasis which, Bergson will much later say, humanly manifests itself in fixed, local, and tribal cultures, moralities, and religions and the other to spirit, which is free and creative and which humanly manifests itself in open and universal civilizations.[13]

It is important to see that precisely because of this dualism Bergson is resistant to German vitalisms and pantheisms. It is not, he says, that evolution creates, but that it is the site of a self-grounded creative process.[14] This latter seems to be impelled towards transcendence and indeed, it would seem, is impelled *by* transcendence. All the same, this spiritual

---

11. I am making an implicit allusion to Peircean semiotics here.
12. Sertillanges, *Avec Henri Bergson*.
13. Bergson, *The Two Sources of Morality and Religion*.
14. Sertillanges, *Avec Henri Bergson*.

urging is also held back by the habituating drag within nature. Indeed, it is because Bergson does not wish to ascribe the spiritualizing *élan vital* to matter that he refuses any notion of finalism or teleology, which might suggest that the vital impulse was merely preordained within matter from the outset. Yet this refusal leaves the creativity of spirit after all subservient to unmotivated choice and preference, however much this may be positively habituated. In consequence, the relationship of "transcending" spiritual impulses to actual transcendence is in Bergson wholly unclear.

It is here that Péguy offers most qualification. For him, if presence involves freedom, then our freedom is in turn wholly bound up with the answering freedom of God. To be free from the constraints of matter, of mere habitude and identical repetition, is to be lured by desire for God, is to meet with a specific "descending" and surprising new proposal which one actively adopts at every turn. Thus, for Péguy, there is no horizontal natural freedom without vertical supernatural grace, such that liberality of motive and grace of style always coincide, for example with respect to our handling of money.[15] His gloss upon Bergson at this point effectively renders the Bergsonian philosophy coincident with that of the other contemporary heir of French spiritualism, Maurice Blondel.[16] For Péguy as for Blondel, the inherent unfinishedness of the human action and its excess over any rational grasp implies precisely a constitutively existential search for something beyond given nature in order to complete it— the supernatural as "over natural," not as "extra natural," as he puts it.[17]

And more than the philosopher of Aix, the poet of Orléans is clear that in fact this completion is arriving at us, and in fusion with our achieved freedom, all the time. Within this perspective, as in that of Bergson's teacher Félix Ravaisson (for whom the "always already" of natural habit could only be initiated and sustained by grace),[18] grace has become fully ontologized, fully integrated into physics and philosophy.

This invocation of grace also allows Péguy to overcome Bergson's concerns about embracing a merely immanentist vitalism. For it permits one to conceive a teleology that is eschatologized: for which the final end is not unambiguously pre-given at the outset, such that it might be latent

---

15. Péguy, "Victor-Marie, comte Hugo," 282. Any suggestion that such aestheticizing of grace is alien to its original concept or to the Greek New Testament use of it is, of course, false.

16. See Milbank, *Theology and Social Theory*, 210–20.

17. Péguy, "Victor-Marie, comte Hugo," 224.

18. See Milbank, "The Mystery of Reason."

and pre-determined, but rather is superadded from above and is continuously superadded as gift. In this way, the vertical structure of fulfillment is in keeping with the horizontal: as with the fulfillment of prophecy, so with the arrival of grace, a habitual tenor is sustained, but also surprisingly transcended.

Péguy also overcomes the slightly Manichaean dualism that lurks within Bergson and that is consequent upon his imperfect escape from immanence—since immanentist philosophies always have to compensate for the loss of the pole of transcendence by introducing some absolute factor within the immanent order itself, which dualistically subordinates everything else within that order. Thus in Bergson's case the danger is that the spatial is somehow less real than the temporal—which is more extreme than the mere ontological secondariness of the spatial, in keeping with Augustine. For the poet, by contrast, there is nothing inevitable about spatialized degeneration into fixed habit: this is entirely the contingent consequence of the fall, and in his long poem *Ève*, a protracted series of rapturous quatrains captures the paradisal reality of a pre-fallen rural France. Even in a postlapsarian world, nothing lies outside the order of redemptive restoration. Thus, Péguy notably insists that creation is not just transcendental "background," as one might say that duration is for Bergson: it is rather each and everything, just because it is the all of everything.[19] No spatial instance therefore falls outside the providential sway.

For Bergson, process seems to be primary over instance, even if it generates an anarchic quantity of creative instants. But it is difficult for him to conceive of a privileged instant and so of an originating event, even though such a notion would seem to be required if time is primary and time necessarily involves contingent beginnings—even for processes only constituted, as Ravaisson taught, by habit, rather than being obedient to prior laws. It is also the notion of an event, or of a series of non-identically repeated events, that permits a certain stronger integration of time and space. It additionally allows one to think of a particular tradition or institution, such as that of the church, as having a universal scope and significance. In his final conversation with Sertillanges on the eve of World War II and his own death, Bergson announced that he was going to concede this significance of the church and the location of Christian mystics only within its tradition, yet this would seem to involve a major adjustment in his entire philosophy.

19. Péguy, "Dialogue de l'histoire et de l'âme charnelle," especially 640–42.

But Péguy, on the eve of World War I and his earlier violent death, had already made this adjustment (which has proved very significant for the recent philosophy of Alain Badiou and his followers). In consequence, time as creativity and creation itself as the process of continuous participation in radical divine origination becomes more real in the philosophy of the poet than in the poetry of the philosopher. For it is no longer the case that all creative originations are "on a level" with relation to process. In Bergsonian terms, this tends to result either in an antiliberal politics of continuous violent disruption (as with Georges Sorel or indeed also with Gilles Deleuze) or in an overly liberal one of pure equal formal rights to creative freedom (as with the later Bergson himself).[20] By contrast, Péguy is able more realistically to insist that even radical politics is situated within specific traditions and that French revolutionary rights cannot be prized apart from French citizenship and all the things which that specifically entails.[21] No longer then, does one have to choose between resignation to material habit on the one hand, or a lone search for creative freedom on the other; instead one realizes that one's own unique expressiveness is always linked to the elaboration of a situated cultural legacy.

And one can suppose that something like this pertains within the natural world also. Thus Péguy suggests that the physics of "moistening" (which applies, he says, at the molecular level) reveals, beyond hydrostatics, a kind of process more fundamental than mechanism. Water bubbles can only receive external watery influence when they burst and are open to it. Therefore, it is not just a matter of continuous process and new creative irruption. There is also an eventful interplay between necessary closure and receptive openness. Péguy suggests that, even for Descartes, our knowledge of the world also fits into this pattern. Logic reaches out into reality, but this must "come forth from its citadel" as experience, like a beleaguered party that is being rescued by a relieving army, if reality is to be really encountered by thought at all. To know something therefore is not a matter of ineluctable processes, either rational or material, nor of their obscure correlation (to invoke a recent philosophical concern) but rather of an eventful interchange in which something higher, namely reason, mysteriously supervenes upon something lower, namely matter,

---

20. See Kennedy, "Bergson's Philosophy and French Political Doctrines."
21. Péguy, "L'Argent suite," 987–89.

only so long as this lower reality mysteriously opens itself out toward it or "elicits" it, to deploy an older scholastic language.

In the case of both physical and cognitive occurrences, this is possible precisely because the reality of time as always "presence" is inherently the reality of something unfinished, open to something yet to come. As we have already seen, Péguy rescues this Bergsonian mode of transcendence from the merely aleatory by suggesting that such openness (perhaps even in the sub-human) is nothing other than a natural desire for the supernatural, always in reality coincident with the actual arrival of grace. In this way, for Péguy, creation as constant happening of participation in the creative act also occurs as the constant event of the return of the creation to God, whether or not interrupted by the fall. To be original and to originate in any degree is entirely at one for the French poet with the receiving of inspiration that is the receiving of grace.

Péguy's Bergsonian Theology

It is clear then, that Péguy's philosophical modifications of his philosophical master involve a fusion of philosophy with theology. How though, inversely, does the poet re-conceive Christian theology in terms of Bergsonian philosophy? It should already be clear that this is in terms of the primacy of time.

For Péguy, if reality is first of all duration, then this fits with the doctrine of creation *ex nihilo*. As for Augustine, Aquinas, and Descartes,[22] this emergence from nothing applies to the whole of creation yet also constantly characterizes it from instant to instant. The emergence from nothing is continuous and therefore creation is temporal (remembering that for the fathers and the scholastics there was also a "time of the angels"). But a decreation, a return to nothing, is, in consequence, says Péguy, also continuous, and this is the horizontally negative mark of the positive vertical return of all things to God. As we have seen, for Péguy in the wake of Bergson, this also means that every creature, at every instance, since entirely constituted by the divine act of creation, is itself an actively receptive participant in the divine creative action. Its horizontal bestowal of itself forward in this participation is also its vertical return to

---

22. In the case of Descartes, however, *creatio continua* has a semi-occasionalist role, since Descartes thinks we cannot immanently account for the continuity of time. This does not apply to Bergson and Péguy.

God upwards by grace—or at least the share of all creatures in the human return to God by grace.

This coincidence of temporal process with divine descent reaches its apogee in the incarnation. Here the crux of Péguy's theology lies in the simple argument that if God became man, then also eternity became time, and the eternal city is given a paradoxically temporal foundation.[23] Traditionally it has been insisted that God is not taken down into time, but rather that time along with humanity is taken up into God. But all that this rubric is intended to secure is the truth that in the incarnation the eternal Creator is not changed into the moving creation. It remains nonetheless valid, in the light of the personal coincidence in Christ of the divine and human natures and of the communication of idioms, to suggest that the complete taking up of time into eternity must inversely imply a complete personal manifestation of the divine in the course of time. Péguy's main theological point is that this has always been insufficiently insisted upon. Thus, he develops a theology that is radically kenotic, though with no suggestion whatsoever of divine alteration.

Because God has submitted himself to time he has submitted himself to a free human *fiat* in the case of Mary's assent to the annunciation, which he says is like a beautiful night of June where evening meets morning and prophetic promise is overtaken by the beginning of fulfillment. He has also submitted himself to a process that is not over once and for all. Thus, God incarnate is submitted to human judgement, not just of the Jewish and Roman courts, but also of the textual critics and the historians, and he is also handed over to natural processes of ageing and decay.

He has also, as we have seen, by assuming human nature inevitably within the natural being of one human person, submitted himself, as the "body of Christ," to a whole series of non-identical repetitions. Péguy is here cogently original in realizing that since Jesus was utterly contingent and not in every way "the best at everything,"[24] we cannot actually say that later interpretations and performances of his life are, as

---

23. Péguy, "Dialogue de l'histoire et de l'âme charnelle," 666, 687.

24. This point is not in contradiction with the affirmations that 1. Christ as particular human individual nonetheless perfectly manifests universal human nature; 2. Christ is only personified, given existence, and so *ultimately* united as an individual by his divine personhood (even if, as Aquinas seems eventually to concede, one has to see a certain unity and being as inherent to human nature as such) and 3. That as a divine person he possessed the infinite divine awareness and capacity. The latter is still paradoxically and for us incomprehensibly manifested and exercised in the necessarily *limited* mode of a single human life.

human, less perfect than his own. Most controversially (and perhaps this could now affect how Christians respond to the figure of Mohammed) he implies that we cannot be certainly sure that Jesus's refusal of military action and removal from coercive political processes has clear axiomatic value for every saint in every instance, as opposed to something that was appropriate in a particular set of circumstances. Indeed, this refusal indicates a peaceful eschatological overcoming of coercion that holds more permanent validity. Yet we cannot be certain that manifesting such reserve is the priority in *every* circumstance, Péguy would seem to imply. Thus as Catholic tradition attests, the notion of the saintly Christ-like King or warrior, including even the female warrior Joan of Arc, becomes thinkable. In accordance with a double pattern that has already been described, Christ is both the absolute and exemplary founding and fontal One, and yet also a mere one that precedes the two and three, etc., of a never-ending and differentiated series.

Péguy suggests different classifications of the saints in this series. For the "classification of Caesar," Christ and the martyr Polyeuctus (eponymous hero of Corneille's play) are in the same category of saints who have rendered unto Caesar what is Caesar's, but Joan and Saint Louis are in the category of saints who have also tried to fulfill the role of Caesar. And yet for a *deeper* mode of classification, Christ and Joan are in the *same* category of saints who have had to undergo the anguish of betrayal, of being handed over to martyrdom by their own side—by the Jews to the Romans, by the French to the English and the Burgundians—whereas Polyeuctus and King Louis are in the "joyful" category of saints who have simply been martyred by their enemies—the pagan Romans and the Saracens respectively. What is significant here is that it is Joan who is the "shifter"; Joan who in a sense has undergone a more entire experience of sacrificial death even than Christ, by dying at once for nature and Caesar in a liberating mode, and for her supernatural witness, and by suffering both spiritual and political betrayal.

It is surely here that Péguy enters into the most difficult and controversial terrain, where the *cultus* of Jeanne d'Arc appears to reconfigure our conception of Christianity as such. But as he suggests in relation to Plato, Descartes, and Bergson, one should not respond to great thoughts simply by embarking on debate and argument. Instead, one should see that their greatness consists in opening up a hitherto unexpected problematic: in the case of the three philosophers, absolute truth, order, and temporal reality respectively. Bergson saw himself as circumventing the usual philosophical debates between empiricists and rationalists by refusing their initial move of abstraction from the "immediate givens" of consciousness, which turn out to imply an inner intuitive and emotional identity with temporal process that stretches forwards and backwards in an unlimited manner and with unlimited variations. Because of this lack of determinate limit, he was able to trump Kant's skeptical denial of a constitutive metaphysics based upon a wholly uncritical confinement of intuition to the merely sensory, which is supposed transcendentally to correlate with *a priori* categories. Instead, his metacritical uncovering of a more fundamental and integrating intuition imposes a new and ecumenical if problematic bias in favor of constitutive metaphysics after all.

Similarly, Péguy is circumventing the usual debates about Christian involvement in politics by pointing out that Christ himself was neither lay nor clerical, nor just a merely hidden or alternatively a merely public figure,[25] and that by entering into the entire temporal and inter-related *series* by becoming incarnate, he disallows the divisions of religious and lay, private and public, eternal and temporally relevant and even non-coercive and coercive as *primary*, whatever relative validity they may well possess. In a real sense then, as with his ontologization of grace, Péguy's point of view has to be described as *integralist*, even if his "left integralism" is staggeringly different from the Maurrassian right-wing variety—and also far more genuinely integralist. For Péguy's integralism involves what will soon be called against Maurras the "primacy of the spiritual," but taken by him as entirely permeating the material and the political. Where the anti-Bergsonian and anti-Romantic founder of Action Française wished to subordinate religion and the church to a populist nationalism, cultural particularism, and positivistic centralized control, the founder of the *Cahiers de la quinzaine* (later perpetuated in a new guise by Emmanuel Mounier as the famous journal *Esprit*) regarded the true cultural and political spirit of France—however over-emphasized by him— as opening up to the historically universal and the eternally salvific.

In this respect, the French poet fully embraced the traditional Christian qualified acceptance of both legal coercion and military defense (which were originally seen as inseparable). But one mark of his integralism is the peculiarly non-hypocritical mode of his embrace. Thus,

---

25. Péguy, "Un nouveau théologien," 411–23. Péguy defends his concern with the hidden youthful years of Joan of Arc's life as a *fully historical* and not just mythical and poetic concern, by analogy to the historicity of the larger and unknown, secret and private, but equally vital part of the life of Christ.

since this "dirty work" has to be performed by some Christians, we cannot necessarily or always accord them a subordinate status of holiness—as indeed the church has sometimes implicitly recognized by sanctifying kings. But what is more, if the only ultimate justification for anything is the promotion of grace and charity, then the only justification for the acceptance of just coercion and warfare has to be not merely their need for keeping the secular peace, but also the need of this peace if in reality the gospel is to be communicated, practiced, and defended. One aspect of this recognition occurs in *Le mystère de la charité de Jeanne d'Arc*, where Joan argues that a state of anarchy puts even victims in danger of spiritual as well as physical despair.[26] Another is Péguy's pondering of the mystery of the providential link between Rome and the spread of Christianity. It is soldiers, he insists, who first mark out the ground in which culture can flourish: without Rome, no Virgil and no preservation of either Plato or the Gospel.[27] It is in this sense that Péguy recognizes just coercion and even ambivalent, conquering violence as an integral part of the salvific temporal process that Christ inaugurated.

We have already seen that the poet integrates grace into his metaphysics. But it is inversely true that he insists, like Aquinas, that nature must be fully satisfied within his theology: indeed he declares that supernatural virtue is really but the "infinitization" of certain ordinary human values of courage, fearful prayer, mutual honoring, and magnanimous co-existence.[28] It is for this reason that he celebrates the Baroque and Jesuit-educated Corneille over the more strictly classical and Jansenist-educated Racine. The latter's superbly streamlined prosody is but a "black magic" that always portrays finite beings as cruel and grace as extrinsic and arbitrary.[29] Corneille, in total contrast, presents the martyr Polyeuc-

---

26. Péguy, "Le Mystère de la charité de Jeanne d'Arc." And see Milbank, "There's always one day which isn't the same as the day before."

27. Péguy, "L'Argent suite," 902–4.

28. Péguy, "Dialogue de l'histoire et de l'âme charnelle," 729–33, 749–50, 775–76.

29. However, one could argue that Péguy is unfair to Racine's later sacred drama, *Athalie*, written for the schoolgirls of Port-Royal as one of only two plays (the other being *Esther*) composed after his Jansenist renunciation of the theatre. Although there is indeed much darkness and cruelty in the play on all sides, there is still something more like a Pascalian rather than simply Jansenist affirmation of God's mercy eventually prevailing over his wrath, and of the commitment of the followers of the true God to human justice and compassion. Above all, the wicked Queen Athalie is lured to her doom only by a genuine softening of her heart towards the captive Temple child Joash who will prove (for all his eventual adult backsliding) to be an ancestor of the Messiah.

tus as caught up in a romantic as well as religious drama and as fully realizing the demands of honor, which his pagan adversaries could fully understand, besides the novel lure of grace.[30] Indeed, the play shows that it is exactly a shared scrupulosity as to honor and respect for the role and commitments of other human beings that smoothly elicits a nonetheless radically new respect for Polyeuctus's recognition of a new and absolute claim of eternal truth and goodness. Just as Joan is for Péguy more saint because she is also a heroine, so for him Polyeuctus is also more martyr because he is a perfect lover, nobly respectful of his wife's divided reflections and ready to leave her in the good care of his pagan rival Severus after his death.

What is favored here is therefore a radical synergism, traceable to the root of a radical *kenosis*. Natural human life, however sinful, is not closed off against grace, by virtue of its very nature. Because it represents such natural openness at its *acme* and many anticipations of grace's full arrival, paganism has been far from the worst state of humanity. That is rather represented for Péguy, not by sinfulness, which merely falls short, but by any mode of closure, however virtuous, any system that constantly inters the present in the past, as the newspaper culture of modernity most of all tends to do with its instant historicization of yesterday. (A hundred years after Péguy, the instanteity of social media achieves this from second to second and not just from day to day—what contemporary *Cahiers* might seek to counteract this?) A closed and rigid morality, lacking the suppleness of presence, is worse than moral transgression, because, unlike the latter, it can be erected into a system of totalizing false rule. It is surely for this reason that Péguy avers, in Nietzschean tones, that "virtue" and "morality" (meaning a fixed Kantian obedience to given norms?) was invented by weak "malingerers," in contrast to the military code of a "Christian way of life," that is always on the march, moving strongly and hopefully forward.[31]

Thus, worse than sin, for Péguy, is the refusal of the arrival of the new instant and above all the refusal of the arrival of a future, which can dynamically restore and heal the broken past, which is only ontologically real for memory and ruined survival. This is another reason why the poet favors the dramaturgy of Corneille. Like Shakespeare (though of course the monoGallomaniac Péguy does not mention this) it is overwhelmingly concerned with forgiveness and reconciliation. It is often a drama of lost

---

30. See Corneille, "Polyeuctus."
31. Péguy, "L'Argent suite," especially 929.

and later reconciled children. It is also, as Péguy says, one in which the concerns of love, friendship, and honor are given equal weight to those of public duty, and wherein the final tragicomic dénouement is only brought about when their inherent harmony is re-established through the decrees of wise, usually monarchic ruling.[32] The perspective here is again an integral one insofar as mercy is not presented in contrast to justice, any more than grace is shown to arrive with an alien Jansenist impact. Instead, forgiveness becomes possible when the interests of honor are satisfied, when justice is served and when concealed and humanly uncontrollable erotic desire is unconcealed (as all occurs in *Le Cid*)[33] and allowed fulfillment, if mutually entertained. The pardoners involved here are indeed also the victims and the weak, but they are more supremely the rulers and the strong, since only in their case is forgiveness clearly not a mere opportunistic recourse, and only in their case can it be offered as reconciliation supervening upon justice, just as real grace supervenes upon nature and coincides with true finite liberty. Integral, complete forgiveness is, one might say, for Péguy always specifically political pardon.

It is in virtue of this kenotic, synergic, truly integralist vision, that Péguy is always concerned with polity as a whole—whether this be church, kingdom, republic, Beauce farmstead, or Parisian family. The kenotic basis of such integration is confirmed when he says that the government of the House of France is a direct imitation of the government of the House of Nazareth.[34] For him all of these social realities may be implementing the rule of Christ and all are in that case components of

32. Beside the essay on Descartes in this book, see "Victor-Marie, comte Hugo," 276–303. It is important to realize that Corneille's still Baroque dramaturgy aligns, as John Cairncross argued, with a mixed constitutional approach to government for which the king was but the aristocratic first amongst equals. Péguy explicitly supports such a politics against the implicit alignment of Jansenism with an encroaching Machiavellian absolutism (for all the fun-and-glory loving Louis XIV's distaste for that grim credo). He also sees this as already anticipated by the medieval practice of Philip the Fair, and thinks that Joan's tragedy partly resulted from her peasant assumption that the late medieval kings were still like Saint Louis and the true sacral monarchs of old. It is just because real constitutional and sacral monarchy had already vanished from France that Péguy thinks that the French Revolution was justified. Indeed he sees it, after Victor Hugo, as inaugurating a new and valid civic sacrality and as being paradoxically the work of men of the *ancien régime* more loyal to a deep antiquity than the Machiavellian distorters of the role of the Crown. Inversely, the reactionaries of his own day, like the supporters of Maurras, are seen by Péguy as after all very modern, heirs only of the decay of the revolutionary *mystique* into mere *politique*.

33. See Corneille, "The Cid."

34. Péguy, "Un nouveau théologien," 413.

the *ecclesia* in the widest sense. Their temporal and secular purpose does not for him weaken this belonging, because he refuses, for partly socialist reasons, the prevailing eschatological model according to which the prime purpose of the church is the saving of individual souls taken in isolation. For him this is to ignore the significance of time and the truth that grace is given for the sake of the unfolding centuries, even though these periods cannot be taken as ones of progress and all are equally near the time of Christ from the perspective of duration, as well as of eternity. The point, nonetheless, of this unfolding, is the necessary inclusion of all—of each and every one as making up the redeemed creation, as the parables of the lost coin, sheep, and son would seem to indicate.[35] For this reason, the constitution of a family, of a farmstead, of a race and of a polity are for Péguy not incidental to the work of salvation itself.

There is a crucial sense here in which, as a philosemite and Dreyfusard, Péguy re-Judaized conceptions of the Christian body, precisely in order to be more faithful to the implications of the incarnation. We have seen how he unsqueamishly emphasized the dependence of Christianity upon Roman military success and *yet* it is also true that he fully shared an Augustinian ambiguity about any conflict tending toward imperial domination, contrasting this with a more supposedly "Greek" and "French" conflict of honor, much more focused on the defense of truth come what may, or on an appeal to a divine verdict on such a trial by combat. In the case of the Jews he goes further by honoring and respecting a people and tradition scarcely concerned with success at all and resigned (as he saw it) to ceaseless defeat and yet survival despite defeat through a suffering loyalty to inherited truth. Christians, for Péguy, are situated between the Jewish and the Roman insofar as they are prepared to suffer temporal defeat for the sake of truth, but are equally more inclined than the Jews actively and "childishly" to rebel against injustice and seek to overcome it. Of course, he thinks that this Christian idiom is most represented by the revolutionary French and their extension of revolution into benevolent empire in the name of the triad of philosophical truth, order and felt reality.[36]

---

35. See Milbank, "There's always one day which isn't the same as the day before."

36. Péguy, "Dialogue de l'histoire et de l'âme charnelle," 759–61. Obviously one may find Péguy's commitments here questionable, in various degrees. One can note, however, the coincidence with the Gallophile Chesterton in terms of both admiration for Napoleon and belief that an aggressive and authoritarian German militarism had to be militarily opposed.

Péguy and the Post-Christian

The defense of Bergson in these two final essays is directed against the soon-to-be-successful attempt to have him put on the Papal *Index* and the opposition to his philosophy on the part of neo-Thomists like Péguy's erstwhile assistant in his socialist bookshop, the then-young Jacques Maritain.

Péguy avers that the word "index" did not figure in his childhood catechism, but allows that such signs and warnings may have their place if one thinks of them on analogy with the signposts on the way to Chartres—the pilgrim route he once walked in order to pray for his sick son with his friend, the author Alain-Fournier and author of a now-famous novel also concerned with childhood, time, ageing, and memory, *Le Grand Meaulnes*. The signs are not needed for peasants, who know the way, but nonetheless serve well as ritual markers, which embellish the route and so actually lift it *above* utility as opposed to serving a purpose of utilitarian direction.

The manuscript breaks off soon after this, on the eve of Péguy's death at the first battle of the Marne, but the ironic implication would appear in part to be that the Christian life is after all a Bergsonian passage and movement through time, though one now more reconciled in Catholic terms with space, as we have seen. Papal guidance may be useful, so long as it is embedded in the more fundamental liturgical and non-juridical process that it merely aids. As to neo-Thomism, it tends to miss the point that all defenders of spirit in a materialist age that eschews heroism and genius as much as sanctity are now allies, and that this defense of spirit is not a victory secured once and for all, any more than is any other victory within time. What is more, Aristotle as the articulator of a "spatial" classification must be regarded (and here Péguy seems somewhat unfair compared to a predecessor like Ravaisson) as himself a lone first "modern" within antiquity—perhaps in contrast to Plato, for whom the finite was always in elusive motion.

But the most crucial point is that Bergson, although himself a modern, has nonetheless discovered the key to diagnosing the key modern illusion, which is the suppression of reality in the mode of temporal presence. One can infer that for Péguy this Bergsonian discovery has become possible just *because* of the modern exacerbation of the betrayal of time, even though no one before Bergson had a sufficiently clear sense of the epistemological and ontological primacy of duration. To intuit the latter is indeed for Bergson to intuit directly the presence of God within the world, since duration is a self-propelled "melody," a whole prior to its elements, and rests on no immanent material basis. Later Bergson conceded to Sertillanges that, as such a musical work, duration could be regarded as the creation and image of the transcendent "composer" God, thereby giving it the status of something like the figure of immanent shaping wisdom in the Bible, lying within and yet before all of God's created ways.

To the degree therefore that modernity suppresses duration more entirely by burying presence and seeking to control the future, this is equivalent to its refusal of God and of the divine presence. But the suppression and the refusal are not for Péguy primarily the work of philosophy. They are rather the public work of the dominance of money and aggregating technology. For it is money that most of all seeks to accumulate, save, and invest present moments and that does so in order to "secure" an indefinite future, which is always the day after tomorrow. To save, says Péguy, is never in reality to preserve, but rather to destroy the thing that one has exchanged for mere lucre. Today, of course, this is much more fearfully apparent.

In this way, by understanding money and capital to be the suppression of presence as spirit and freedom, Péguy achieves nothing less than an alternative critique of capitalism to that of Marx, which rather understands money in terms of the suppression of the concrete and material by the abstract and spiritual. By comparison, Marx's critique looks naïve and it is unsurprising that later, more sophisticated materialists like Gilles Deleuze and Eric Alliez have sought to accommodate the poet's alternative insight. Marx's critique is naïve, because it thinks in basically spatializing terms and so of human relationships whose merely spatial and consequently material character is arbitrarily taken for granted. The already distorted ontological idiom in which alienating relationships become possible is not here properly accounted for.

At times, all the same, Marx indeed saw that abstract financialization was something that the merely distorted human relationships involved in capitalism already *assume*, but Péguy much more consistently adopts this perspective. Thus, in order that mere things be exchanged for mere abstractions, it must be the case that the integral qualitative multiplicities of time have already been both suppressed and divided. Living emotions are docketed and numerated as "over," but stockpiled in a way that serves the interests of one of the only two remaining emotions, which is avarice. The other is venality, which is unleashed as a ravenous appetite for the future, since the reserving of realities on a quantified scale paradoxically also "liquifies" them and materializes them in aggregative fashion. That which can eminently be measured (indeed one could add, as for Descartes) is commensurate with a "sheerly" concrete space of pure extension that can now be dominated and rearranged at will. It is just for this reason that Péguy thinks that one facet of the dominance of money is the embrace of a mechanistic and utilitarian philosophy—he compares this coincidence to a Spinozist aspectual duality. To put it simply, one can say that an ever-more-dominant financial market and a ravaged earth are the two exactly overlapping modes of the one modern political substance.

For these reasons, the betrayal of time, the dominance of money, and the ignoring of the spiritual and the divine are for Péguy one and the same thing. It is then no longer any use for the church in the modern age to persist in initially trying to convert sinners—there are no conscious sinners left, for if there were then God and the opening to grace would not have been suppressed. Something astonishing has now occurred: despite the manifestation of God himself in time, people have lost their "feel" for this reality, exactly as if they had lost their taste for bread and for "the color of the sun." Yet this can seem less astonishing if one realizes that even the supreme event of the incarnation can fall prey to the human capacity to relegate the most extraordinary events to the level of the ordinary, if they happened to have occurred a long time ago.[37]

In any case, the focus on the saving of "any old" individual souls, rather than the attempted inclusion of the vital spiritual and creative *contribution* through spiritual labor of *each* and everyone, has always been part of the problem of the perverse inversion of the "mystical machine"—the deploying of it in terms of the elevated interests of the clergy, whose prestige is linked to the saving of "any old" individuals, instead of in the interests of the laity and their collective solidarity within time. Yet today, the correct operation of this machine is the only *possible* way forward for mission. Péguy is surely uncompromising: for the church now to make an impact, it must make integral war upon modernity. He says that this is "literal war," with surely the disturbing implication that this could sometimes truly involve violence. Such a war on modernity has also to be a socialist war on capitalism, for the reason that we have seen. And yet it is surely a war waged not just by a Christian socialism but by a church socialism,[38] since Péguy is clear that the truly revolutionary class

---

37. Péguy, "Dialogue de l'histoire et de l'âme charnelle," 722, 744–45.
38. This conception is very close to that of Anglo-Catholic socialist tradition from

of independent artisans scarcely exists any longer, and he regards both the proletariat and the intellectuals as likely to surrender to state social democracy (and an allied pacifism, indifferent to international justice, as with Jean Jaurès), which for him, as for the real, older French socialist tradition, has nothing to do with socialist mutualism at all.

And yet for Péguy there is a special joy, grace, and privilege in being a Christian in the dire circumstances of modernity. For one thing, we must simply accept that even the church as bearer of eternal truth is subject to the habitual decay of ageing, attendant upon all natural processes: God himself has mysteriously invited this by becoming incarnate. Although this boredom even with God manifest is the final and apparently irreparable disaster, it is after all only the disaster of the death of the God-man on the cross, after which he was re-manifest as the new springtide of resurrection.

For another, the now-compulsory call to arms makes it clearer that the Christian struggle has always really been an integral one.[39] It includes a struggle against money, the betrayer of time, named by Péguy as the Antichrist, which could only have arisen after Christ as the absolute refusal of presence which Christ most supremely offers as liberal gift in abundance. What this indicates is that modernity, the post-Christian, is not quite such a novelty after all. There is rather a sense in which the post-Christian is as old as the Christian, or is even paradoxically pre-Christian, beginning with Herod and the slaughter of the holy innocents.[40] The modern betrayal of time is both foreshadowed and actually begun in the betrayal of Christ as the very consummation of time and the event in coincidence with eternity. And this betrayal of Christ was from the outset for money, which Christ himself taught was the root of all evil.

Christ, betrayed for money, already experienced on the cross the anguish of modernity, the closure against time, against the One Father and against grace. And the instance of the incarnation was itself occasioned by the ultimate character of all sin as being after all a closure also against the offer of forgiveness in advance, the refusal of the very pertinence of the categories of infinite justice, sin, and reconciliation.

---

the East End slum ritualist Stewart Headlam in the 1890s, through to Conrad Noel, the 1930's Vicar of Thaxted in Essex and beyond. But this is unsurprising, as its ultimate roots lie, back through John Malcolm Ludlow who was brought up in Paris, in the French Catholic socialism of Pierre Buchez.

39. Péguy, "Un nouveau théologien," 517–49.

40. Péguy, "Le Mystère des saints Innocents."

Thus, even though it required Mary to come out from the citadel of finite captivity and to open the gates in order to allow God in, her very doing so is already the beginning of the divine entry, "on a perfect June night," just as the permeation of a bubble by further moistening is at once a breakout from within and a benign intrusion from without.

For this reason the albeit unique situation of the post-Christian is also for Péguy nonetheless the typical human situation, the situation of infirmity, misery, and poverty that Christ arrived to both accommodate and redress.[41] It is the problem of sin as the hardening of hearts, of an "illiberal" lack of honoring respect for the sincere (even if mistaken) views of others, of a modernist indifference even as to one's own commitments,[42] and above all the flight from the living moment and its demand for continuous artistry from each and every one of us. But the demand remains and our contemporary Christian agony of undergoing its totally unaware refusal by most of our contemporaries is the divine agony in which we but slightly share. And the witness of the cross and resurrection is the witness to the universal saving power of this anguish, in the end for each and every one of us, else the divine integrally kenotic purpose of redemption would not have been accomplished in time, which is now the time of eternity.

For this reason then, for Péguy the modern Christian enjoys the advantage of clarity. This clarity calls her to a new degree of creative striving in unity with receptive openness, which will also involve a new degree of redemptive suffering. It also calls her to a new degree of militancy and of political besides spiritual struggle. Yet all this must be joyfully undertaken, in the mode of an inevitable ageing which nonetheless always seeks to retain and repeat the original freshness of the very earliest lost times.

John Milbank

Bibliography

Bergson, Henri. *Creative Evolution*. Translated by Arthur Mitchell. Mineola: Dover, 1998.

———. *An Introduction to Metaphysics*. Translated by T. E. Hulme. London: Palgrave Macmillan, 2007.

---

41. Péguy, "Un nouveau théologien," 469–70.

42. Péguy, "L'Argent," especially 821. "Liberty is a system of deference" says Péguy (against all *Guardianista* delusions in advance).

———. *Matter and Memory*. Translated by N. M. Paul and W. S. Palmer. New York: Zone, 1990.

———. *Time and Free Will: An Essay on the Immediate Data of Consciousness*. Translated by F. L. Pogson. Mineola: Dover, 2001.

———. *The Two Sources of Morality and Religion*. Translated by R. Ashley Audra et al. Notre Dame: University of Notre Dame Press, 1977.

Corneille, Pierre. "The Cid." In *The Cid/Cinna/The Theatrical Illusion*, translated by John Cairncross, 30–109. London: Penguin, 1975.

———. "Polyeuctus." In *Polyeuctus/The Liar/Nicomedes*, translated by John Cairncross, 41–120. Harmondsworth: Penguin, 1980.

Kennedy, Ellen. "Bergson's Philosophy and French Political Doctrines: Sorel, Maurras, Péguy and de Gaulle." *Government and Opposition* 15.1 (1980) 75–91.

Milbank, John. "The Mystery of Reason." In *The Grandeur of Reason: Religion, Tradition and Universalism*, edited by Peter M. Candler Jr. and Conor Cunningham, 68–117. London: SCM, 2010.

———. *Theology and Social Theory*. Oxford: Wiley-Blackwell, 2006.

———. "'There's always one day which isn't the same as the day before': Christianity and History after Charles Péguy." In *Theologies of Retrieval: An Exploration and Appraisal*, edited by Darren Sarisky, 9–36. London: T. & T. Clark, 2017.

Péguy, Charles. "L'Argent." In *Oeuvres en prose complètes III*, edited by Robert Burac, 785–847. Paris: Gallimard, 1992.

———. "L'Argent suite." In *Oeuvres en prose complètes III*, edited by Robert Burac, 848–996. Paris: Gallimard, 1992.

———. "Clio, Dialogue de l'histoire et de l'âme païenne." In *Oeuvres en prose complètes III*, edited by Robert Burac, 997–1214. Paris: Gallimard, 1992.

———. "Dialogue de l'histoire et de l'âme charnelle." In *Oeuvres en prose complètes III*, edited by Robert Burac, 594–783. Paris: Gallimard, 1992.

———. "Le Mystère de la charité de Jeanne d'Arc." In *Oeuvres poétiques et dramatiques*, edited by Claire Daudin et al., 397–559. Paris: Gallimard, 2014.

———. "Le Mystère des saints Innocents." In *Oeuvres poétiques et dramatiques*, edited by Claire Daudin et al., 775–927. Paris: Gallimard, 2014.

———. "Un nouveau théologien: M. Fernand Laudet." In *Oeuvres en prose complètes III*, edited by Robert Burac, 392–591. Paris: Gallimard, 1992.

———. "Victor-Marie, comte Hugo." In *Oeuvres en prose complètes III*, edited by Robert Burac, 161–345. Paris: Gallimard, 1992.

Racine, Jean. "Athaliah." In *Iphigenia/Phaedra/Athaliah*, translated by John Cairncross, 233–317. Harmondsworth: Penguin, 1970.

Sertillanges, A. D. *Avec Henri Bergson*. Paris: Gallimard, 1941.

Acknowledgments

TRANSLATING A GREAT WRITER from one language to another is a difficult enterprise, fraught with pitfalls, foreseen and more often unforeseen, and in the case of a writer as idiosyncratic in his own language as Charles Péguy, it can be downright hazardous. This translation has benefitted greatly from the careful scrutiny of two francophone philosophers, who are thoroughly familiar with Péguy in the original French: Lucien Pelletier of the Université de Sudbury and Alexandre de Vitry of the Université de Paris–Sorbonne. Their clarifications and suggestions in several instances about what Péguy was saying in French have been invaluable; as for any errors or infelicities in expressing this in English, the responsibility is entirely mine. My thanks also to Graeme Ward for his help with Péguy's Latin and Greek phrases.

I am grateful for the courteous help received from the staff of the Centre Charles Péguy in Orléans, France, where I consulted a number of manuscript sources important to this translation, especially the Péguy–Bergson correspondence.

Annette Aronowicz's remarkable commentary on Péguy's reflections on history, "The Secret of the Man of Forty," which constitutes the Appendix to this book, is reprinted with the permission of the journal *History and Theory*.

I am thankful for the encouragement and advice I received at the very beginning of this undertaking from Benoît Chantre, President of the Association Recherches Mimétiques, and for the support of Conor Cunningham and John Milbank in getting the translation to publication.

It has been a pleasure working with my Wipf and Stock editor, Robin Parry, whose capacity for combining a keen sense of grammatical precision with an openness to Péguy's idiosyncratic grammatical style has been a boon to this project.

My deepest thanks, finally, to Nancy for her loving support in this and in all things.

1

Introduction

> In truth . . . it's really a scandal; and so it's a mystery; and it's really the greatest mystery of the temporal creation: that the greatest works of genius are thus handed over to foolishness (our *messieurs* and dear fellow citizens); that for their temporal eternity they are . . . perpetually passed on, dropped, . . . delivered, abandoned into such hands, such poor hands: ours . . . . It is dreadful . . . to think that we have every license, that we have the exorbitant right, that we have *the right* to make a bad reading of Homer, to dethrone a work of genius, that the greatest work of genius is delivered into our hands. . . . And above all, that letting it fall from our hands . . . we can bring about its death through forgetfulness. What a dreadful risk, . . . what a dreadful adventure; and above all, what a dreadful responsibility.[1]

CHARLES PÉGUY WAS ACUTELY aware of the responsibility and the risk inherent in the requirement, due to the historicity of human temporal existence, that all aspects of life—material, political, cultural, spiritual—depend on a continual handing on and renewal. Though he might not have been thinking of his own fate, his observation about the vulnerability of works of genius to being mishandled, badly read, or simply forgotten is certainly illustrated in his case. In his native France, Péguy's *oeuvre* early fell victim to the left *versus* right, secular *versus* religious polemics that have so characterized French intellectual life in the twentieth century, and have tended to marginalize also other thinkers, such as Albert Camus and Simone Weil, who do not fit comfortably into the

---

1. Péguy, *"Clio,"* 1013–15.

conventional categories of the progressives or conservatives. Péguy was not forgotten in France after his death in 1914 so much as he was dismissed by convenient association—with the Action Française and its brand of conservative nationalism. This dismissal is comparable to the early dismissal of Nietzsche as a prophet of German national socialism or of Dostoevsky as a reactionary Orthodox apologist for Russian imperialism. Much more profound readings of Nietszche and Dostoevsky have long been in practice, and there are definite signs that a more adequate reading of Péguy is underway in France. In addition to scholarly commentaries that might be cited, one could point to the widely discussed recent novel by Michel Houellebecq, *Submission,* in which Péguy's poem *Ève* is declaimed at length by one of the characters (to whom the author is clearly not unsympathetic), and Péguy's Christian vision is upheld as a possible, if unlikely, option for the reanimation of a France torn between nihilistic secularism and growing Islamization.[2]

The reception of Péguy in the English-speaking world has not been so markedly characterized by bad reading, or even by forgetfulness, since his work has been little known at all. This betokens the potential for a fresh reading, unencumbered by the ideological baggage associated with his work in his native France. Péguy's cultural, intellectual, and spiritual itinerary renders him an outsider: a peasant who attended the elite École Normale in Paris, a Dreyfusard and socialist who converted to Catholicism, a poet and philosopher, essayist, polemicist, and publisher, a patriotic Republican and an admirer of the medieval saint Joan of Arc—and staunchly fervent in all of these commitments. To those who saw contradiction and inconsistency, especially between his Christianity and his socialism, he responded that his position came, rather, out of a steady *approfondissement* of what was given in both traditions. Péguy defies any easy conventional categorization, remaining now, as he was for his

---

2. See Houellebecq, *Submission,* 129-37. The more recent French reconsideration of Péguy owes much to Gilles Deleuze, particularly his *Difference and Repetition,* in which he placed Péguy alongside Nietzsche and Kierkegaard as a great thinker and practitioner of repetition. Also significant for the French return to Péguy, especially as a political thinker, have been works by the philosophers Alain Finkielkraut, *Le Mécontemporain,* and Pierre Manent, *La Cité de l'homme.* For an illuminating discussion of the relation between Deleuze and Péguy, see De Vitry, "De Deleuze à Péguy," in *Charles Péguy.* The other articles in this book are also representative of the best current French scholarship on Péguy; of particular relevance to this translation of the *Notes* are Riquier, "Péguy, 'Bergsonien,'" Le Guay, "Péguy et Maritain," and Chantre, "La logique enchantée." See also Chantre's recent book, *Péguy.*

contemporaries, a *mécontemporain*. But as Charles Taylor has remarked, it is Péguy's unique kind of spiritual itinerary that is most significant for our age, beset as it is by a universal "fragilization" of belief: "Charles Péguy is a paradigm example of a modern who has found his own path, a new path. . . . We can see how Péguy confused his contemporaries, and was almost impossible to place. This left socialist Dreyfusard, a believer in revolution and in the Republic, passionately insisted on the need to root one's action in the millennial, including Catholic, past of France. So is he a reactionary? But he also passionately denounced the clerical anti-Dreyfusard party, precisely for their desire to re-impose old forms: monarchy, clerical dominance, in their outmoded form, without ever considering how the tradition had grown and changed."[3] The very qualities that have rendered Péguy's work so vulnerable to mis-readings render it at the same valuable to a Western modernity in a state of cultural and spiritual crisis that goes far beyond the conventional polemics of left *versus* right, progressive *versus* conservative. Perhaps above all, he offers us a way to come to terms with the past that neither rejects it outright nor attempts to reproduce it mechanically, but rather points to a creative appropriation of tradition. This, however, is not the place to make a case for Péguy. That case can only be made convincingly by his work itself. Always admiring of those with the courage to measure their ideas against the best of others', this is how he would want it.

Péguy's writing is so little known in the English-speaking world largely because it has been so little translated. Some of his major poetry is available in excellent translations,[4] but with one notable exception, none of his considerable body of prose essays has had anything like a complete translation.[5] For those unable to read Péguy in French, the essay offered

---

3. Taylor, *A Secular Age*, 744–55. For other recent significant scholarship bringing Péguy's thought forward in the English-speaking world, see John Milbank's extensive foreword to this translation of the *Notes on Bergson and Descartes*, and his preface to *Beyond Secular Order*, as well as discussions of Péguy in the work of other "Radical Orthodox" theologians; for instance, Cunningham, *Genealogy of Nihilism*, chapter 8, and Pickstock, *Repetition and Identity*, 85–107. An excellent literary-critical and historical contextualization of Péguy's prose essays is provided in Roe, *The Passion of Charles Péguy*. Notable also is George Steiner's eloquent essay on Péguy, "Drumming on the Doors." Roe's book contains an extensive bibliography of works in French and English by, about, and related to Péguy.

4. Most notably, *The Portal of the Mystery of Hope*, translated by David Louis Schindler Jr.

5. The one available translation of more than aphoristic fragments of Péguy's prose work is Dru, *Temporal and Eternal*, containing versions of *Notre Jeunesse* (translated

here will signal a new voice in regard to questions of politics, literature, philosophy, and religion—some specific to his time, but most, perennial. The voice will be fresh, but also sometimes disconcerting, and not always easily accessible. One reason that Péguy has been so little translated is the extremely challenging style of his original French. The French writer, François Mauriac, on being told of a projected English translation of one of Péguy's works, remarked that he wished someone would first translate it into French, a remark aimed not at the quality but at the unique difficulty of the writing, and a remark that can only inspire a certain trepidation in the would-be translator. Some of the difficulty is obviated by keeping in mind that Péguy was first and foremost naturally a poet, who thought and wrote like a poet, even when writing prose, and even prose about philosophy. Awareness of the poetics integral to Péguy's thought and style must be brought to bear on that constant challenge facing any translator: achieving a just balance between readability and fidelity to the text. Péguy's prose, with its tendency, as in his poetry, towards continual repetition-with-variations, presents the translator with a strong temptation to prune, reduce, or smooth out for the sake of readability. I have resisted this temptation precisely because, in Péguy's case, the style is not merely a subjective quirk, but an integral expression of ideas about time, human freedom, and creation that are central to his thought. In this regard, it seems only right that the English-speaking reader of his prose should share the experience of the French reader. My decision for fidelity to the text and therefore to the author's thought, entails a translation that attempts as much as possible to imitate rather than re-package the original. This might mean that more effort is required of the reader, but together with this effort, the assurance of closer proximity to Péguy's original work and his intentions for this work. While in an endeavor so fraught with pitfalls as translation, "success" must be a relative term, I would consider this translation a success if the reader comes away from it with the sense that she has heard Péguy's voice rather than the translator's, a sense that might well be induced by those jolts sometimes occasioned by the strangeness of a style and thought that are anything but "ready-made."

---

as "Memories of Youth") and *Clio, Dialogue de l'histoire et de l'âme charnelle* (translated as "Clio 1"). While able translations by a scholar with a good understanding of Péguy's thought (see his *Péguy*), they are not really complete, because they have been substantially abridged, so much so that Dru styles his work as an "adaptation" rather than a translation.

As the French philosopher Pierre Manent has noted, access for non-French readers to the thinking of Péguy can be especially challenging because "nearly everything he wrote about is buried deep in French history . . . linked to an explicitly French perspective."[6] However, the ostensible subjects of this particular essay, Bergson and Descartes, are well-known outside France; furthermore, Péguy's concern with questions of philosophy and religion that transcend the particularities of time and place will quickly become evident to the reader. Yet the incarnational (or as he would put it, "temporally eternal/eternally temporal") nature of his thought itself means that he comes at the eternal or universal through the particularities of the temporal[7]—and these particularities are for him primarily those of his native France. Therefore, the non-French reader will be in need of some explanatory notes. I have tried to keep these notes to the minimum required for understanding Péguy's argument, striving to avoid as much as possible the interposition of excessive scholarly apparatus between the thoughtful reader and the actual text. The notes are thus limited to translation of Péguy's citations, which are frequent, from other languages, primarily Latin and Greek, and the identification where appropriate of their source; to the identification of people, places, and events alluded to in the text, both contemporary with Péguy and from earlier history, where these might not be already familiar to the reader; and to some miscellaneous items of information for which the reader might be grateful. On occasion, too, I will note Péguy's use of a French term, if it is unusual (or invented); but, with very few exceptions, I have refrained from pointing out the many plays on words, unfortunately almost always untranslatable, with which the text abounds.

The French edition of Péguy used for this translation of his last major prose work, the "Note sur M. Bergson et la philosophie bergsonienne" and "Note conjointe sur M. Descartes et la philosophie cartésienne," is the *Oeuvres en prose complètes III* (1992), the third volume of the magisterial Gallimard *Pléiade* edition of his prose writings, which contains all the scholarly apparatus of notes, variants, index, chronology, and bibliography indispensable to those who might wish to pursue the detailed study of Péguy's entire *oeuvre*. My own explanatory footnotes owe much to the notes of the third volume's editor, Robert Burac.

---

6. From Manent's "Foreword" to *Temporal and Eternal*.

7. As Charles Taylor notes, Péguy's "Christian thought is animated by his profound rejection of modern excarnation" (*A Secular Age*, 751).

Background

Péguy's last major prose essay arose most immediately out of his concern to defend the philosopher Henri Bergson, who was about to be placed on the Catholic *Index*. The issue of the *Index* was, however, merely the most publicly visible culminating point of a deeper well of criticism that had been developing for years, indeed, virtually in tandem with Bergson's growing fame and influence in France and beyond, which reached its high point from 1907 to 1914. This criticism came from both the left and the right in France. On the more or less "official" left were the academic intellectuals, especially the historians, sociologists, and scientists of the Sorbonne, who were closely associated with the secular government of the Third Republic, and who saw themselves as defending the hard-won gains of scientific reason against both religious and political reaction; and on the more philosophical (and, for Péguy, more thoughtful) left, there was above all the figure of Julien Benda, Péguy's personal friend and collaborator on the *Cahiers,* an atheist of Jewish background, who excoriated Bergson's thought as a vague non-philosophy that substituted murky sentiment for clear reason and the influence of which in France was a betrayal of the Cartesian inheritance that was the glory of French thought. On the right, there was again a discernible twofold division between the more political and the more philosophical critics: the former were represented by the conservative nationalists of the Action Française, led by Charles Maurras, who after having first flirted with Bergson's thought insofar as the concepts of "intuition" and *élan vital* could appear to serve an anti-Republican agenda, turned against his philosophy in the name of the "classical" and Catholic heritage of France; and the more profound critics, who attacked Bergson's anti-rationalism on behalf of Catholic (that is, neo-Thomist) intellectual reason, were represented, above all, by Jacques Maritain, another personal friend of Péguy and a fellow-convert.[8]

---

8. Maritain was an eighteen-year-old student of philosophy when he met Péguy (who was nine years older) in 1901. He became a collaborator, a devoted fellow-socialist, and a close family friend of the older man. Both men came to Catholicism, unbeknownst to each other, at about the same time: Maritain (from a Protestant background) in 1906, and Péguy about a year later. Their conversions, however, marked the beginning of a deep rupture in their relationship, as it became increasingly clear that their understandings of what it meant to be Catholic were radically different—a difference expressed in Péguy's critique of the *parti dévôt* ("devout party") in the second *Note.*

Péguy's own relationship to Bergson went back far earlier, to his time as Bergson's student at the École Normale in 1898, and then as a regular attender of Bergson's lectures at the Collège de France in the years after. As will be clear from Péguy's essay, he regarded Bergson as one of the very greatest philosophers, in the same league as Plato and Descartes. According to the testimony of Péguy's friends at the École Normale, he was "overwhelmed" by Bergson's teaching; for him, "philosophy began with Bergson";[9] and the subsequent trajectory of his own work was profoundly influenced by his sustained encounter with Bergson's thought, especially as this was expressed in *Time and Free Will* (1889), *Matter and Memory* (1896), and *Introduction to Metaphysics* (1901). Péguy credited Bergson for liberating him from the scientistic positivism and historicism that had come to dominate French intellectual life by the latter part of the nineteenth century, through the writings especially of Ernst Renan and Hippolyte Taine and their academic epigones at the universities. As will also be clear from this essay, Bergson's ideas not only helped him think his way out of the dominant dogmatic rationalism, but also helped him think his way into a renewed Christianity.

Over the years Péguy developed a personal relationship with Bergson, as well, corresponding and meeting with him frequently. His loyalty to his former teacher was unwavering, even when it was accompanied by a critical stance towards Bergson's third major work, *Creative Evolution* (1907), and even when it was not always entirely reciprocated, as when Bergson declined to write a foreword for Péguy's projected *Oeuvres choisies* (1910), likely because the academic philosopher was reluctant to be too closely associated in the public mind with the decidedly unacademic and controversial Péguy. Although their friendship became somewhat more distant after this strain, they maintained regular contact, by letter and in person; and Péguy, for his part, did not hesitate, when the time came, to compromise himself for Bergson by defending him vehemently against his critics, both among leading secular intellectuals and within the leadership of the Catholic Church. It is clear from Péguy's correspondence at the time that he did not consider Bergson, by reason of his temperament and ambitions, to be sufficiently capable of defending himself.[10]

9. Grogin, *The Bergsonian Controversy in France*, 146–47.

10. As Péguy wrote in a personal letter to Bergson in March, 1914, "Only I have a pen hard enough to reduce a Maurras, only I have a hand heavy enough to hold in check at the same time the anti-Semites and the fanatics; will I see for the first

The opposition to Bergson began to crystallize in attacks mounted in the same year that his fame reached its apogee. When he became a serious candidate for election to the prestigious Académie Française in early 1914, the Action Française attempted to undermine his candidacy by characterizing his philosophy of intuition as a variant of Germanic romanticism that threatened to undermine the classical Cartesian reason that was the essential strength of French culture. This criticism was, moreover, accompanied by a more or less explicit anti-Semitism aimed at the philosopher's Jewish background.[11] In the same year, Bergson's writings became the target of the compilers of the Catholic *Index*, in large part due to the critical efforts of Maritain and other neo-Thomists. When it became clear that Bergson's writings were indeed to be placed on the *Index*, Péguy immediately began work on a written response to this development, which he published in April 1914 as the *Note sur M. Bergson et la philosophie Bergsonienne*. His work on a sequel (much longer), the *Note conjointe sur M. Descartes et la philosophie cartésienne*, was left incomplete when he was called up in the French general mobilization for war in August 1914; his death in battle the next month meant that the second essay was published only posthumously.

It is worth remarking that after reading the first *Note*, Bergson was moved to write in a letter to Péguy that "you have admirably understood and rendered . . . what I would like to have done."[12] This would likely have much pleased Péguy, who thought of himself as someone who could take Bergson's thought to places that Bergson himself would not dare.[13]

---

time in my life, a battle fought and maybe jeopardized, without my being there?" It is worth noting that in a letter a few years earlier (September 1912) to his friend, Joseph Lotte, he said of Bergson, "Bergson does not want to be called a poet. He applies himself to showing that his philosophy really is philosophy and even the philosophy of a professor of philosophy. . . . At bottom, he lacks courage" (*Henri Bergson, Péguy Correspondance*).

11. For an excellent account of the political and cultural context of Péguy's defense of Bergson, see Roe, *The Passion of Charles Péguy*, chapters 4, 5.

12. Letter of May 4, 1914. This year seems to have brought about a renewed closeness between the two men, after a four-year period of some distancing, since it was to Bergson that Péguy entrusted his family before going off to war.

13. In the same letter to Lotte (quoted earlier), where he refers to Bergson's lack of courage, Péguy goes on to say, "At bottom, I am as much a philosopher as he is . . . ."

A Word about Structure and Style

The reader might at first be disconcerted by what seems an absence of structure in Péguy's two *Notes*. This begins with the titles, since the first note is at least as much or more about Descartes than about Bergson, while the second starts with a brief discussion of Descartes only to return again and again to Bergson. Yet the apparent absence of structure can be seen to be the most appropriate vehicle for Péguy's ideas about language, philosophy, creativity, and reality itself. The repeated setting-off on a line of thought that moves far from the original point, then the repeated taking-up again of what seems the same theme, and within these large repetitions the constant small repetitions of words and phrases that are similar but not quite identical—this Péguyan rhythm of writing has a strange power to move the reader, once he has ceased to worry about a straightforward, linear structure and allowed himself to be carried along by the flow of words. As Péguy himself once remarked: "Ah! words! words! There is nothing comparable, neither music nor painting can rival words."[14] It might be true that Péguy was primarily a poet rather than a philosopher or theologian, but this distinction does not account entirely for the zigzag rhythm of his prose. In the first *Note*, he says the following about Descartes, that supposed paragon of logical coherence:

> It is a singular journey that Descartes proposes to us. . . . A singular journey this Cartesian journey . . . . One descends, one stops, . . . one leaps, . . . one touches a point that will be the definitive point of arrival, and is for the instant a momentary point of departure, one re-ascends, one comes back to the stopping-point, one re-descends to the definitive point of arrival. One sets out, descends, stops, leaps, re-ascends, re-descends, arrives. One goes, leaps, comes back, goes again. It doesn't matter. Because a journey is singular, because it is interrupted, discontinuous, and even because it is partially backward, that is not a reason for not making it.[15]

This description of Descartes's "singular" journey, based on the accumulation of various verbs used by Descartes himself throughout the *Discourse on Method*, could easily be applied to the journey on which Péguy himself takes the reader, and it signals Péguy's view that a truly great philosophy,

---

14. Quoted in Roe, *The Passion of Charles Péguy*, 203.
15. See below, 42–43.

whatever its epigonal practitioners might claim, is not primarily a matter of the strictly linear logical development of ideas.

The repetitive rhythm of Péguy's writing serves various purposes. Most obviously, it ensures that the reader "gets the point"; one cannot take a point in and then simply move on to the next one in a progressive manner until the conclusion of the argument is reached. Rather than flitting about briefly in the upper regions of the consciousness until it is filed away (and frequently then forgotten), the idea gets appropriated into the very being of the reader, as it were. The repetition also serves to break apart the usual *habit* of reading, where habit is most often the enemy of fresh understanding. Péguy's repetitive style is, however, more than an instrument aimed at readers, because in relation to his thinking it is an end as well as a means. As he himself declared: "I don't ask of you what you are saying. I ask of you how you are saying it. . . . That alone proves."[16] With reference to the long succession of water lilies painted by Monet, Péguy raised the question of which should be considered the best—and answered that "good sense" and logic would dictate the last. But, as Gilles Deleuze observed, Péguy's own answer is the *first*, and this because it is the *maximum* point from which the entire series of water lilies is derived; in this sense it already repeats all the others. For Deleuze, in declining to see the final water lily as the culmination to which all the preceding ones have led, Péguy offers a correction to the modern belief in indefinite temporal progress. One can agree with Deleuze while noting, however, that more needs to be said, for, as Péguy himself notes, Monet went on from the first to paint "twenty-five and thirty-seven" more. Why did he continue, even as an old man, to paint them if the first was the maximum? In this question, I think, we approach the heart of Péguyan repetition, as a response to the challenge posed by the passage of time itself and the inevitable ageing or wearing out (*vieillissement*) of what is so astonishingly new, fresh, original that it seems an irruption of the eternal into time. The challenge for him was to know how to age, how to repeat many times—whether an event, an idea, a spiritual experience, a grace—while remaining faithful to the first, original time, without losing the astonishment and the newness. What he called the problem of "temporal insertion" required a combination of genius and patient craft, insight and practice, interior memory and skill.[17]

16. Péguy, "Un poète l'a dit," 820–21.

17. For more discussion of Péguyan repetition that goes beyond Deleuze's interpretation, see Riquier, "Péguy, 'Bergsonien,'" 171–77. And for thought-provoking

Péguy's repetition is the opposite of what we usually mean when we speak of someone "endlessly beating the same old drum," and is indeed meant to counteract just that kind of repetition, the endlessly stale verbiage that inundates modern "news" and modern life. His writing does not simply go over the same worn paths, only taking us back to where we began; the movement is not linear, but nor is it simply circular. As Maurice Blanchot observed in regard to the unique rhythm of Péguy's prose: "What we call repetition is actually the indefinite return of a form that seeks to grow through insistence, through its alliance with duration, through the fact that it imposes itself and, by dint of patience and length, is drawn from something else to become more than itself."[18] One might think of the pattern of Péguy's writing as an ever-deepening spiral, rather than a straight line; when we are brought back to the point, it is with enhanced insight.

In turning from questions of style to content (with the proviso that these are not easily separated in Péguy), the ostensible subject of the two *Notes*, a defense of Bergson's philosophy, might appear to be very specific. Yet, while it would be overly dramatic to claim that Péguy, as if with a presentiment of his imminent death, took the opportunity to write a sort of literary testament, it is certainly the case that in the *Notes* he addresses *all* of the questions most central to his thought; hence a major reason for my choice of this particular prose work for translation. However, it would not do justice to the careful orchestration manifest in the *Notes* to regard the discussion of Bergson merely as a convenient hook on which Péguy hangs themes that preoccupy him but have little to do with Bergson. It does become clear that the subject of Bergson is a kind of springboard for the exploration of themes central to Péguy's thought that seem to draw us far away from Bergson; but the way that Péguy keeps returning to Bergson, just when it seems he has been abandoned entirely, demonstrates that he wants his larger explorations to be seen as creative applications of Bergson's thought, which go further than Bergson himself does, yet remain tied to his leading ideas. This demonstration of the importance of Bergson to our thinking about the most important questions, both timely and timeless, thus only constitutes further evidence in defense of his philosophy as philosophy.

---

discussions of the theological implications, see Cunningham, *Genealogy of Nihilism*, chapter 8, especially 197–208; Milbank, "'There's always one day which isn't the same as the day before'"; Pickstock, *Repetition and Identity*, 85–107.

18. Quoted in Roe, *The Passion of Charles Péguy*, 203.

Further, the profound suggestiveness of Bergsonian philosophy in Péguy's hands for understanding both the spiritual desolation of modernity and the temporal-eternal tension of Christianity, with the consequent interplay of sin, grace, and freedom enacted within history, is meant to support his claim that Bergson is Christianity's best modern philosophical ally. That perennial question of the relation between faith and philosophy is thus a primary theme of Péguy's *Notes;* but there is an astonishing wealth of other themes as well, awaiting the discovery of the attentive reader, open to the "singular journey" that follows.

An Overview of the Text

There can be no substitute, in the form of a close textual commentary, for the reader's own journey through the text. Péguy's work is especially resistant to any interpretation that might pretend to stand in its place because of the peculiar power of his style, which is inseparable from his meaning, and indeed *is* in a real sense the meaning itself. Yet although vehement in his own dismissal of the "baseness" of much scholarly representation of difficult creative works in the form of scientific analysis and commentary, which often just caters to the laziness of readers, he was, as we shall see, willing to affirm the importance of "signposts" along the way of a traveller's journey—whether the journey on foot from Paris to Chartres, or the journey of faith itself, or the journey through a significant text. As we shall also see, he was willing to erect such signposts himself in his commentary on Corneille's text, *Polyeucte*. It is in the spirit, then, of pointing to some signposts that might prove helpful to the reader in moving through the *Notes* that I offer the following remarks. To repeat, however, the signposts should not be taken as markers succeeding each other in a straight, linear path; the reader will come back to them more than once.

The First Note

The primary concern of the *Note on Bergson* is *the relationship between Bergson and philosophy*. Péguy, like Nietzsche or Dostoevsky, is an agonistic thinker for whom ideas enter into an arena of combat or duel (his writing is suffused with military imagery), and are frequently personified through identification with a particular individual. It is no surprise, then, that his treatment of Bergson's relation to philosophy takes the form of a defense of Bergson from the attack of a philosophical rationalism inherited from Descartes and personified particularly by Julien Benda. The defense of Bergson is engaged on three principal fronts.

1) *The nature of philosophy.* Péguy argues that the philosophical enterprise itself is illuminated by Bergson's idea and practice of *approfondissement*, "deepening." Philosophy is not a matter of systematizing reality in a once-and-for-all geographical map that is exhaustively complete and true, to the exclusion of other systems as false. It is, rather, an exploratory venture, or a plurality of ventures, which yield different discoveries about the inexhaustibly complex nature of reality. It is more akin to geology than geography; the only worthwhile discoveries are those achieved through penetrating as deeply as possible into the particular aspect of reality grasped by the original insight of the explorer. In the ensuing contestation of philosophies, there are no "winners" and "losers," at least among the true philosophers, who are true to themselves; there is only the contest nobly engaged, in which each contestant measures itself against the others by displaying itself as it most profoundly *is*. Cartesian rationalism, then, is not *the* form of philosophy itself, but one possibility among others, and it is precisely Bergson's thought that enables us to realize the diversity of the philosophical enterprise.

This dethroning of Cartesian rationalism as the only form that philosophy can take opens up the space for Péguy's affirmation of the cognitive value of passion, emotion, and intuition in the human exploration of reality, and therefore of the value of literature for philosophy,[19] a value he proceeds to demonstrate not only by references to Greek tragedy and Homeric epic in the first *Note*, but also by his own use of Corneille's *Polyeucte* in the second.

2) *A critique of "intellectualism."* This critique identifies the only "losers" in the great philosophical contest: those "intellectuals" (from whose number he seems to exempt Benda himself) who do not really think but merely pass on ready-made ideas, substituting their lazy mediocrity for the courage and creativity of the true philosopher. The attack against Bergson mounted by the intellectuals relies on the ready-made distinction, dear to romantics and anti-romantic classicists alike, between reason and passion, leading to the truism that reason is clear

---

19. This value is given full philosophical elaboration in Martha Nussbaum's *Upheavals of Thought* (especially Part 1), which, like Péguy, points to the primacy in this regard of ancient Greek tragedy.

while passion, emotion, intuition are obscure, if profound. It is again a Bergsonian concept, that of the "ready-made" (*tout fait*) as distinct from the "being-made" (*en faisant*), that illuminates the crucial difference between philosophy and ideology, the philosopher and the intellectual, and more generally, between the authentic and inauthentic human being. In his powerful critique of the ready-made ideas of ready-made people in the ready-made modern world, Péguy stands with Nietzsche's call to "become who you are" and Kierkegaard's observation that we are "born original, yet it comes to pass that we die copies." Yet, again drawing on Bergson, Péguy also shows how the habitual embracing of the ready-made is an inevitable feature of the universal law of *vieillissement* (ageing, withering, hardening) that pervades life itself, material, mental, and even spiritual, due to the irreversibility of time. It is Bergson's philosophy, according to Péguy, that reveals the metaphysical dimension of the distinction between authentic and inauthentic existence.

3) An analysis of the "rational" method of Descartes. Passing from the ready-made Cartesianism of the intellectuals to a true philosopher, Descartes himself, Péguy offers a remarkable analysis of Descartes's *Discourse on Method*, revealing above all, in a manner that anticipates Heidegger's analysis in *Being and Time*, the *already founded* character of Descartes's finding of reality through his method. As Péguy puts it: "Experience did not come out to meet him only at the beginning of the more particular things; it came out to meet him at the beginning of the beginning." Yet Péguy then goes on to say "it doesn't matter. Descartes, in the history of thought, will always be that French cavalier who set off with such a dashing step."[20] In his frankly admiring affirmation of Descartes's audacity and his genius, Péguy illustrates his Bergsonian vision of philosophies in a competition in which the important thing is not who is right or wrong, who wins and loses, but to enter the contest and to bring to it, with courage and genius, the insight one has been given to offer. Descartes's focus on the habitual disorder of human thought brought about a philosophical revolution; while Bergson's focus on the habitual itself promises an even more comprehensive revolution.

20. See below, 58.

The Second Note

The primary concern of the *Note on Descartes* is *the relationship of Bergson to Christianity*. Again in accord with the agonistic character of Péguy's thought, this concern takes the form of a defense of Bergson, this time against the theological rationalism represented by early-twentieth-century neo-Thomists such as Jacques Maritain. Maritain, like Benda, viewed Bergson's thought as giving priority to feeling over intellect, and as therefore detrimental to a Christian faith able to understand and present itself in a way that does justice to the highest demands of reason.[21] Those worried about the popularity of Bergson among young Catholic seminarians in France took Maritain's criticism as justification for the placing of his works on the *Index*. In response, Péguy sets himself the task of showing that it is precisely Bergsonian concepts that are most helpful to a Christian faith seeking understanding; most helpful among the modern philosophers, certainly, and in at least one crucial regard, more helpful than Thomas Aquinas. I say "Bergsonian concepts" because it becomes increasingly clear in this second *Note* that Péguy is using Bergsonian language to develop and express his own thought, or as he would put it, "going further" than Bergson himself does in certain directions (itself perhaps the most appropriate way to remain faithful to Bergson's own thought). He discusses four principal ways in which Bergsonian concepts illuminate Christian understanding.

1) *The proper approach of the Christian to intellectual engagement with the non-Christian is illuminated by Bergsonian "approfondissement."* Julien Benda makes a reappearance at the beginning of this second *Note*, not only as an invisible opponent as in the first *Note*, but as a character, the interlocutor of another character, Péguy himself. This time it is not his Cartesian rationalism that is most significant, but his Jewishness, and the fact that he is one of the few, along with Péguy himself, who really "knows what he is talking about" when he talks about Bergson. While Bergson is in the background and is supposedly the subject of the discussion as the two men go for a walk together in the Latin Quarter, Péguy's actual focus is on one (himself) as the personification of Christian sensibility

---

21. Maritain's criticism of Bergson was first expressed publicly in a series of lectures given at the Institut Catholique de Paris on "La philosophie de M. Bergson et la philosophie chrétienne," in 1913, and published in 1914 as *La philosophie bergsonienne*. For an English-language version of this critique, see Maritain, *Bergsonian Philosophy and Thomism*.

and experience and the other (Benda) as a personification of Jewish sensibility and experience. Péguy notes what they have in common—their interest in Bergson and their deep unease at France's unthinking slide into modernity—but his discussion has much more to do with differences, differences that have deep roots in their traditions.

Like the moving portrait-memoir elsewhere in his writing of Jewish fellow-Dreyfusard Bernard Lazare,[22] these pages devoted to the Jewish background of his interlocutor should dispel any thought that Péguy shared the anti-Judaism current among the nationalist right in France at this time. They demonstrate, rather, an application of Bergsonian *approfondissement*, allowing and encouraging a deepening of what the other truly *is*, just as one moves more deeply and faithfully into one's own identity. This is not "identity politics" as now conceived, with its endless resentful claims and counter-claims against others, but a different sort of contest that Péguy has in mind. Bergsonian *approfondissement*, whether in the realm of philosophy or religion, entails for Péguy a confrontation with others best expressed in the image of the duel. His discussion of the duel as a measured confrontation between equals displaying what they truly are in contradistinction to the confrontation in which the goal is simply to dominate the other might seem excessively idealized when he applies it to two types of warfare throughout history, and especially when he applies it to the differences between French and German approaches to waging war. When his discussion moves from the level of politics and war to the contest of philosophies and religions, however, we can see the unfolding of a suggestive metaphysical pluralism, in which mutual measuring and especially self-measuring rather than domination is the intent. For Péguy, the encounter of religions is not a matter of a zero-sum confrontation, in which one vision of reality wins at the expense of the other, or replaces the other; instead, different visions measure themselves against each other by being themselves what they are at their best, and allowing the others to be what they truly are at their best. Such mutual measuring does not, however, preclude the possibility of persuasion or conversion, as we shall see.

Thus, in addition to the *repetitive* rhythm of Péguy's thought, its *dialogic* nature should also be emphasized. For Péguy, as for Dostoevsky, the truth and power of an idea can only be measured insofar as it takes on life through becoming incarnate in a time and place, thereby entering

---

22. Péguy's account of Bernard Lazare is found in "Notre Jeunesse," 57-65.

into the arena of other competing idea-incarnations. The dialogue of ideas, whereby they measure themselves against each other, is thus also a dialogue of persons, whether actual (Benda, Maritain) or fictional.

Péguy's movement into a lengthy interpretation of Corneille's tragedy, *Polyeucte*, is explicable in light of this affirmation of metaphysical polyphony. In the confrontation between the noble pagan, Severus, and the newly converted noble Christian, Polyeucte, Péguy sees the consummate artistic expression of how the non-Christian should be faced by the Christian (as the reader will see, he also sees it in the historical confrontation between the French King Louis IX and the Muslim Sultan of Egypt, Baibars, during the Seventh Crusade). This confrontation of equals, equally respectful of each other, to the point of solicitude, illustrates a metaphysical polyphony that is *not*, however, a mere relativism. Péguy (again like Dostoevsky) is unapologetically emphatic about the Christian voice being the finally true one. But he is equally emphatic that the Word, in taking on flesh, gave itself up to the temporal process of reading and misreading, understanding and misunderstanding, and above all, endless dialogue, which cannot finally persuade by attempting to foreclose on or to finalize the free consciousness of the other. According to him, such an attempt would not only violate human freedom, but also the operation of divine grace.[23] In the contest of the Christian with the non-Christian, Péguy affirms the practice of immanent critique, although he himself would call it the practice of winning not only for oneself or even for God, but also for the other, so that a crack is opened in the armor of the other's habitual consciousness, which might allow for the penetration of grace.

2) The operation of grace and human opposition to grace is illuminated by the Bergsonian critique of habit. Péguy has already drawn on Bergson's distinction between the "ready-made" (*tout fait*) and "being-made" (*en faisant*) in the first *Note*; but in the second *Note* he applies the concept with a comprehensiveness and depth that goes beyond Bergson. Compelling in its rhetorical power though the entire *Note* is, it is perhaps most compelling in the pages that Péguy devotes to the (literally) deadening effect of habit. At the corporeal level, habit signifies the unavoidable human

---

23. Péguy's upholding of a pluralistic dialogism that yet is not relativism, beautifully expressed in his comments on Corneille's *Polyeucte* in this second *Note*, bears comparison with Mikhail Bakhtin, who points to Dostoevsky's refusal to "finalize the free consciousness" even of his own fictional characters with whom he disagrees (for instance, Ivan Karamazov, in *The Brothers Karamazov*). See *Problems of Dostoevsky's Poetics*, 78–100, 251–66, 270–72.

subjection to the irreversibility of time, as the repeated habitual gradually replaces the living life of the human being. Péguy's evocation of the rigidifying effect, unto death itself, of habit must stand as one of the most original accounts of a biological phenomenon. Yet his primary concern is with death at another level, the spiritual death of a soul impervious to the "moistening" of grace. Péguy's discussion of habit and grace might be viewed as a Bergsonian unpacking of Leonard Cohen's lines in his poem-song, "Anthem," about there being a "crack" in everything, which is just how the light gets in. But what of those whose habit-generated armor is so complete that there is no crack? While showing that Bergson's critique of habit can best illuminate the meaning of the traditional Christian teaching that spiritual death is a "hardening" and the final rejection of repentance is a final hardening,[24] here again Péguy goes beyond Bergson. In his *Creative Evolution*, Bergson had consigned matter to the process of inevitable entropy, but had posited another principle at work in life, the *élan vital*, which in its upward ascent ensures the overcoming by the soul, if not the body, of ageing and death (*vieillissement*). Péguy, however, in this *Note* especially, makes clear why he repudiated *Creative Evolution* as conceding too much to the modern belief in progress. As he insists against Bergson, the soul too falls into habit and grows old. There might be hope in the face of this reality, but there is no quasi-automatic overcoming thanks to a salvific *élan vital*.

Against Bergson's concession to a progressive modernity, Péguy observes that it is precisely modernity that is most impervious to grace, impervious in a way that pre-Christian antiquity was not, because centuries of Christianity have turned even grace itself into a habit. While *individuals* might still be open to moistening by grace, modern post-Christian *culture* is not, not in the way that ancient culture was open to its eruption (this is why, according to Péguy, Corneille sets his *Polyeucte* in the ancient Roman empire). Divine grace itself is subject to the conditions of temporality, and therefore *vieillissement*.

3) *Bergson's philosophy of time—particularly the ideas of "vieillissement" and the "presence of the present"—illuminates three further fundamental concerns of Christianity.*

i) The problem of "temporal insertion" as unavoidable for Christianity because of its incarnational nature: "et homo factus est." The vulnerability of grace itself to the wearing-out effect of time is, for Péguy, one

---

24. This notion of "hardening" appears to be based on Péguy's reading of Paul in Romans 2:5.

implication of Christ's taking on of human nature, "without any cheating"; another, to which his reflection proceeds, is the vulnerability of sanctity to this process. Péguy's particular admiration for Joan of Arc is a consistently strong feature of his life and thought, evident long prior to his conversion. One reason for this was her embodiment of a sanctity characterized by an aura of youthfulness; for, according to him, sanctity, while remaining sanctity, can nevertheless appear worn-out, withered. Sanctity, like heroism or genius, must find ways to renew itself temporally through a continual return to its source.

Péguy's meditation on Joan of Arc does not shy away from the perennial question: How is Joan's taking up of the sword against the English invaders compatible with Christ's own non-resistance to violence? Again he points to the incarnation; Christ's taking on of humanity "without any cheating" implies (as has been noted) that he gives himself over to the inevitable temporal process of understanding and misunderstanding, interpretation and misinterpretation, reading and misreading—above all, in the modern period, to the continual skeptical interrogation of enlightened critics, so that his trial and crucifixion are never-ending. He also gives himself over to the unavoidable limitations of historical time and place. Jesus is a saint, the "first" among the saints; but not necessarily the comprehensive model for all saints everywhere and at all times. As Péguy puts it, rejoining now the concept of polyphonic *approfondissement,* Jesus allows the other saints *to be what they are,* in the manner most appropriate to their own time and place, which might entail even their taking up the sword. Péguy's reflection on the temporal dimension and therefore diversity of sanctity offers also a fresh insight into the question of Christianity and just war.

ii) *The nature of the passage from Hebrew prophecy to Christ's fulfillment of prophecy.* Péguy here addresses the question of how the relationship between Hebrew prophecy and the event of Christ should be understood, noting the general failure to understand it properly by treating the connection as a chronological and causal one, wherein the prophets predict the future and the Gospels put those predictions into the past tense. Drawing on what he considers Bergson's liberation of the present from domination by the future and past tenses of time, Péguy locates the key to the relationship between Hebrew prophecy and Christ in that "secret point" of the present in which the passage happens. He identifies this secret point with the annunciation to Mary, the final instant of promise and *at the same time* the first instant of the keeping of the promise; an end that is simultaneously a beginning, the two held together in the secret point of the present. Here, in this secret point, we come as close as we ever will to that event or happening (*événement*), which in Péguy's thought is that first source containing already the entire series of repetitions, akin to Monet's first water lily, but here the departing point for so many *Ave Marias*, including all those Joan of Arc would say.

iii) The theological virtue of hope. In the second of the trilogy of long poem-discourses devoted to Joan of Arc, "The Portal of the Mystery of Hope," Péguy has God speak (through Madame Gervaise) at the outset in a manner that is, well, surprising: "Faith doesn't surprise me. / It's not surprising . . . / Charity . . . that doesn't surprise me. / It's not surprising . . . / But hope . . . that is something that surprises me. Even me."[25] That humans can nevertheless hope is "surprising" to God; it is also what God loves the best, for it is, Péguy argues in this second *Note*, the Christian virtue most indispensable to the other two, faith and charity. This indispensability is cast, again, in Bergsonian language: hope, which he personifies as a child, is the primary weapon available to human beings against the *vieillissement* that pervades life because it is the great *dis-habituator*. Its capacity to penetrate the protective armor built up by habit creates space for grace, for the freedom to receive grace, for living life itself; it interrupts the inexorable decline into spiritual death. For Péguy, Bergson's philosophy offers hope, not because of any *élan vital*, as evoked in the temporal progressivism of his *Creative Evolution*, but because he reveals in his philosophy of time the metaphysical basis of the present by fixing on and never letting go of the "presence of the present." In thus liberating the present from the enslavements of the past and the future, from being merely a middle term between the past and the future, he also liberates human freedom and life itself. In placing human beings *in the present*, Bergson's philosophy actually reinstalls them in the "only situation and position that is Christian," for they are put back into "the precarious and transitory, and into that state of undress, which is truly the human condition."[26] The same philosophy that the Catholic Church is about to place on the *Index* is, according to Péguy, the one modern philosophy that restores the possibility of Christianity.

4) What must be resisted in modernity, and why, by all who wish to avoid spiritual death is illuminated by Bergson's philosophy of time.

---

25. Péguy, *The Portal of the Mystery of Hope*, 3–6.
26. See below, 204.

Responding successfully here and now to the challenge of "temporal insertion" required, in Péguy's view, as clear an understanding as possible of the temporal situation, which he most frequently characterizes by the word "modern." Throughout both *Notes*, Péguy's creative application of Bergsonian concepts takes always two directions: towards a re-thinking, or better, re-memoration, of Christianity, and towards a critique of modernity meant to shed light on the darkness of its spiritual desolation. Like certain other Christian critics of modernity (one thinks of Dostoevsky, or more recently, Ivan Illich), Péguy sees it not as a series of more or less accidental and rather isolated developments of an external nature (especially technological and political), but as a whole civilizational paradigm that is profoundly anti-Christian while at the same time partially a stepchild of Christianity.

What is most unique about the analysis of modernity that he develops in the second *Note* is his focus on its metaphysical basis in a certain understanding of time. According to him, the whole "mechanism" of modernity—economic, political, psychological—hinges on a certain making disappear the present, motivated above all by the desire for tranquility. In this focus on the modern eclipse of the present moment, Péguy draws again on Bergson's philosophy of time. When thinking of trenchant critics of modernity, Bergson does not usually come to mind, but his concepts of the presence of the present and time as duration become, in Péguy's hands, the basis of an analysis of the modern totality that is at once comprehensive and penetrating. The modern eclipse of the present, or what Péguy will call its "rigidification," is for him the key to the generation of a set of interlocking structures, material and intellectual, that have their most reductive but also most powerful expression in the undisputed mastery of money in the modern age. For Péguy, money is the modern name of the Antichrist.

Péguy's criticism of the "devout party"

Most of the defense of Bergson's philosophy as an ally rather than an opponent of Christian faith is directed, in a positive manner, toward the ways in which it illuminates Christian understanding. Towards the end of the second *Note*, however, Péguy launches an attack directly on what he calls the "devout party," those intellectual Catholics, such as Maritain, who style themselves modern-day "scholastics" for whom Thomas

Aquinas, above all, is the theological touchstone and in whose name they dismiss Bergson. Péguy makes it clear that his quarrel is not with Thomas. In keeping with his refusal to reduce competing metaphysics to a zero-sum, either-or, judgment, he does not hold that Thomas Aquinas was wrong or has been replaced or superseded by Bergson; Thomas is, after all, "a great saint of the past, a great doctor of the past, a great theologian of the past." However, he is "without a hold in the present, without a way in...."[27] This lack of "a way in" is not merely because Thomas was not familiar with modern science, but because he was not required to come to grips with modernity itself as a spiritual phenomenon; and the eternally-temporal/temporally-eternal nature of Christianity obliges it always to consider its eternal truths in relation to its temporal situation, just as the temporal reality must be considered in light of the eternal truths.

Péguy argues that the entire approach of the new scholasticism to restoring Thomist theology betrays a fundamental, if inadvertent, acquiescence in the modern paradigm, precisely because it is not sufficiently Bergsonian in its thinking; and in failing to grasp the complexity of the problem of temporal insertion, to give the temporal its due, it betrays the incarnational dimension of Christianity. Moreover, the devout party's anti-liberal stance, dismissive of "freedom" and "justice" because of the way in which these terms have become shallow republican slogans, fails to recognize that freedom and justice are *also* Christian imperatives. Focusing on the eternal, they give up the temporal field, the one on which the battle must be fought, to those powerful modern forces arrayed against the spirit. Moreover, and this is where Péguy is most vehement in his criticism, they turn their guns[28] against the one who could, at this point in history, be most helpful to the side of the spirit.

The urgent tone of Péguy's rhetoric as he castigates those who divide the weakened spiritual forces of modernity reflects his sense of crisis. But, though writing on the cusp of World War I, the crisis he identifies goes far beyond the threat of war, to encompass the destruction of human nature itself. In the face of a vast mechanism so hostile to the human spirit, unprecedentedly powerful in its expression, as money, Péguy insists on the need for a common front: philosophy (in the true sense) *and* faith, Athens *and* Jerusalem, wisdom *and* sanctity, Jew *and* Christian, Catholic *and* Protestant. Needless to say, this is not a call for a facile synthesis,

---

27. See below, 221.

28. Péguy's writing is so suffused with military imagery that sometimes the commentator cannot help using it.

since in the case of each spiritual form a proper *approfondissement* is presupposed.

Péguy's "confession"

In the final pages of the second *Note*, Péguy sets up a dialogue between himself and a Catholic Monsignor about the *Index*. This is a return to the original issue that precipitated these *Notes on Bergson and Descartes*. It signals also Péguy's move towards the *approfondissement* of his own Catholicism. The turn away from the critique of modernity seems also to be a turn back to his own "corner of the earth," as he refers to the catechism of his childhood (in which there was no mention of the *Index*). In these final pages, the tone is no longer apocalyptic, nor even stridently agonistic. The more gentle Péguy in dialogue with the representative of official Catholicism is unfailingly respectful, even at times affectionate and lighthearted. This might seem surprising, given the combative default mode of his writing and his fraught relationship with the Catholic Church even after his conversion, culminating in his own coming under investigation by the Vatican.[29] Péguy's demeanor in the dialogue is that of a humble, if obstinate, child of the Church, wishing to get beyond the controversies of the day to what Catholicism *is*, and also what it is in distinction from the Judaism and Protestantism known to him from close personal acquaintances. As he hints, the dialogue is intended as his own partial *profession de foi*. Given the incarnational emphasis in his understanding of Christianity, the reader should not be surprised that the subject of the discussion is less intellectual than corporeal, less about ideas than about a way, the way of life symbolized by the road from Paris to Chartres, with its signposts for those who walk it as Péguy did.

---

29. The inquiry into Péguy's orthodoxy, begun in June 1914, was probably precipitated by his first *Note* on Bergson, published earlier the same year. However, there was already the difficulty posed by Péguy's loyalty to his pre-conversion civil marriage to a woman from a staunchly secular and republican family; his acceptance of her refusal to have their children baptized, or their marriage solemnized in the Church, led to his own exclusion from participation in communion. For an account of Maritain's ultimately unhelpful role in these personal difficulties, see Le Guay, "Péguy et Maritain," 182–84.

Chronology

1873 (Jan. 7): Charles Péguy was born in Orléans, France. His father, a veteran of the Franco-Prussian war, died the same year, and Charles was raised by his mother and grandmother, who were of peasant background and had no formal education.

1894: Péguy was admitted to the École Normale Supérieure for studies in philosophy. In the same year, Alfred Dreyfus, an officer of Jewish background in the French army was found guilty of treason, in passing secret documents to the Germans.

1895: This year marked a "conversion" to socialism, which he said in a letter to a friend was "perhaps the greatest event of his moral life."

1897: Péguy founded a socialist circle at the École Normale (which excluded Christian socialists). In the same year, he completed work on his first major poem-play, *Jeanne d'Arc*, and married Charlotte Baudoin. Due to the marriage, he was required to leave his formal academic program at the École Normale.

1898: Péguy assumed a leadership role among the "young socialists" protesting the verdict against Dreyfus and calling for his exoneration. In the same year, he founded the socialist publishing house and bookstore, Librarie Georges Bellais (using money inherited by his wife); and he began to sit in on the courses of Henri Bergson at the École Normale.

1900: With the failure of the Georges Bellais enterprise, Péguy established a new journal, which he published himself, *Cahiers de la quinzaine*. During the next several years, the journal published essays, reviews, poetry, and prose fiction by authors significant, or soon to be significant in French letters, including Romain Rolland, Jean Jaurès, André Suarès, and Péguy's own major writings. He continued to audit the courses of Bergson, who was now lecturing at the Collège de France. His regular attendance at Bergson's courses was maintained for several years, until the outbreak of World War I. These Friday lectures were, according to Péguy, the "best employed hour" of his week.

1905: In the wake of the Tangier coup involving the German Kaiser, Wilhelm II, Péguy believed war with Germany to be imminent, so much so that he interrupted work on the *Cahiers,* and prepared himself to be called up for active duty (he was in the reserves). Later resuming work on the *Cahiers,* he published his account of the crisis, *Notre Patrie*.

1907–8: During this period, as he confided to two close friends, Jacques Maritain and Joseph Lotte, Péguy "rediscovered" (*retrouvé*) Christian faith.

1910–12: These three years saw the publication of the three parts of Péguy's poetic trilogy centered on Joan of Arc: *Le Mystère de la charité de Jeanne d'Arc, Le Porche du mystère de la deuxième vertu, Le Mystère des saints Innocents.*

1912: Péguy (in company with the novelist Alain-Fournier) made the first of three annual pilgrimages on foot to the cathedral at Chartres in accomplishment of a vow for the healing of his seriously ill son, Pierre.

1914: Bergson's works were placed on the Roman Catholic *Index Librorum Prohibitorum* ("Index of Prohibited Books"). Péguy published his defense of Bergson, *Note sur M. Bergson et la philosophie Bergsonienne* in April of that year. He then worked on a continuation of the argument in the much longer *Note conjointe sur M. Descartes et la philosophie cartésienne,* which he abandoned in mid-sentence when he was called up in France's general mobilization for war. On September 5 he was killed at Villeroy by enemy fire on the eve of the Battle of the Marne. The *Note conjointe* was first published posthumously in 1924.

2

Note on Bergson
and the Bergsonian Philosophy

To the memory of our old teacher, M. Humbert,
who taught us such good philosophy at the Orléans lycée.

ALL THESE DEBATES THAT have arisen for the past two or three years about and for and against Bergson and the Bergsonian philosophy would have been greatly clarified (but was clarification wanted?) if they had consented to examine what we understand by intellectualism. They pretended to believe that the quarrel with intellectualism was a quarrel with *reason*, with *wisdom*, with *logic*. And with intelligence.

The philosophy of Bergson is almost as badly understood by its adversaries as by its partisans. And that says a lot. First, reason is not wisdom, and neither the one nor the other is logic. And the three taken together are not intelligence. These are three—and four—orders, three—and four—realms, and there are many others. Now, the revolution, the Bergsonian inspiration, did not consist in displacing these realms but in bringing about in them an interior transformation. And it is not surprising that this philosophy, which is a philosophy of the interior, ends not in displacing the realms through an exterior movement, through an external translation, through an extrinsic substitution, but in renewing them, deepening them, bringing them to themselves by effecting an internal revolution.

NOTE ON BERGSON AND THE BERGSONIAN PHILOSOPHY

The Bergsonian philosophy is not a physics of transfer, a mechanics, a kinematics of translation. It is an organics. And even a re-organics. And it is a dynamics.

There are orders, there are realms, there are *kingdoms*, there are disciplines. There is faith; there is love; there is art; there is philosophy; there is ethics; there is science. And doubtless there are others. And it would even be necessary to say that there are not only realms: there are provinces. And they are perhaps as separate as the realms. For there is perhaps nothing as contrary to the plastic arts as the musical arts. And there is perhaps nothing as contrary to the mathematical "sciences" as the natural "sciences." And within *ethics*, I would perhaps set apart a *civics*, which would have my preference.

Bergsonism is not a geography, it is a geology.

It is not a matter of whether Brittany is really Provence and Queen Anne really King René. It is a matter of Lorraine being truly Lorraine and the Île de France being yet more fully the Île de France and truly being the heart and the head.

Bergsonism is not at all a philosophy of metathesis and metonymy.

Or, to speak in Platonic (and pre-Platonic) terms, it is not a question of whether the one is really the other. It is a question of deepening the one, and deepening the other.

Bergsonism does not make compartmentalized maps.

Just as the revolutions in anatomy and physiology in the natural sciences did not consist in opposing the animal *kingdom* to the vegetable *kingdom* or *vice versa*, but in striving *at the same time* in both disciplines for a certain reorienting of thought in relation to two parallel realities, so the Bergsonian revolution in philosophy has not consisted in opposing or displacing the various realms of knowledge and being. It has consisted in striving *at the same time* within all the realms, the orders, the disciplines for a certain reorienting of thought in relation to these parallel realities.

We must thus not say that Bergsonism is a pathetic philosophy,[1] nor a philosophy of the pathetic, nor that it opposes the pathetic to logic or mathematics or science or reason or wisdom, nor that it tries or proposes

---

1. This is a reference to an anti-Bergsonian essay written by Julien Benda ("Une philosophie pathétique"), which was published by Péguy in 1913, in *Les Cahiers de la quinzaine*. Note also Péguy's use of "pathetic" (*le pathétique*) does not generally have the negative connotation of "pitiable," "inadequate," as in English, but reflects its ancient Greek etymology, pathos, i.e., suffering passion.

to substitute the pathetic for all this. It is from the inside of the pathetic that it operates, as at the same time from the inside of logic or mathematics. For there is an intellectualism of the pathetic, just as there is an intellectualism of logic, or mathematics, or all the others. And everywhere it is the same.

We must renounce this idea that the pathetic forms an inferior domain. It is like the other domains, as in Molière, it is inferior when it is inferior, and it is not inferior when it is not inferior. It is not an exception to the general rules of rank. It is not inferior because it is the pathetic. It is inferior when it is of inferior, base quality. When it is a base pathetic. It is not inferior when it is not of base quality. One will never make me say that comedy is an inferior genre. As for tragedy, I confess that I know nothing human that is superior to the *pathetic* in Sophocles and for a demi-chorus from *Antigone* I would give the three *Critiques* preceded by a demi-*quarteron* of *Prolegomena*.² And by this I do not mean only, which is understood, that I would give them in regard to beauty, *sub specie pulchri*,³ but that I would give them away no less in regard to truth, to reality, *sub specie rei ac realitatis*.⁴ And I mean that there is in this *pathetic* infinitely more and otherwise than in that *critique* a *knowledge*, an analysis of nature, of human reality and fate.

We must renounce this idea that passion is murky (or obscure) and that reason is clear, that passion is muddled and reason is distinct.⁵ We all know passions that are clear as fountain-springs and reasons, on the contrary, that always get tangled up in their own baggage train. One cannot even say that passion is rich and that reason and wisdom are poor, for there are passions as flat as billiard tables, and wisdom(s) and reasons as full and ripe and heavy as grapes.

---

2. *Le quarteron*, an old French term meaning an "insignificant band" or alternatively "a quarter of a cent." The three *Critiques* and the *Prolegomena* refer to the major philosophical works of the German philosopher, Immanuel Kant.

3. "From the perspective of beauty." Péguy frequently injects Latin (and also Greek) words and phrases into his French text; this is in part a reflection of his classical education at the École Normale Supérieure, and in no small measure an implicit protest against the modernizing French educational reforms of the Third Republic, beginning in 1902, which aimed at replacing the classical humanities with the sciences and social sciences (history and sociology, in particular).

4. "from the perspective of the real and reality."

5. *Claire* and *distincte* were, of course, Cartesian criteria of truth; and it is Descartes whom Julien Benda upholds against Bergson's "pathetic" philosophy of feeling.

We should renounce once and for all this idea of constituting once and for all hierarchies of the different orders, the different domains, which would be not only ranked but fixed in their ranking. This solution is a solution of laziness, this fixation is a fixation of laziness. It is in the interior of the different orders, the different domains, that we must seek, search after, recognize hierarchies, subordinations, parallel coordinations. Of value, merit, clarity, obscurity, distinctness, depth. Hierarchies that are parallel, comparable, corresponding, and probably intercommunicative.

Here again some or other people make a mistake, or rather deceive. But it is the same mistake and the same deception. Instead of acknowledging that there are profound passions and superficial passions, the novelists want it to be passion as such, which is itself, in its essence, profound. They want that it has only to show itself, to be passion, in order to be profound. Because they themselves want to have only to show themselves, to treat, even just to speak of passion, in order to be profound and mysterious. And on the other hand, against this the anti-novelists, the critics, want it to be criticism as such, that is in itself, in its essence, clear. They want that it has only to show itself, to be criticism, in order to be clear. Because they themselves want to have only to show, to treat, even just to speak of criticism, in order to be clear and enlightening. But I, who have no system and who for this reason will not make my fortune (even intellectually), am compelled to confess that I see criticism that is turbid and pathos that is exceedingly clear, just as I see criticism that is profound and pathos that is exceedingly superficial.

At bottom, the novelists would like only to have to be novelists in order to be profound. No, my children, it is necessary *as well* to be profound novelists. And the critics would like only to have to be critics in order to be clear. No, my good sirs. It is necessary *as well* to be clear critics.

At bottom, it is the same debate everywhere. It is the secret of the *situation characterizing history and sociology* and above all historians and sociologists themselves *in modern times*.[6] The historians want only to have to be historians in order to know the past. The sociologists want only to have to be sociologists in order to know human societies. One instant, your lordships. Knowledge of the past, and of societies, and of human beings is also necessary in this matter.

The poets are infinitely more reasonable (one expected as much); they acknowledge readily that it is not enough to write verses to be a poet.

6. Péguy's essay, "De la situation faite à l'histoire et à la sociologie dans les temps modernes" was published in the *Cahiers* in 1906.

And if they didn't acknowledge it, everybody would certainly acknowledge it for them.

It is as if it were enough to dress up as a soldier to be brave. So, it is not enough to dress up as a novelist and pathetician[7] to be profound. And it is not enough to dress up as a critic to be clear.

So it is necessary to cease attaching qualities and hierarchies to certain orders as if they were ready-made tunics, but pursue in parallel manner the search for these qualities and hierarchies, as they are, as they are given, without a ready-made idea, inside the different orders. And, so to speak, climb up the whole way within the different orders.

It is necessary to be stupid, it is necessary to not be systematic, and this also is indispensable in order *not to make* one's career: one must say what one sees. I see that the pathos of the Greeks and the French, being classic, is infinitely more clear than German critique, which is romantic. Or rather, the pathos of the Greeks and the French is clear and German critique is not. And the critique of the Greeks and the French, being classic, is profound, and German pathos, being romantic, is not.

Nothing is so lucid as the invocations and lamentations of *Antigone*. Nothing is so lucid as the stanzas of *Polyeucte*.[8] On the other hand, nothing is more profound than a Platonic analysis and critique, nothing is more profound than an analysis and critique of Pascal.

So let us cease attributing certain qualities to certain orders, like overcoats. Let us search instead in parallel manner within the different orders, and let us know how to recognize the analogous qualities.

Let us cease also to consider, in isolation from their context within the various orders, as contradictory in themselves qualities that are contradictory only according to the categories of the intellectuals. Where has one ever seen that the clear excludes the profound, or the profound excludes the clear? They exclude each other in textbooks, in didactic material, in educational manuals. They do not exclude each other in nature, nor in that other nature, which is grace. Neither in nature nor in that second and superior nature, which is the nature of grace. Isn't Homer, who is the greatest clarity, also the greatest depth? The elderly Priam at the feet of Achilles, who is, if I may be permitted to speak thus, the maximum of the pathetic and the classic and so to speak the maximum of the antique,

---

7. Péguy's French word here, *pathéticien*, is already a neologism.

8. Corneille's dramatic play *Polyeucte* (1642) will be the subject of extensive discussion by Péguy in the second *Note*.

being the maximum of antique supplication, doesn't he give us at once the maximum of clarity in the maximum of depth?

It is the romantics who invented the notion that it was necessary to be obscure in order to be profound, and that there was a ligature, a ready-made outfit, tying the turbid or obscure to the profound. And their contrived turbulence, their artificial agitation (intellectual), only ever allowed them to achieve superficial profundities. When Hugo followed his own nature, his classical genius, he was profound and clear. When he knocked himself out in order to be and while being a romantic, he suffered like a dog just to achieve a mysteriousness in plain brown wrapping paper.

(I do not wish to impassion the debate, and to make it personal, and to hurt anyone. But we have even at the *Cahiers,* a critic who is at the same time a novelist. I do not see, when he is a novelist, that he divests himself of clarity, and, when he is a critic, that he divests himself of his profundity.)[9]

As the romantics could not deny the clarity of the classics, they set about compensating by means of profundity. They wanted to make themselves specialists of profundity. But those who are profound never said to themselves they were going to be profound.

And they never said it to others.

Thus the romantics pretended that there was a contradiction in nature between the lucid and the profound, so that the classics being evidently clear, it was understood automatically that they were not profound. As though the verses of Racine most filled with light were not also the most mysterious.

The profound and the mysterious is not inevitably dark and tormented. Nothing is so pure as the fold of the mantle of the ancient prayer.

Of all the ideas that have ever taken the form of maxims, I believe that the most false is without doubt this: *for passion, everybody is good.* If I wanted to speak Christian language, I would say that not everybody is good even for sin. There is a choice, an election, even in regard to sin. The natures that are *good for sin* are of the same nature, the same order,

---

9. Péguy might be referring here to Romain Rolland.

as those that are good for grace. Both grace and sin are two operations of the same kingdom. Many are called, few are chosen. And outside there is an immense crowd, which as a whole is good for neither, neither sin nor grace. For sin and grace together are two operations of salvation, hermetically articulated one upon the other. And outside there is the immense crowd of those who are not even capable of sin, whom I would name the intellectuals or "intellectualists" in the order of sin; of grace; of salvation.

I am convinced that it is the same in all the orders and that there are very few beings who are good for happiness, as there are very few beings who are good for affliction. And outside, there is the immense crowd of beings who as a whole and from the same inclination, the same incapacity, the same sterility, the same infecundity, are good for neither happiness nor affliction. And whom I would name intellectuals in the order of happiness.

Very few are intended, for those who know their Christianity. And outside, there is this immense kingdom of dis-grace,[10] which consists in not even knowing what one is talking about.

It is this way with passion. Love is more rare even than genius. It is as rare as sanctity. And friendship is more rare than love. To say that for passion everybody is good is as false, and I would say also as foolish and as unimaginative and as hastily said, as to say: For sculpture everybody is good, or: For mathematical analysis everybody is good. There are intellectuals everywhere and there are intellectuals for everything. That is to say: there is an immense crowd of people who feel with *ready-made* feelings, in the same proportion as there is an immense crowd of people who think with *ready-made* ideas, and in the same proportion as there is an immense crowd of people who desire with *ready-made* wills, in the same proportion as there is an immense crowd of "Christians" who repeat mechanically the words of prayer. And one could go on for a long time passing through all the domains, and could say: in the same proportion as there is an immense crowd of painters who draw according to ready-made lines. There are as few painters who really look, as there are philosophers who think.

---

10. The use of a hyphen here and throughout this translation is meant to convey that Péguy's play on the French words *grace-disgrace* intends a more direct opposition between grace and what counters grace than would be conveyed by the more usual English meaning of disgrace as a matter of public shame. Péguy's use of the word does not, however, preclude the usual English sense.

This denunciation of a universal intellectualism, that is, a universal laziness consisting of always making use of the *ready-made* will have been one of the great conquests and the *instauratio magna*[11] of the Bergsonian philosophy. It is true that the immense majority of people think with ready-made ideas, with learned ideas. But it is also true, in the same way and everywhere, that the immense majority of people see with ready-made vision. With learned vision. There is a universal and, so to say, untiring laziness. It is work that tires, but laziness, tiredness does not tire. The denunciation of this laziness, this tiredness, this constant intellectualism lies at the threshold of the Bergsonian discovery.

One says to me: What is this "discovery" that consists only of denouncing an old habit? What is this new thing that only consists in denunciation and in revealing a hereditary flaw? What is this *positive* that consists in not falling into the *negative*? What is this *more* that consists simply in not falling into the *less*? What is this acquisition, this *conquest*, that consists in not losing the oldest territories?

And as for me, I ask: Do you know of many others? To prevent human beings from sliding down certain slopes, is this not the work of a giant? To prevent human beings from sliding down certain slopes of feeling, certain moral slopes, certain slopes of behavior, is this not the work and the greatest part of the secret of so much art and of the greatest morality? To unchain human beings, to prevent, to dis-habituate human beings from sliding down certain mental slopes, certain slopes of thought; if only one succeeded, let us be convinced that there we would have, we have had, the material, the object of a very great logic, a very great morality, a very great metaphysics. Freedom, which we say is the first good, is generally obtained only through an operation of unchaining. Why would the real, which is perhaps a more profound good, not also be obtained through an operation of unchaining? And why would an operation of unchaining not be an operation of extreme importance? The French Revolution was an operation, an enormous historical event, because it seemed to unchain the world from a seeming political servitude. And finally the whole immense apparatus of the incarnation and redemption, was it not set up in order to unchain human beings, in order to prevent them from *remaining fallen* into enslavement, and I almost want to say,

---

11. "Great Renewal," which is the original Latin title of the work by the English philosopher Francis Bacon (1561–1626), in which he proposes the method of "induction" for scientific inquiry.

into the habit of original sin? For sin had become above all an immense habit. And slavery is, so to speak, the most habitual habit.

We must attend, moreover, to this expression: the *ready-made* [*tout fait*]; if it recurs constantly, as is natural and to be expected, in Bergson's philosophy, it is made to recur in two quite sensibly different senses, which I do not think have been sufficiently distinguished. When Bergson opposes the *ready-made* to the *being-made* [*se faisant*] (I would like to know how he could have spoken in other terms, and really, much lack of good will would be necessary not to recognize in the past participle and the present participle the heirs of two fine Greek semi-passive participles), he is setting up an opposition, recognizing a metaphysical tension pertaining to the order itself of duration [*la durée*], and emphasizing the opposition, the profound, essential, metaphysical tension, between the present and the future and the present and the past. This is a distinction pertaining to metaphysics. (It is this profound and chief Bergsonian idea that the present, the past, and the future are not only time but being itself. That they are not only a matter of chronology. That the future is not only the past for later. That the past is not only the future made old, the future inside time. But that creation, as soon as it passes, descends, falls from the future into the past through the ministration, the accomplishment of the present, changes not only in date but in being. That it changes not only according to the calendar, but in its nature. That the passage through the present is the taking on of another being. That it is the divestment of freedom and the putting on of memory.) However, when this same philosopher speaks of the *ready-made* in the sense of ready-made ideas, of ready-made thought, he uses the word in the same sense as one speaks of ready-made clothing as "off the rack" instead of "made to measure." It is a distinction of making, of process, of cutting, of technique. The Bergsonian philosophy wants us to think "to measure" and not "off the rack."

Especially as clothing "off the rack" is always second-hand clothing. It is new second-hand clothing rather than old second-hand clothing. But it is still second-hand clothing. It is *for the occasion* that it does the job, or is supposed to. This is not by a prior adaptation proper to it, a prior cutting out proper to it; not at all by a unique adaptation, an intended cutting out.

It is one of the great sources of sophism and error, or, to remain within our simile, I will say: It is one of the largest retail outlets of sophism and error, this negligence, this omission, this failure to consider, I mean this negligence that consists in not considering, in neglecting to consider that the wholly "new" is not necessarily the wholly "original." Much misunderstanding arises from this, and many mistakes of judgment, many errors of judgment. It is generally believed that it is sufficient for an idea to be new in order to be original. It is believed that it is sufficient for an idea to be new to have never been served up before. What an error. It has been served up by its manufacturer. When a tree for a theatrical stage setting, when a theatrical love affair, comes straight from its manufacturer, it is all the same an old tree, all the same a ready-made tree, all the same merely of the theatre. For all its newness, it is not for that a real tree, a tree of the countryside. It is not for that a new tree in the world. This is not a question of different degrees, but of different orders. Homer is original this morning, and nothing is perhaps so old as today's newspaper. This is a question of nature and essence. Just as in Bergson's philosophy the future and ultimately the present do not differ from the past only chronologically, but essentially and metaphysically, so a ready-made idea is ready-made in itself and essentially. It is fabricated ready-made. A ready-made idea comes into the world like a tree of the theatre comes into the world, ready-made and a stage-set tree. It is all of cardboard, of wallpaper. It is totally alien to germination, to fecundity, to conception. There are people who reinvent, beings who relive, thoughts that reconceive again the oldest ideas. And there are people who *make* ideas that are *ready-made*. There are ideas that are ready-made *while they are being made*, BEFORE THEY ARE MADE, as ready-made overcoats are ready-made *while they are being made*, as stage-set trees are ready-made and stage-set trees *while they are being made*. It is a question of nature or of artifice. It is a question of grace or of dis-grace. Trees of the theatre are not trees of nature diminished, spent, grown old and no longer good for anything else. They are trees of another order. They are other trees. They are not natural trees flattened out on a frame. They are trees that came into the world flat. Thus, a ready-made idea comes into the world flat and ready-made.

"Is this all?" one will say to me. This is far from all. But I will say all the same that if there were only this and nothing to consider but this, even this would be of the utmost importance, and would make a great philosophy. Cartesianism is a great philosophy. Cartesianism is one of the three or four great philosophies of the world. Now what has made the fortune of the Cartesian philosophy? I am not saying this fortune is illegitimate. I am saying: What has made this fortune?

Let us leave aside the academic Pharisaisms, the solemn publication of textbooks, the re-editions of the collected works.[12] Let us leave aside the academic celebrations. Let us leave aside the official commemorations, and the centenaries, and the circumspections, and the false scholarly respects. All that also smacks of the ready-made, of ready-made ideas. Let us be Bergsonians, both in regard to the story of Cartesianism and the story of Bergsonism.

What has made the fortune so high and so great and so justifiable of the Cartesian philosophy? Those who have read the complete writings of Descartes beyond the explications of the textbooks know that all the fortune of Descartes and of the Cartesian philosophy has been made by four or five lines in the *Discourse on Method*. And that is all. And those four or five lines, those four or five phrases are precisely precepts for, so to speak, a mental ethic, some *anterior* principles of intellectual hygiene, rules of *method* finally, he says it himself, not principles or revelations or conclusions of a system. This is again, in a sense, a matter of unchaining and liberation. It is even also a denunciation. As the Bergsonian philosophy begins by being a denunciation of the *ready-made*, so the Cartesian philosophy began by being a denunciation of *disorder*. The Cartesian philosophy has been essentially a philosophy of order, as the Bergsonian philosophy is essentially a philosophy of reality. Whether *subsequently* Descartes succeeded in imposing order and even the idea of order, for always, on the thinking universe, and even on himself, that is another question, an ulterior question. Whether *subsequently* Bergson succeeded in imposing on the thinking universe, and even on himself, for always, respect for the purely real, that is another question, an ulterior question. They are human beings. Did they achieve, will they achieve, a total success? One does not see that philosophers are destined to succeed totally any more than Caesar or Napoleon. But it would be easy to demonstrate that Bergson is an infinitely better Bergsonian than Descartes was a good Cartesian. I see everywhere in Bergson concern for the purely real. And in Descartes I see very great disorders.

The *Discourse on Method*, or more exactly, *Discourse on the method of conducting one's reason well and of searching out* or of discovering *truth in the sciences*. It is a program, alas, and almost an electoral program. And it has been almost as little realized as an electoral program. When, instead of rereading the program, and especially the title of the program,

---

12. Another new edition of Descartes's collected works, the *Oeuvres complètes* in twelve volumes had been published in 1913 (Adam et Tannery).

and especially the beginning of the title of the program, we consider the results, what do we see? We see that Descartes was a great philosopher, a great metaphysician, a great mathematician, a great scientist. But great among others, of the same rank as others, of the same sort and same nature as others, of the same order as the others, of the same order of certainty and of the same order of work; not at all a man without peer, a man outside the bounds, a man to whom a method, suddenly and abruptly appearing in the world, delivered a secret that was infallible and totally certain. It is with this discourse on method as it is with the famous rules of Bacon.[13]

Bacon's tables have never brought about an invention or a discovery. There is no example of an invention or a discovery having been made by an official. Inventors and discoverers follow entirely different instincts; they pursue entirely different ventures. Inventors and discoverers have never been functionaries of the patent office. Bacon's tables have only ever served the professors who demonstrate how an invention (and a discovery, but that is always an invention), should have been made *after* it has been made. As for Bacon, he never invented anything, except the tables according to which others invent. He never discovered anything, except the tables according to which others make discoveries.

Or rather, the tables according to which others had invented, the tables according to which others had made discoveries.

Bacon's tables have only ever served the historians of inventions in explaining how inventions had been made *after* they had been made. And even how it was inevitable that they be made, and made thus. It was not that way at all. But the essential was that there be a history, and perhaps above all that there be historians.

Bacon's tables are perhaps made for the conductor. And for the inspector of conductors. They are certainly not made for the tram driver.

I will not say the same about Descartes. He himself invented. He himself made discoveries. However, the Descartes who invented, the Descartes who discovered, Descartes the philosopher, metaphysician, mathematician, physicist, physiologist, psychologist, and other things, was a philosopher and geometrician and mechanicist and physicist of genius who did not proceed directly from the *Discourse on Method*, who

---

13. The reference is to Francis Bacon's *Instauratio Magna*, where he explicates his "inductive" method of summoning the objects of scientific investigation to appear before the tables of the judicial court: the tables of presence, of absence, and of degrees.

was not in direct connection, and so to speak, continuing creation[14] with the *Discourse on Method*. Whatever he thought about it himself. He was a metaphysican in his rank, in his place, which was high, a geometer in his rank, a mechanicist in his rank, a physicist in his rank, among the greatest; not at all a metaphysician, a geometer deduced and continually deduced, not a metaphysician, a geometer, a mechanicist, a physicist upon whom a secret of method, suddenly appearing in the world, conferred this promised outward infallibility. And I see today that they are coming back to the hypothesis of Cartesian vortices in astronomy and in celestial mechanics and physics,[15] and I am truly happy about that, for it was a beautiful stroke of genius (of the *divining power* of genius), and I will be still more happy when they have come back to this in physics in general. But if they do come back to it (the German says: if they *will* come back to it), that will not be because the idea of the vortex is clear and distinct; it will be because it is more useful and will embrace more closely new aspects of physical reality. It will not be in accord with the *Discourse on Method* that they will readopt the hypothesis of Cartesian vortices. It will not even be in accord with Cartesian physics. It will be, if I may say so, in proportion to the physical, period. And for the sake of the physical, period. They will take up again the hypothesis of Cartesian vortices because it will better account for the facts, the observations, and the calculations that *start from* facts and observations. They will not take it up again as a matter of taste but because of its efficacy. One only ever takes up again what is efficacious. They will not take it up again because of its virtue but out of a great necessity. They will not take it up again in order to ensure orderly thought (after two centuries, and soon two and a half centuries, they have ended by realizing that the laws of attraction and universal gravity were generally applicable and perfectly calculable, but that the hypothesis itself of attraction at a distance and gravity at a distance was perfectly unthinkable, which is to say finally that Newton is metaphysically unthinkable). (For one can hardly see how an ether could be a perfect conductor of attraction and gravitation, could instantaneously *conduct* attraction and gravitation at a distance, could make

---

14. This might be an allusion to a distinction made by Bergson in his *Creative Evolution* (chapter 4) between the "continued creation" of Descartes, the action whereby God preserves in existence the world of creatures as already created, and his own concept of "continuing creation," which allows for evolutionary change.

15. *la mécanique et la physique célestes* are traditional terms for what would now be called astrophysics.

instantaneous transpositions of forces like "attraction" and "gravitation.") They will not take up the hypothesis of Cartesian vortices again in order to safeguard order or to safeguard thought or to safeguard discourse or to safeguard method. They will take it up because reality is more like that, or appears to be more like that, or they discover it to be more like that.

The hypothesis of Cartesian vortices will not be taken up again because it will be in conformity with the *Discourse on Method*, but because it will be, or they will think it to be, in conformity with the discourse of reality. The hypothesis of Cartesian vortices will not be taken up again because it will be in accord with Descartes, but because it will be thought to be in accord with reality.

Did Descartes himself deduce his metaphysics, his physics, his physiology, his entire system *starting from* his method? He did not even deduce the whole thing starting from his principles. He did not even deduce the whole thing starting from his *I think*. He himself said that it was necessary for experience to come out to meet deduction. By this he understood, and quite explicitly, that deduction, either mathematical or logical or metaphysical, or philosophical in general, could and sometimes (or often) did end in double or multiple possibilities, possibilities that Leibniz called "indifferent," that is, possibilities such that the last solution deduced, the solution found at the end of the deductive path, leaves us, so to speak, suspended before two or more equally effective solutions, before two or more equally realized or realizable solutions, before two or more solutions accounting for the details. It was in order to arbitrate among these equal solutions, equal in the sense that they equally satisfied the conditions of a final deduction, that Descartes had experience re-intervene. He acknowledges, he affirms that proceeding backwards, *recurrens, regrediens*,[16] experience comes into play again (starting from facts, phenomena, observations, experiments), that it goes out to meet that deductive path that had been, so to speak, on the cutting edge of chance.

Reality, at every point, is like a city under siege. The royal army has gone to its relief. However, the royal army cannot break through on its own, and it is necessary that a *sortie* sally forth to meet it and give it a hand. At this intermediary point between humankind and the world, at this intermediary point between the mind and reality, at this point where a connection is established between the army of relief and the relief

---

16. Literally "running back, reverting."

belonging to the place itself, at this point for Descartes the knowledge of truth is effected. And one must not doubt that for him it is effected absolutely and this knowledge of truth is absolute. No one has anything more to say. The mind comes from one side. The object of the mind comes out to it from the other side. Neither the mind nor the object has anything more to say.

One will permit me to open here a note within this note. It is impossible not to remark, with a shock, how this Cartesian theory is so closely similar, how it parallels the Christian and Catholic theory of grace, what we have the right to name the mechanism of grace. As it is necessary that experience come out to meet reason, so by a movement perfectly comparable and perfectly parallel, it is necessary that freedom come out to meet grace. The human being also is this besieged city. Sin also is this perfectly regulated blockade. Grace also is this royal army that comes to the rescue. But it is necessary also that human freedom make a *sortie, erumpat*,[17] and that it goes out to meet this army of rescue. This is what Péguy was saying when he said that by the creation of human freedom, and the playing out of this freedom, God made God's self dependent on humanity.[18] For one should not consider only the frontier outpost. One must also consider "Versailles and Saint Denis."[19] If the outpost is not rescued, it is lost. But if it does not rescue itself by this sortie, it loses itself.

This is a twofold disaster. If at the point of connection the sortie from the outpost does not give a hand to the army of relief, the army of relief will also not give its hand to the sortie from the outpost.

If one army does not find the other coming out to it, the other will also not find it.

When we fail, we fail for two. The human failure makes even God fail. When grace does not find freedom coming out to meet it, freedom also fails to find grace. The dereliction is inevitably a double one. When the human misses God, God misses the human. When the outpost loses itself, Versailles also, the kingdom also, loses an outpost.

17. "should sally forth."
18. Péguy says this, for instance, in his poem, "The Portal of the Mystery of Hope," "He who loves places himself, by loving, / By that very act, from then on, into dependence, / He who loves becomes the slave of the one who is loved" (81).
19. A line from the *chanson, Auprès de ma blonde*, dating from the Franco-Dutch war of the late seventeenth century. Versailles, the royal palace, and Saint Denis, the cathedral where many of the monarchs of France are buried, could between them be considered the political-religious center of the *ancien régime* of France.

NOTE ON BERGSON AND THE BERGSONIAN PHILOSOPHY 41

Moreover, I noticed in regard to experiments, that they become more necessary as one becomes more advanced in knowledge. For in the beginning it is better to make use only of what presents itself to our senses of its own accord and which we could not ignore, provided we reflect just a little on it, than to search for unusual and contrived experiments. The reason is that the most unusual ones often deceive one when one does not know yet the most common causes, and that the circumstances on which the unusual ones depend are almost always so specific and so minute that it is very difficult to notice it. But the order I have held to in this has been the following. First of all, I tried to find in a general way the principles or first causes of everything that is or can be in the world.

. . . Of everything that is or *can* be, there precisely is the fissure.

. . . without considering anything for this effect except God alone who created it, and drawing these principles moreover only from certain seeds of truth that are naturally in our souls. After this I examined which ones were the first and most ordinary effects that could be deduced from these causes; and it seems to me that in this way I found the heavens, stars, an earth, and even, on the earth, water, air, fire, minerals, and other such things that are the most common of all and the most simple, and thus the easiest to know. Then, when I wanted to descend to the more particular ones, so many different ones were presented to me that I did not believe it possible for the human mind to distinguish the forms or species of bodies that are on the earth from an infinity of others that could be there if it had been the will of God to put them there, nor as a consequence to make them useful to us, *unless one goes ahead to causes through effects,* and makes use of many particular experiments. After this, repeatedly passing my mind over all the objects that ever presented themselves to my senses, I dare say that I have never seen anything in it that I could not explain with sufficient ease through the principles I had found. But it is also necessary for me at admit that the power of nature is so ample and so vast, and that these principles are so simple and so general, that I observe almost no particular effect without my first knowing that it can be deduced from them in several different ways, and that my greatest difficulty ordinarily is to find on which of these ways the effect actually depends; for, to this end, I know of no other expedient than to search once more for some experiments that are such that their outcomes are not the same, that it is in one of these ways rather than another that one ought to make the explanation. What's more, I am now at the point where, it seems to me, I see quite well what angle one should take in order to make the most experiments that can serve this effect: but I see also that they are of such a nature, and such a great number, that neither my hands nor my financial resources, even if I had a thousand times more than I have, would be enough for all of them; so that, according as I henceforth have the wherewithal to do more or less of them, I will also advance more or less in the knowledge of nature: this I promised myself to make known through the treatise I had written, and to show in it so clearly the utility that the public can gain from it, that I would oblige all those who desire in general the good of humanity, that is, those who really are virtuous, and not by a false pretense, or only by reputation, to communicate to me those experiments they have already done as well as help me in the search for those that remain to be done.[20]

Who does not see that by such a breach all the non-deduced can enter forcefully? (If on every occasion the deductive path must be left at a certain point of suspension, and a leap must be made—where, in which direction, and how does one know it must be in this direction?—and the point of reality be found from where one must return to the point of suspension.) However, a great philosophy is not one that has no breaches. It is one which has citadels.

A great philosophy is not one that is never defeated. But a paltry philosophy is always one that does not enter the fight.

It is a singular journey that Descartes proposes to us. (But he is really forced to do so.) A singular journey this Cartesian journey. It is properly the interrupted journey, the discontinuous journey. One descends, one stops (or is stopped), one leaps (where, and how?), one touches a point that will be the definitive point of arrival, and is for the instant a momentary point of departure, one re-ascends, one comes back to the stopping point, one re-descends to the definitive point of arrival. One sets out, descends, stops, leaps, re-ascends, re-descends, arrives. One goes, leaps, comes back, goes again. It doesn't matter. Because a journey is singular, because it is interrupted, discontinuous, and even because it

---

20. This lengthy direct quotation is from Descartes's *Discourse on Method*, in Péguy's edition referred to in the next chapter, footnote 1. The italics are Péguy's. For an illuminating suggestion as to why Péguy reprints such lengthy extracts from texts on which he is reflecting, see the Appendix by Annette Aronowicz, 252.

is partially backward, that is not a reason for not making it. A risky journey does not matter if the effort is fruitful, if the adventure is rewarded. Which amounts to saying that a great philosophy is not a philosophy that is uncontested. It is a philosophy that wins out in certain ways. A great philosophy is not a philosophy without reproach. It is a philosophy without fear.

A great philosophy is not a *dictée*.[21] The greatest is not one that has no flaw.

A great philosophy is not one against which there is nothing to say. It is one that has said something.

And it is even one that had something to say. Even if it could not. Say it.

It is not one that has no defects. It is not one that has no empty places. It is one that has full places.

It is not a question of confounding. It is in the schools that it is a question of confounding. It is not even a question of convincing. In convincing there is vanquishing, as Victor Hugo liked to repeat.

To confound the adversary in regard to a philosophical question, what vulgarity.

The true philosopher knows very well that he is not situated *opposite* an adversary, but *alongside* the adversary, and others, in the face of a reality always greater and more mysterious.

And this even the true physician knows also. That he is not situated opposite a contrary physician, but alongside the contrary physician, in the face of a nature always more profound and more mysterious.

To attend a philosophical debate or to participate in one with this idea that one is going to conquer or bring down one's adversary, or that one is going to see one adversary confound the other, is to demonstrate that one does not know what one is talking about. It witnesses to a great incapacity, baseness and barbarism. It witnesses to a great absence of culture. It demonstrates that one is not from that country.

If the *Discourse on Method* has a meaning, then it is precisely that one must go *step by step* and with extreme prudence. In effect, it leads to a walk, a progression, a reasoning that requires one *to leap* between the point of suspension and the point of arrival.

21. A dictation exercise common in the French school (*lycée*) system, which places emphasis on the exactly correct transcription of a text read out by the instructor.

If the *Discourse on Method* has a meaning, then it is precisely that the movement from the mind to the object is a deduction, a continual *degression*. A continual *going*. In effect, the real Cartesian journey is a going, then a return and going again.

When I was a child, in the provinces of the Center,[22] whenever our games involved measuring out a distance on the ground, for example in "prisoners' base," we were careful not to measure by leg strides, because we thought that, even involuntarily, leg strides could be unequal. We measured (and counted) foot-to-foot, that is fairly and carefully placing the heel of the right foot against the front sole of the left foot. And so from there alternately. It was the *straw-hay* distinction of the *ancien régime*, becoming under the Republic and the government of reason, the *left* and *right*. And it was straw that became the left foot, and hay that became the right foot. But in the past they counted and measured by *straw-hay*, not by *left-right*. Now Descartes is someone who in the second part of the *Discourse on Method* wishes to advance only foot-to-foot, but in the fourth part, positioning himself, *going* to position himself by the *I think* at the heart itself of being and the self and thought, proceeds to what is perhaps the most prodigious leap in the history of metaphysics.

Will I say that he cheated a little and perhaps needed sooner than he said to have experience come out to meet him in order to help him to what would be his event? He believed that he deduced the heavens, the stars, an earth. He believed that he deduced water, air, fire, minerals, and other such things. Perhaps if he had never seen the heavens, he would not have so easily deduced them. Perhaps if he had never seen the heavens, he would never have *found* them. And the same in regard to a few other such things. Perhaps if he not had a certain experience of the heavens, he would not so easily have had such a knowledge of the *event* of the heavens. He wanted to rely on experience coming out to meet him only when he wished to descend to more particular things. Yet one is allowed to wonder if experience did not come out to meet him right at the beginning point of the heavens. One is almost allowed to wonder if experience did not come out to meet him right up at the premise of God.

We who have seen, and see every day, all the progress and development of physics since Descartes, what can we make of such a qualification,

---

22. That is, the center of France; Péguy grew up in the Beauce region.

and consequently such an affirmation, that the heavens, the stars, an earth, and even on the earth, water, air, fire, minerals, and other such things would be the most common of all things and the most simple, and therefore the easiest to know? Very few physicists today would dare speak of *easy to know*. Was I not right to speak of a certain electoral program, and of a certain tone of the electoral program, in Descartes? But what is it to say this, if not that I find here further support for what I suggested at the beginning of this note, that the method of Descartes has had such great success not because it is good, but because it is a method. It is because of this that it is eternally inscribed in history.

It is not because it is victorious, it is because it enters the fight. It is not because it arrives, it is because it departs.

It is solely, at bottom, because it is resolute. We follow those who march. And it is because it marches in the French manner. *"My second maxim"*; it is a maxim of his own moral code, but what I am claiming is that his method also is a morality, a morality of thought or a morality for thinking; or if you wish, everything is morality with him. Because everything here is conduct and the will to proper conduct. His provisional morality is a provisional morality for the conducting of conduct (everyday, personal and social). His method is a foundational morality for the conduct of thought. But the one and the other [conduct and thought] are conjoined and follow exactly the same pattern: *"My second maxim was to be the most firm and the most resolute in my actions as I could be . . ."*

At bottom, his great maxim of method is also to be the most firm and the most resolute in his thoughts as he could be. And perhaps his greatest invention and novelty, and his greatest coup of genius and force is to have deliberately conducted his thought as an action.

". . . and to follow no less the most doubtful opinions once I had determined on them . . . ."

To follow no less the most doubtful opinions once he had determined on them . . . this is what will scandalize every person who is not a philosopher and every person who has no culture. Because in the two poles of this phrase, in the two phases of this maxim, it is *determined* that is stronger than *doubtful*, determined that is more important than doubtful, determined that carries the day. *Vim patitur.*[23] It is determination,

---

23. "The violent take it by force" (Matthew 11:12).

assurance, resolution that conquer. His resolution is not less mental than moral. It is not less a matter of mental conduct than of moral conduct. It plays no less a role in the former than the latter. In the moral, it is supposedly provisional. In the mental, it is introductory and foundational. Everywhere it is most profoundly of his type[24] and his genius.

> ... than if they were very certain: imitating in this the travellers who, finding themselves lost in some forest should not wander this way and that, or what is worse, remain in one place, but always walk as straight as they can in one direction, and not change course for feeble reasons, even if at the outset it was perhaps only chance that determined them to choose it: for, by this means, if they do not go exactly where they wish, they will finally arrive at least somewhere where presumably they will be better off than in the middle of a forest.[25]

The whole question is precisely to know whether thought also is not better off anywhere than in the middle of a forest. What I am saying is that exactly because his moral maxim was provisional, because it did not fit into his system, because it was not finalized, because, so to say, it was not official, exactly because he was less cautious in uttering it, it is what delivers to us his secret. His secret really is to go always in the same direction and, at the end of the day, to arrive somewhere.

The whole question is indeed to know whether thought itself is not subject to certain general conditions of humankind and of being, which are organic conditions, one of which would be precisely that anything is better than going in a circle.

To set out, *to walk in a straight line*, to arrive somewhere. To arrive rather than not to arrive. To arrive where one was not going rather than

---

24. Péguy's French word here, *race*, can be translated as "type," "culture," "ancestry," "people," "tradition," or "race," the last in its meaning of a group of people having the same culture, interests, characteristics, or as Péguy would have it, providing the support or material for the political-social-historical incarnation of an "idea." Here it is worth quoting the French philosopher, Alain Finkielkraut: "When Péguy speaks of race, he is not designating a physical category or the hereditary traits of a collective entity; he is affirming the intimate connection between a people and an idea." See Finkielkraut, *Le Mécontemporain*, 115. For Péguy, it is no doubt felicitous that *race* is closely related to *racines* ("roots"). My translation as "type," "culture," "ancestry," "people," "tradition" or "race" throughout this work depends on the precise context.

25. The quotations are from Descartes's *Discourse on Method*, the same edition as noted above.

not to arrive at all. Before everything, to arrive. Anything rather than merely to wander. And that the greatest error is to remain merely errant: there you have his very nature and the ancestry of his secret.

I would not want to make him suspect of that *pragmatism* for which the Bergsonian philosophy has so often been reproached (wrongly, in my view, and one day I will demonstrate it), but finally it is evident that the Cartesian philosophy is a system of thought where *arrival* is of eminent value, and even of unique value. Anything rather than not to have a lodging this evening.

L'espoir d'arriver tard dans un sauvage lieu.[26]

If the method of Descartes had been good, in the sense he himself understood it, that is, if it had had in itself, or if it had led automatically to a certain certitude, which he was announcing, and which was truly of a genuine infallibility, it would not have led immediately and almost at the same time to propositions that appear to us today so scandalous. (For instance, the declaration that the heavens and earth are easy to know.) Where is the evidence that was supposed to solve everything? And what is this evidence that was supposed to be universal and does not go beyond its author, that was supposed to be eternal and does not survive its author, that is perhaps not even as real as its author? What is there to say except that a great philosophy is not one that resolves the questions once and for all, but one that poses them; that a great philosophy is not one that pronounces, but one that demands.

Descartes promises a method of certitude, and immediately after and almost at the same time he falls into propositions that soon appear scandalous to us. Or rather, he reaches propositions that soon appear scandalous to us. But a great philosophy is not one that renders decrees. It is perhaps one that renders services. It is in any case one that institutes proceedings.

A great philosophy is not one that pronounces definitive judgments, that installs a definitive truth. It is one that introduces uneasiness, that provokes a shock.

The world has perhaps not followed the Cartesian method, and Descartes certainly did not follow it. But the world and Descartes have followed the Cartesian shock.

26. "The hope of late arrival in a wild place." The line is from Alfred de Vigny's poem, "La maison du berger."

A great philosophy is not one where there is nothing to take up again. It is one that has taken up something.

A great philosophy is not one that is invincible in its reasoning. It is not even one that once, at one time, has conquered. It is one that at one time has entered the fight.

And the paltry philosophies, which are not even philosophies, are those that make a pretense of fighting.

It is very much a matter of confounding and convincing. When it is all over, no one is confounded, also no one is convinced. But some are signed up, some are enlisted. The others are not.

This proposition of Descartes that the heavens, the stars, an earth, water, air, fire, the minerals and other such things would be the most common of all things and the most simple, and therefore the easiest to know, straight away seems ludicrous to us. It doesn't matter. What is necessary to know is whether the opening words of this *Discourse on Method* have been the point of origin of an immense shock wave, an immense circular wave in the ocean of thought, on the surface of the ocean of thought.

A great philosophy is not one that is the best in composition, the best dissertation. It is in philosophy classes that one conquers by reasoning. But philosophy doesn't go to philosophy classes.

A philosophy is also not a court of law. It is not a matter of being right or wrong. It is a sign of great vulgarity (in philosophy) to want to be right; and yet more to want to be right against someone else. And it is a sign of the same vulgarity to attend a philosophical debate with the thought only of seeing one of the two adversaries be right or wrong. Against the other. Speak to me only of a philosophy that is more resolute, like that of Descartes, or more profound, or more attentive, or more pious. Or more unbound. Speak to me of an austere philosophy. Or of a happy philosophy. Speak to me above all of a certain *fidelity* to reality, which I place above everything.

A great philosophy is not finally one that ensconces itself all at once on all the positions on all the fields of battle. It is only one that, one day, fought truly for a corner of the wood:

Heureux ceux qui sont morts pour quatre coins de terre.[27]

---

27. "Happy are they who have died for four corners of earth," from Péguy's poem, "Ève."

Napoleon no longer occupies the Eylau cemetery,[28] and he no longer pitches his tent at the foot of the pyramids. But *there was* the Egyptian campaign, the Russian campaign, *the German wars,* and there was the French campaign.

I do not wish in this simple note to enter into the depths of the Bergsonian debate. If I can do it one day, I will speak as a Christian and a Catholic. I will speak without authority, but I will not speak without understanding and without comprehension. That the battle that has arisen around Bergson is at this point furious, is in the order of things. But that it has arisen in such a backwards manner defies belief. One would accomplish a great deal, one would perhaps accomplish everything, if only one compelled the combatants to occupy their true lines of battle. *Acies suas, non alienas, non contrarias, instruere.*[29]

Today I want only to underline the distinction of times. In the same way that Victor Hugo was classical at first and romantic in a later time, so a philosophy can have several times and generally does belong to several times. There is also history. Whatever one thinks metaphysically of the Cartesian *system,* when Descartes made his method shine forth, *cum irrupisset,*[30] when he made his *method* irrupt, he won his place in eternal history. Whatever one thinks metaphysically of the Bergsonian *system,* when Bergson made his *method* burst forth, he won his place in eternal history.

It would be in vain to fall back on the notion that Descartes's method is a positive one and Bergson's is purely negative. Descartes's method is only positive in appearance. And I would say in apparatus. It essentially comes to climbing back up a slope violently, and making the mind climb back up it. I will say making the human being climb back up it. And the Bergsonian method essentially comes to climbing back up a slope in a vital way, and making the human being and the mind climb back up it in a vital way.

In the same sense that Cartesianism has consisted in remounting the slope of disorder, Bergsonism has consisted in remounting the slope of the ready-made.

---

28. The cemetery was an important site within the Battle of Eylau (1807), fought in what was then eastern Prussia, ending in a costly victory by Napoleon over Russian forces.

29. "To draw up in their own lines, not in others', not in those opposite."

30. "when he broke out."

All great philosophy has a first time, which is a time of method, and a second time, which is a time of the metaphysical. When we say that Platonism is a philosophy of dialectic, and Cartesianism is a philosophy of order, and Bergsonism is a philosophy of the real, we are taking all three in their time of method. When we say that Platonism is a philosophy of the idea, and Cartesianism a philosophy of substance, and Bergsonism a philosophy of duration, we are taking all three in their time of the metaphysical.

Cartesianism was a violent rupture. Bergsonism was a rupture, an unbinding that was vital and so to say tenacious. There is certainly in Bergsonism a tenacity that there is not in Cartesianism. But that is perhaps because the rupture, the unbinding carried out in Bergsonism was that much more threatened, more precarious, and on the other hand that much more indispensable than the rupture carried out in Cartesianism. We are infinitely more bound to the slavery of the ready-made than to the slavery of disorder. The slavery of the ready-made is infinitely more ready to recapture us than the slavery of disorder. And the consequences are infinitely more disastrous. In disorder itself there can be coups of good fortune and even coups of order. In what is worn out there is no longer either grace or an outpouring. Of all there can be of bad, habit is the worst. Cartesianism held in check only one habit, the habit of disorder. Bergsonism has undertaken to hold in check habit as such, all organic and mental habit.

And this in all the orders, in all the disciplines that we indicated at the beginning of this essay. One has seen battles won in disorder and even through disorder itself, through panic moving forward. One has never seen tiredness and old age yield works of novelty through error.

There can be in disorder a certain fecundity. Habit and old age try in vain to play the young man.

This is what we call a revolution, this great effort momentarily crowned. The man in his armchair who sees a revolution, a mental revolution, and who says: "Not so clever," has said nothing. In this order, the question is not whether it is clever; it is whether, at a certain moment in the history of the world, it has penetrated within. The greatest revolutions, in all the orders, have not been brought about with and through extraordinary ideas, and it is the same peculiarity of genius only to proceed through the simplest ideas. Only normally the simple ideas wander about like dream fantasies. When a simple idea takes on flesh, there is a revolution. The Cartesian revolution consisted in halting the decline, in climbing back up the slope of habitual disorder. The Bergsonian revolution has consisted in halting all the decline, in climbing back up the slope of all habit, organic and mental.

It is this way in all the orders. What is most opposed to salvation itself is not sin, it is habit. Thousands of creditors repeat mechanically the terrifying words: *Et dimitte nobis debita nostra, sicut et nos dimittimus debitoribus nostris.*[31] Were one of them all of a sudden, suddenly illuminated to take seriously these words, to let them penetrate within, that would instantly be the greatest revolution there could actually be, for it would be a revolution in the regime of money, a subversion of the regime of money. And this would be a person saved as well.

Everything is in the incorporation, in the incarceration, in the incarnation. And here again, in this matter, we are compelled to speak the Bergsonian language, and will never speak another. Everything is in the insertion, and insertion is extremely rare. Of God there has been only one incarnation, and even of ideas there are very few incorporations. When, instead of considering an idea in the air, it is all of a sudden taken seriously, this is what is and makes a revolution. And history counts only three or four of these great upheavals.

Discourse on the Method for Rightly conducting *One's Reason and for Seeking Truth in the Sciences.* Bergsonism also is a method for rightly conducting one's reason. Bergsonism also has its reason. Bergsonism also is a party of reason. We cannot see what a philosophy would be that would not be of the party of reason. Bergsonism even intends to serve reason yet better, for it intends, so to speak, to serve it yet *more closely.* Every philosophy is obviously and essentially a rationalism. Even a philosophy that would be, or would like to be, against reason, will be all the same rationalist. A philosophy can only ever bring reasons. Cartesianism was in its principle an effort to *conduct* reason in the seeking of truth *in the sciences* (but by *sciences* Descartes evidently meant a portion of what we name *metaphysics,* or at least the metaphysics of the sciences). Bergsonism has been in its principle an effort to *conduct* reason in the grasping of reality (in the sciences, in the metaphysics of the sciences, in metaphysics). Platonism had already been in its principle an effort to conduct reason by means of the dialectic of the ideal—or if one likes, of the *ideas*—to

---

31. "And forgive us our debts as we also have forgiven our debtors" (Matthew 6:12).

the very source of being. Bergsonism has been an effort as great, an effort of the same order, and I would say an effort in the same sense. There is no more a philosophy against reason than there is a battle against war, art against beauty, faith against God. Bergsonism has never been either an irrationalism or an anti-rationalism. It has been a new rationalism, and it is superficial metaphysical systems that Bergsonism has undone (materialist metaphysics, medico-legal metaphysics, neuro-physiological metaphysics, sociological metaphysics, and so many others), which were so many hardenings, ossifications, stiffenings, ankyloses, were literally the amortization of reason. All these metaphysical systems were acts of sabotage through the hardening of reason. They were bone splinters and bedsores. Bergsonism is so little against reason that it not only brought into play again the age-old articulations of reason, but also brought new articulations out of it.

The famous rules of Bacon have not introduced any fecundity into the history of the world. We owe to them strictly speaking, nothing. Not one invention, not one discovery, not one movement of thought. All those who since the first beginnings of Greek thought had made an invention, a discovery, a movement of thought, had applied the rules of Bacon without knowing they were doing so. All those before Bacon. However, since Bacon, every person who might arise one fine morning with the firm proposition of applying the Baconian rules, and who would have only this firm proposition, who would bring into play only this firm proposition, this person would not produce for all that one invention, one discovery, one movement of thought. And we have never seen an invention, a discovery, a movement of thought come forth from contemplation of the rules of Bacon. And there you have a nice application, and not the least important, of the tables of presence and of absence, and of concomitant variations.

If I were a great philosopher, I would perhaps not have the right to recount the following story. All the more because it is not really a story, but a soldier's saying. But I am only a poor moralist. So, when there was, in the 131st regiment,[32] one who worked himself up too ostentatiously (to undertake an action, to speak a word), there was always another who would say coldly: *Above all, do not forget to breathe.* All those who have done something in the world are types who did not forget to breathe. But

---

32. This was the regiment in which the young Péguy did his military service in 1892.

one has done nothing in the world solely because one proposed to oneself not to forget to breathe.

Discourse on the method for rightly CONDUCTING, it is really, literally, a method for avoiding loose conduct, or bad conduct. And so, if you want, it is nothing, because one has always wanted to avoid loose conduct in the realm of thought, and if you wish, it is everything, because it is one of the three or four great upheavals ever produced in the history of thought. If you wish, it is nothing because it has always been a matter of avoiding loose conduct in the realm of thought. And if you wish, it is still less than nothing, because we have not avoided it more after than before, and Descartes himself did not avoid it more than any other (and it is in this sense that I said Bergson is an infinitely better Bergsonian than Descartes is a good Cartesian). And nevertheless, if you wish, it is everything, because it is Cartesianism.

And yet in this discourse on method, there is only one part out of six, the second, which consists of rules of method. Seven and a half pages in all. And even in this second part, it is only the heart of it, twenty lines in all, that consists of rules of method. It is these twenty lines that revolutionized the world and human thought. Valmy also was a small battle, an artillery duel, I mean it was effected with small numbers, and even not effected at all, with almost no dead and wounded.[33]

It is a prejudice, but an absolutely ineradicable one, that wants a rigid reason to be more a reason than a supple reason, or rather that wants a rigid reasoning to be more rational than a supple reasoning. It is a prejudice that has status and that flourishes all along the line. It rules, it is ineradicable in all the disciplines we looked over at the beginning of this note. It is the same prejudice that wants a rigid logic to be more logical than a supple logic. And a rigid scientific method to be more methodical, and more scientific, than a supple scientific method. And above all, a rigid morality to be more of a morality and more moral than a supple morality. It is as if one were saying that a mathematics of the straight line is more mathematical than a mathematics of the curve.

It is evident, on the contrary, that it is the supple methods, the supple logics, the supple moralities, that are the most severe, being the most

---

33. The Battle of Valmy (1792) was the first major victory of revolutionary France, against Prussian troops marching on Paris.

closely woven. Rigid logics are infinitely less severe than supple logics, being infinitely less closely woven. *Rigid moralities are infinitely less severe than supple moralities,* being infinitely less closely woven. A rigid logic can allow folds of error to elude. A rigid method can allow folds of ignorance to elude. A rigid morality can allow folds of sin to elude, while a supple morality, on the contrary, will hug, will expose, will follow closely the twists and turns of the elusions. It is a supple logic, a supple method, a supple morality that follows, gets at, traces out the twists and turns of flaws and deficiencies. It is a supple morality that exhausts the twists and turns of weakness. It is in a supple morality that everything appears, is exposed, is pursued. In a rigid compartmentalization one can get away with gaps, hollowness, false folds. Rigidity is essentially unfaithful, and it is suppleness that is faithful. It is suppleness that exposes. Contrary to all we believe, to all we commonly teach, it is rigidity that cheats, it is rigidity that lies. And it is suppleness that not only does not cheat, does not lie, but does not allow for cheating and does not allow for lying. Rigidity on the contrary permits everything, flags nothing. In a modern trunk you can pile up all the linen veils of ancient supplication. If these veils make false twists inside the trunk, nothing of it will appear on the lid.

A widespread or rather global misinterpretation that one sees taking hold in regard to Bergsonism, to the ancient and the modern, the classical and romantic would collapse once we separate the rigid from the firm and hard. It is in the rigid moralities where there can be niches for particles of dust, microbes, mold, and hollows of rot, it is in the corners of rigidities, in trusted vaults, that gather what our Latin-speakers called *lues* or *situs,*[34] the mold and filth arising from immobility, filth born from having been left there. And it is a supple morality on the contrary that demands a heart perpetually held to account. A heart perpetually pure. *Nous sommes lavés d'une telle amertume.*[35] In the same way, it is the supple methods, the supple logics that require a mind perpetually held to account, a mind perpetually pure. It is the supple moralities and not the rigid moralities, that practice the most implacably hard constraints. The only ones that never go absent. The only ones that seek no excuse. It is the supple moralities, the supple methods, the supple logics that fulfill perfect obligations. It is for this reason that the most decent person is not

---

34. "diseases," "decay."

35. "We are cleansed from such a bitterness," from Péguy's poem, "La Tapisserie de Notre Dame."

the one who submits to obvious rules. It is the one who stays in his place, works, suffers, remains silent.

3

Conjoined Note on Descartes and the Cartesian Philosophy

"But the order I have held to in this has been the following." We shall see later what this order has been. We have the time to see it. What matters, what has marked the world, is this resolve to hold to an order. And to have announced it in such terms. "First of all I tried to find in a general way[1] the principles or first causes of everything that is or can be in the world, without considering anything for this effect except God alone who created it, and drawing these principles moreover only from certain seeds of truth that are naturally in our souls. After this I examined which ones were the first and most ordinary effects that could be deduced from these causes; and it seems to me that in this way I found the heavens ... "

Well, then, I say: It doesn't matter. We know he did not find them, the heavens. They had been found before him. Or rather, they had found themselves all by themselves. Creation had need of its Creator in order to be, to become, to be born, to be made. It did not need humanity, either to be, or even to be known. The heavens were well found all by themselves.

---

1. Here Péguy inserts the following footnote in his text, "I don't need to say that I am citing Descartes according to the least scholarly edition I could find. It's not for a veteran typographer like me to be told what a scholarly edition is." Péguy put in many hours himself setting the type by hand for the *Cahiers* that he published. The note here might be a reference to his declining to use an edition of the *Discourse on Method* recommended to him by Jacques Maritain (see the editor's note in *Oeuvres en prose III*, 1792). Péguy cites throughout this *Note* the same edition of Descartes's *Discourse on Method* as in his first *Note* on Bergson.

They never lost themselves. And they do not need us in order perpetually to find themselves in their orbits.

They had been found before him. They had found themselves before him. I say: It doesn't matter. The audacity alone interests me. The audacity alone is great. Has there ever been an audacity so beautiful; and so nobly and modestly cavalier; and so decent and so crowned with a wreath; has there ever been such great audacity and assault on fortune, has there ever been a movement of thought comparable to that of this Frenchman who *found* the heavens? And he did not find only the heavens. He found "stars, an earth." I do not know if you are like me. I find it prodigious that he *found an earth*. Because, after all, if he had not found it.... And not only an earth, but "even, on the earth, water, air, fire, minerals, and other such things that are the most common of all and the most simple, and thus the easiest to know. Then, when I wanted to descend to the more particular...," then, but only then, he did not find them and he needed the discrimination of experience to come out to meet him. Until then (he says, he believes), he had no need of it. He was following the royal route, which does not err. It was only when arriving in the forest of Fontainebleau that he hesitated at the crossroad of the Grand-Veneur.[2]

One may ask (we have done it ourselves) if this discrimination of experience had not already come out to meet him and if he had not needed it to come out to meet him much earlier. It doesn't matter. He believes, he wants to have deduced all this, and even from God, barely passing through principles or first causes, barely getting help from the innate ideas, from those "certain seeds of truth that are naturally in our souls," and that themselves are more or less deduced from the principles and from God. We know that he would not have found the heavens and the stars and an earth if he had not heard of them. I will say more. We know that he would not have found the very principles or first causes "of everything that is or can be in the world" and that he would not have found the innate ideas, those "certain seeds of truth that are naturally in our souls," if he had not also heard of them, that is, if he had not had, like everyone, a certain *experience* of the operations of thought, I will even say a certain experience of the *event* of the operations of thought. I will say more. We know that he would not have found even God if he had not heard of God and if he had not heard God speak, that is, if he had not

---

2. The Fontainebleau palace, built by French royalty, lies in the midst of the Fontainebleau forest, and the Grand Veneur crossroad, on the route to Paris, is situated a few miles from the palace.

had, like every real metaphysician, like every person born metaphysical (and, it must be said, like every person born Christian and French) a certain experience of God. I will go so far as to say: a certain experience of the *event* of God. Experience did not come out to meet him only at the beginning of the more particular things; it came out to meet him at the beginning of the beginning. It doesn't matter. Descartes, in the history of thought, will always be that French cavalier who set off with such a dashing step.

These great philosophies are immense and happy and profound explorations. Fools believe that these philosophies contradict each other. The fools are right. They do contradict each other. Fools believe that often they contradict themselves. The fools are right. Often they do contradict themselves within themselves. Some of them say the elephant is an enormous animal, others say it is a little less enormous. Yes, my friend, because some are speaking of the African elephant, and others of the Asian elephant.

These great philosophers are explorers. Those who are great are those who have discovered continents. Those who are not great are those who have only thought of being solemnly accepted at the Sorbonne.[3]

There is a certain world, a universe of thought. On the face of this world geographies can be drawn. In the depth of this world geologies can make deeper engravings. The public, so to speak, always believes, and the philosophers almost always believe, that they are quarreling over the same terrain. Neither sees that they are plunging into different continents.

It is already a great deal to have discovered America. It is a great deal to have penetrated to the heart of Africa. Let the one who has discovered America be entitled the "American." And let the one who has penetrated to the heart of Africa be hailed with the title of the "second" or "fifth" or "sixth African." *Sextus aut septimus ille Africanus.*[4] Whereas, if we want the one or the other or each of them all to have discovered "the earth," obviously we will risk smashing the American against the African, and the African against the American.

There is a certain spiritual and temporal eternity of philosophies that comes from this. History will one day have to bring itself to fall in with geography, as geography has fallen in with geology. The temporal

---

3. Bergson's candidacy for the Sorbonne was rejected twice (in 1894 and 1898).

4. "That sixth or seventh African." *Africanus* was an honorary title given to a Roman general for conquering a part of north Africa (i.e., Carthage).

that belongs to you can be rooted out. The spiritual that belongs to you can perhaps be rooted out. Your *having had* the temporal or the spiritual that belongs to you cannot be rooted out. You can renounce the temporal and perhaps the spiritual that are yours. You cannot renounce having had the temporal or the spiritual that were yours. Here there can be no withdrawal. Nothing can take away from Christopher Columbus his discovery of America. It is always the tale of that poor boy who spoke of submitting his resignation from being a *former* student of the École Polytechnique.

It is what we generally like to call historical justice. I do not believe at all in history. I have little belief in temporal justice. And I have always thought the best reparation is not to have been defeated. It is better to speak of a sort of winnowing, so to say infallible, which ensures that at the end of the day the chaff is chaff and the wheat is wheat:

> À vous, troupe légère,
> Qui d'aile passagère
> Par le monde volez,
> Et d'un sifflant murmure
> L'ombrageuse verdure
> Doucement ébranlez:

JEUX RUSTIQUES d'un vanneur de blé, aux Vents.[5] It is by such rustic games, when all is said and done, that the great philosophies come to the great philosophers.

Like the continents, like the great explorations came to the great explorers.

There are immense zones of thought, climates of thought. There is a world, a universe of thought, and within it there are races of thought. A great philosophy is recognizable in this way, which, however, does not go without a certain apparatus.

Two friends are walking together. Two and not three, because with three one begins to blather. With three one is an orator, one is serious, one is sententious, one is eloquent, one is prudent (all the vices). With three one is circumspect or one is rash (it comes to the same thing). One

---

5. "To you, light troop / Who with passing wing / Fly through the world, / And with whistling murmur / the shadowy verdure / gently shake." Péguy takes this verse from a poem of Joachim du Bellay (1525–60), "Rustic Games of a Winnower of Wheat, to the Winds."

is fearful or defiant (it's the same sentiment). One adopts the moral or the immoral stance (it's the same thing). With three, it's the beginning of parliamentarism.[6]

Two friends set out from that small shop.[7] They are going for a walk. The grind of Parisian life, all made of toil, leaves them a little breathing time. They have three quarters of an hour, fifty minutes before them. With three, one is compelled to hold forth; but with two, one can converse. And as the temptation of philosophy is most present for one who has once tasted it, they will talk without conviction about some mundane temporary events, and then they will be compelled to converse about philosophy.

Whether they are of the same temperament of thought has no importance. Obviously it would go better if they were of opposed temperaments. The dialogue would perhaps have more thrust. But (in philosophy) one can get along even with one's friends, and even with one's allies.

Here are our two friends setting off from that honorable shop. Neither one nor the other has any part in the aggrandizements of temporal power. Neither one nor the other has any part in the aggrandizements of spiritual power. Neither one nor the other exercises any public office. They are only what they are. They are worth only what they are worth. Neither has any part in the aggrandizements of intellectual power. The Sorbonne has conferred on them a license to teach, which they use as much as they are able. Which is little. But they have never been made doctors.[8]

---

6. Péguy's word *parlementarisme* is loaded with his barbed criticism of the rhetoric of the left-liberal and socialist politicians of the Third Republic, who betrayed the *mystique* of the Dreyfusard struggle, turning it into the narrow and worn-out *politique* of the bourgeois Republic.

7. The friends are Péguy himself and Julien Benda, who later recalled that during the four years preceding the outbreak of WWI, he and Péguy would meet almost daily at Péguy's *Cahiers* shop/office near the Sorbonne, and then go for a walk that would eventually take them to some café along the Boulevard Saint-Michel, followed by lunch at the Closerie des Lilas. Benda's vehement, sustained criticism of Bergson, in defense of the Cartesian rationalism that had long been the touchstone of French philosophy, was expressed in books such as *Le Bergsonisme, ou une philosophie de la mobilité* (1912) and *Sur le succès du Bergsonisme* (1914), as well as the essay published by Péguy in the *Cahiers* (see the preceding chapter, footnote 1).

8. Péguy's university studies at the École Normale effectively ended with his marriage in 1897. In 1906 he submitted a doctoral thesis proposal to the Sorbonne, but later abandoned the project when it became clear that a university position would never be forthcoming, in large measure because of his ongoing polemic against the

There we have them, the men in the street. An inevitable inclination takes them down the Boulevard Saint-Germain. What would they be speaking about that was more pressing than the problem of being? One is the only adversary of Bergson who knows what he is talking about. The other is, after Bergson, and I would dare almost to say with Bergson, the only Bergsonian who also knows what he is talking about. He was the student, and more than the student, of Bergson at the École Normale. He has maintained for Bergson a filial fidelity.

We will also suppose them of good faith; not through virtue, but through good faith. They thus begin by placing in the same bag the Bergsonians and the anti-Bergsonians. And it is not a bag of "values," I beg you to believe. This operation done, they come back to themselves, to what they are. One is (in philosophy) a fierce critic, of absolute severity. The other is a good Christian.[9] He is even more a good Christian than he would wish. I mean that it costs him more dearly than he would wish to be a good Christian. He who is not a Christian is much stronger in mathematics. He who is a Christian has unfortunately become very strong in many things that do not end with "ics." He who is not a Christian is animated against Bergson with an animosity that is personal, inexhaustible. The other tries in vain to cure him of it. And he is not getting over it. The one (the Bergsonian) constantly has the impression, and says so to the other (the anti-Bergsonian), who also knows it and says it, that a man is missing at their conversation, that they require a man who would come as a third, and that this man is precisely Bergson. He alone presides in thought over their conversation. He alone would know how to judge the game (this serious game). He alone would know how to evaluate, to savor, to appreciate. He alone would know how to be delighted by such a discordance, to enter into such a spectacle, to penetrate such depths. He is missing, and they speak only about him.

One would quite like him to be the judge of the sides. Who would like it? The one; and perhaps even more the other. The partisan can, if need be, do without the presence of the patron. But what is sweeter for the adversary in thought than to feel the presence of the adversary? There

---

"intellectual party" that dominated both the universities and government of the Third Republic. For an excellent detailed account of Péguy's critique of *le parti intellectuel* and of his relationship to the French academic system in general, see Roe, *The Passion of Charles Péguy*.

9. "The one" is Benda, "the other" Péguy himself.

is in this perfect fencing-match a certain strike that can only be *demonstrated* by way of him.

We will suppose them to be in their forties (our two men), that is of another world, another universe, another creation than if they were not. For at forty one has known for five years who one is. We will suppose them rid of everything, having completely forgotten school, without concern for glory, naturally, without the notion of shining, without even the thought of appearances. They follow only their inclination. They love to philosophize as if it were a vice. This is the only way to love.

We will suppose them animated by a certain feeling that renders them equally and profoundly and, so to speak, mutually respectful of thought. They will have that certain peculiar taste for thought that nothing can put off track, and that separates people into the barbarians and the cultivated. They will have this peculiar taste, which is at the same time a gluttony and a profound passion, without parallel. A passion, a certain peculiar taste that nothing can deceive. A passion, which like a vice, gathers together, and from the farthest reaches, the most apparently heterogeneous beings; and the most heterodox. But they understand each other by certain signs. And they hear each other before speaking. And they find each other before looking.

A secret taste gathers them together, assembles them from the most secret corners and preferably from the most contrary parties. I do not speak only of the most contrary political parties. I speak also of the most contrary intellectual parties, of the most contrary spiritual parties. They love the gracious players. They love partners better than partisans. They recognize each other before a word has been spoken. They have a secret taste for the adversary. They have a secret contempt for the partisan. The adversary is not only useful. He is not only the fulcrum and the indispensable foil. He is not only the inevitable accomplice. He is infinitely more and infinitely better. He is not only the amateur. The partisans are amateurs. But the adversary is the professional. He is the one who knows what one is talking about. He loves what one knows so well (the opposing thesis, always present). And he knows so well what one loves, the precious thesis of thought that is infinitely more profound than one can make visible, infinitely more one's godchild and more fondly nurtured than one can allow to be seen. And he knows so well the projecting edges of bad faith, and that to love is to be on the side of the loved one who is wrong.

And that to love is to defend what one knows is indefensible.

We will suppose the two of them illuminated by this mutual regard, agreed in this mutual understanding, animated by this mutual respect. The two of them, one towards the other, are mutually complicit in this: that they know the incomparable dignity of thought, that contrary to the rest of the world, contrary to all the barbarians, they know that nothing is as grave and serious as thought.

They will therefore not be disturbed by what there might be of the comic and apparently detached in their words. The two of them being classical (how can one not be classical?), they know that nothing is as grave and serious as the comic, and that nothing is so parallel and similar to the tragic. Moreover, a long experience of effort and of fidelity has taught them what there is of painful and jealous attachment underlying this circumstantial detachment. And that this is not an elegance and a politeness, but a secret decency and the greatest purity.

They are mutually respectful again in a double and a triple sense. Respectful of thought, in itself, as being of an incomparable dignity and price. Respectful of thought as of a kind of work of art, a sculpting operation that must be guarded from violation as if it were a crime. Respectful of thought as of the most beautiful and most precious and most secret creation. Saluting it wherever it is; not merely a fencing salute, but a cultic salutation denoting singular esteem.

Being respectful of thought, they are naturally respectful of persons. They would willingly be Kantians on this point, even while not loving Kant. Or rather, they would love Kant. But it is he who does not permit himself to be loved. And then Konigsberg is quite far away. *Regis mons.*[10] And Konigsberg is quite harsh. If only he was born at Weimar.[11]

They also have this idea that Kant did not know. That, agreed, he applied himself well. But, all the same, he lacked too much what is necessary, a certain temporalness, living life, and that fortune and grace that consists in being unfortunate in a certain kind of inexpiable way.

They have this idea that Kant is well constituted, but that precisely the great things of the world have not been the things that are very well constituted. That high fortune has never crowned perfect mechanical apparatuses. That the unforgettable successes have never fallen upon impeccable ironwork. That when it is so well constituted, it never succeeds, it never receives that gratuitous accomplishment, that gracious crowning

10. "The mountain of the king" (Péguy is translating the German name into Latin).

11. Weimar, the city of Goethe, was called the "Athens of Germany" by the French writer, Mme de Staël (1766–1817).

of a high fortune. That when it is so well constituted, it is lacking exactly in that it lacks nothing, [it lacks] that *on ne sait quoi*, that opening allowed to destiny, that play, that opening allowed to grace, that withdrawal from self, that abandonment to the current, that opening allowed through the relinquishment of high fortune, that absence of self-supervision—at bottom, that perfect piece of intelligence, that perfect knowledge that we are nothing, that surrender and that abdication, which is at the core of every truly great human being. That surrender into the hands of another, that *letting be*, that *then I don't busy myself with it anymore*, which is at the crux of the most high fortune. Kant busies himself all the time. With Kantianism. This is not the way to succeed in the world. The most beautiful verses are not the ones with which one is busy all the time. They are the ones that have come all by themselves. That is to say, in fact, those that have been left. To fortune.

Respectful, in love with thought, respectful of persons, our two men avoid with jealous care wounding one another. They would perhaps prefer not to pursue in depth the idea most dear to them, to conceal it until another time, to put it off for later, rather than to wound the other. They watch out for this with scrupulous attention, with meticulous cunning, with a tender and melancholy, sly and infallible skill. They are forty years of age. They know that a wound never heals; and that the most imperceptible is also the one that will be fatal. Furthermore, they know that friendship is of a unique price, that it is infinitely rare, that nothing replaces it; that it is infinitely sensitive.

Respectful of thought, respectful of other persons, I will say that from this each has come to respect his own person. Not in the Kantian sense, naturally. Kant is not really the question. Kant in their eyes has become merely an official, an unhappy conscientious professor. He's not really the question. In the same way that they have a pathological fear of wounding each other, each has the same pathological fear of wounding himself. A long experience of pain, an incoercible fever, an incapacity for healing, the ever-present bruising of an imperishable scar has taught them that the wound one inflicts on oneself is the most incurable of all; as it is of all the best placed, the only one well placed. *Par besoin de nous mettre au centre de misère. Et pour bien nous placer dans l'axe de détresse.*[12] They know that the wound one inflicts on oneself is the only skillful and infallible one. And that it hurts. And that it hurts to have a hurt. "To

---

12. "In need of putting ourselves at the center of affliction. And placing ourselves in the axis of distress." From Péguy's poem, "La Tapisserie de Notre Dame."

beat oneself," say the manuals. To beat oneself, they know that this is the only infallible way to be beaten. The only skillful, the only perfect way. The only way that is hermetically sealed, without a crack, without a join, with no way out. The only way that is really terrible and in fact, the only authentic way.

He who is among other things a Christian took seriously all that there was in the catechism. When he was little. That led him far. He did not at all make use of the catechetical rules to berate others; and to examine the conscience of others. He made use of them to do himself much hurt; and continually to make his own examination of conscience. All that he can do, perhaps, is not to regret it.

To beat oneself, the only defeat that is exact and also the only one that is total. The only way to be irrevocably beaten. When one is beaten by the others, they can be mistaken (they are human beings). They do not know well where to inflict the hurt. When one beats oneself, one knows where to hurt oneself with a terrible exactitude.

To beat oneself: to be beaten inexpiably; the worst defeat; the only defeat that counts; the only also from which one never recovers.

Our two men are melancholy. How would they not be? Have I said they are in their forties? One by a year and a few months, the other by a few years. It doesn't matter. When you are on the downward slope, when you are descending that slope that ends at only one point, it doesn't matter whether you have passed by a few months or a few years the summit line, the line that divides our days.

How would they not be melancholy? All that they love is dangerously threatened. Often they ask, not each other, but each of himself, if all is not lost. They see this people of France threatened from every side, betrayed on every hand, betraying itself. They know that there have only ever been two successes in the world; in the ancient world it was the Greek people, and in the modern world it was the French people. It being agreed that the Jewish people is and has been and will always be a long-enduring race and the race itself of non-success, and that the Roman people was destined to make itself the vaulting of an immense rotunda.

How would they not be melancholy? They know that nothing is so fragile, nothing is so precarious as such successes. They see that one was achieved. And it is Greece. They see another was achieved. And it is

France. They ask themselves from where will another ever come? And they well know that there is no place from which another will ever come.

These two successes, the only ones ever produced in the history of the world, appear of infinite value to them. An anxious tenderness, hidden and as if resigned on the part of the Jew (resigned to dispersion), inexpiable and as if frenzied on the part of the Christian, gathers them around the ancient and French cultures as around survivals every day more dangerously threatened. Here is manifest the internal difference of their two peoples. Every Jew come out of a certain fatalism—Oriental. Every Christian (current, French) comes out of a certain revolt—Occidental. Contrary to what people tend to believe, contrary also to the most false, the most specious appearances, the Jewish people (when one knows them well) always find that it is nevertheless good like this, that anyhow it's better than nothing, that one is happy at least to have had this, and that it is even astonishing that one has had it. The Christian, always disconsolate, never has enough. A God died for him. He considers, and always finds, that we are indeed poor wretches.

Have I not said that the two are fatigued? Not perhaps so much with work as with an incurable concern. The deep cut of the incurable concern of the people of Israel, this hole in the marrow, which runs the length of the stem of this long-enduring race. And through Jesus the incurable graft of this concern onto the denser trunk of French strength. Thus was born the most beautiful people of sorrow that has ever come to the world. And this also is the rare success among the few successes. In order to obtain a melancholy of this incurable profundity, so deep-set and so mortally engraved, this graft and this wild stock were required, this people and this other people, this soul and this other soul and this mortal body; the introduction of a virus so ancient into a young and healthy and, it must be said, defenseless body was required. What was required was a virus so acrid and so sacred, macerated in the only Oriental people that was created against the Orient, concentrated and re-concentrated through thirty and forty centuries in secrecy, then abruptly inserted into a new people, into so much innocence and so much purity, into so much grace and defencelessness, into this marrow and this tenderness, into so much newness, so much vigor and blood, such a beautiful temporal body, such beautiful material strength, so much audacity and such an inoffensive soul—all this was required, the process of this unique graft, so that the unique Jewish anxiety would become the unique Christian anxiety, and so that the royal wisdom and royal sadness of King Solomon would become the tragic and more-than-royal anguish of a Pascal. All this was required, this maceration thirty, forty centuries old in the core of a gradually vaccinated people, this abrupt explosion into a healthy and young people that was not expecting it.

Really, it will be said, all this for these two unfortunates who are descending this street and who have only one mania, for philosophizing? See them descending with their knowing airs. Look at them in that rue de la Sorbonne where they will soon be rubbing shoulders only with strangers. *Really*, you are saying, so much ado about these unfortunate men, *philosophi philosophantes*,[13] of the most common kind?

Yes, all this for the one; and all this for the other. For the most common of Jews, Moses brought the Tables of the Law. And for the most ordinary kind of Christian, Jesus died. There are only two sorts of Jews: those who are consumed by the Jewish anxiety and play so many poor comedies in order to deny it (and in order to deny it to themselves); and those who are consumed by the Jewish anxiety and do not even think of denying it. And there are only two sorts of Christians: those who are consumed by the Christian anxiety and play so many poor comedies in order to deny it (and in order to deny it to themselves); and those who are consumed by the Christian anxiety and do not even think of denying it. Neither the one nor the other of these two faiths, neither the Jewish faith nor the Christian faith, are the sort of machinery reserved for extraordinary beings. They are in one sense, and Pascal said it very well, all that belongs to what is most common.[14] The same eternal and essential debate plays itself out in everyday life, in everyday people. Moses is everyday for the Jew. Jesus is everyday for the Christian.

Bearing such high destinies within, our philosophers descend. Here again the difference and the contrast of their two ancestries shines out. The Jew finds it natural to be ill. Son and, so to speak, cell and elementary fiber of a people that suffers through centuries of centuries and that will vanquish the universe through having been ill for a longer time than the others, he says he knows that spiritual work has as its price its own kind of inexpiable fatigue. He even finds this to be just. He even finds it to be

13. "Philosophers philosophizing."
14. Pascal says that "nothing is more common than the good things" in his opuscule, "Of the spirit of geometry and the art of persuasion."

still very good like this. He counts the days when it goes well. He marvels at them. He finds that one still has some good luck. (He does not say it, but he is an old Jew at bottom, and he finds that the Lord is still quite good, in that he is not worse.) He counts the days that he has been able to work. All in all, they have been many.

Sly, rebellious, son of the earth, the Christian lives in constant revolt, in perpetual rebellion. Raised in a house where his mother worked for forty or fifty years, seventeen hours a day, re-caning chairs,[15] he never accepted, he never *acknowledged* that that part of the carcass called the brain was not driven and was not under orders like that part of the carcass called the fingers of the hand. As his ancestors (ancient and immediate, far away and immediate) worked in the vineyards, at harvest time, sixteen, seventeen hours a day, in the full days of summer, in the long days of July, August, and September, from first daylight at almost two in the morning to last twilight almost past nine in the evening—so he would like to carry on, he would like to do as much, he also would like to achieve feats of strength. Hence the accidents. He would like to make dramas and *tapisseries*, dialogues and *Notes* like one canes chairs,[16] so that line comes after line and verse after verse like cord comes after cord. The madman. He would like to do on his work table, on those sixty-six square decimeters covered in green cloth, what his ancestors did in the immense plains of the Loire valley and on the slopes of Saint-Jean-de Braye: days without number and days without limit. Days, so to speak, without ageing. Days with no other limitations than the very limitations of the sun. Days where it was the vine-worker who wore out the vine, where the spine wore out the stock, where the harvester exhausted the harvest. I say more: where the harvester wore out the harvest. Days where people wore out the earth. Where people wore out the age, and all there is of the eternal. That is what he would like to do, the fool. He does not accept his downfall. He knows, but he *does not want* to know that there is in the pen a virus that is not in the trowel and the hoe. He knows, but he does not want to know, he lies to himself (he knows it), he does not want to know that in the pen there is

---

15. Péguy's father died in 1873, shortly before he was born, so he was raised entirely by his mother and grandmother in Orléans. His grandmother came from peasant stock in the Beauce farming region, and his mother supported the family by re-caning chairs in their home, work with which Péguy often helped her when he was a boy. He was the first member of his family to receive a secondary school and university education. For more on Péguy's family background, see Villiers, *Charles Péguy*.

16. Péguy here notes the variety of literary genres he attempted (including the poem, "La Tapisserie de Notre Dame").

a poison, a mystery, a reproof, an exhaustion that there is not in the plow and the harrow. Like his ancestors, he would like to be the king, and like his ancestors, an absolute king. As they commanded their head and the individuals named muscles, so he would like to command the brain and the individuals named nerves. He discovers the difference there. As they battled against back strain, he battles against his liver. He discovers the difference there. He is the first of his people who is forced to go gently. He is the first of his people whom the carcass does not obey. He is the first of his people who is beaten.

The Jew has been beaten for seventy, ninety centuries: in this lies his eternal strength. And in this also lies his eternal victory. The Jew has been wretched since Eve and since Adam, and by the expulsion he has represented the diaspora: this is his eternal patience and a kind of happiness. The Jew has been forced to go gently through centuries and centuries; from this comes the eternal stiffness of their necks.[17] When therefore they set off, the two of them, the Jew tries to calm the Christian, to point out to the Christian that it is still very good this way, that he must, all the same, get used to it. (And the Jew says this to the Christian, but he knows very well that he speaks, in this regard, a foreign language to the Christian, and that the Christian does not even understand him. But he continues all the same, because it is just as well this way, to speak, to say this, to speak thus.) The Christian looks at the days when he is well: there are none of those. He looks at the days when he works: what a meager network. (When he would have so much to say, when he feels himself full of works that will never be carried in procession.) He does not look at the days of happiness: there wouldn't be any; there would not even be so many as those nails in the wall that appear numerous and that are as nothing in the hollow of the hand. Through an obscure need for compensation which is at the bottom of all morality and perhaps of more than morality, through a sort of angry and insidious persistence in applying the *lex talionis* against himself and, basically as an appeasement of the gods, he has not ceased to hope mutely that in sacrificing happiness he would at least have the work. But at bottom he knows very well that one has neither the one nor the other.

Because that would be too beautiful.

17. See Exodus 32:9; 33:3; 34:9.

Jesus was able to graft the Jewish anxiety onto the Christian body. This was necessary in order that the all-consuming nature of this anxiety, attenuated in an attenuated race, blunted in an ancient race, become habitual in a race used to it, would gain in a new race, and almost instantly, a finally incurable depth. And Jesus was not able (or did not want) to graft Jewish patience onto the Christian body. This also was necessary, so that a Pascal might be produced, so that well of anguish, that desert of sand, that abyss of melancholy might be obtained.

And the Jew and the Christian know very well that in the matter of patience the Jew is always more Christian than the Christian. The anxieties of the Jew have become patience-based. They are allied, they are intimately coupled, they are conjoined with patience. The Christian is consumed by dull revolt, by rustic unwillingness, by the sly rebellion of the peasant. He is the peasant who watches the hail ravage his harvest and chew up his grain. He is willing to watch. He is willing that the hail fall. (Above all because he cannot do otherwise.) The next year he will re-sow the grain. Even if there were hail every year, he would re-sow the grain all the next years, all the following years. He only does not want to be content:

> *Nous sommes ces soldats qui marchaient par le monde*
> *Et qui grognaient toujours mais n'ont jamais plié.*[18]

At bottom it is permitted to ask oneself if this constant revolt, this sly peasant rebellion is not more in the Christian order than a certain category of patience. How many types of patience are only ways not to suffer? *Patientiae NON patiendi.*[19] The patiences of suffering, *patientiae patiendi*, the fought-for patiences, the contested patiences, do they not enter infinitely more deeply into the Christian order than so many types of patience that are perhaps only anesthetics and that one must probably place in the category of laziness?

I do not say this about Jewish patiences. They are entirely other. They are too much anxiety-based, too much connected with anxiety ever to enter into the category of laziness. Moreover, the Jews never enter into the category of sin. If they entered into the category of sin, they would

---

18. "We are those soldiers who marched through the world / And who always grumbled but never folded." This is from Péguy's "La Tapisserie de Notre Dame."

19. "Patiences NOT of suffering."

not be Jews, they would be Christians. They would not be of the old law, they would be of the new. All they can do is enter into the category of disobedience to the law of Moses.

I will not say as much of the new law. I will not say as much of the Christians. How many types of patience (secretly proud of being patience, and of having conquered impatience, and of having conquered anger) are no more than a turning of the shoulder in order not to receive a blow. How many types of patience are no more than the most knowing, the most impeccable cheating with pain, that is with the ordeal, with salvation, just as there is another patience (the same), which is the most knowing and the most implacable cheating against the race.

How many types of patience are only anesthetic inventions, infallible defenses mounted against pain, against the ordeal, against salvation; against God. So many dismal and sly abdications of the very condition of humanity. Platitudes calculated so that destiny will pass over, not being able to catch hold at all. Dismal and dull and sly leveling out practiced so that even God will miss the mark.

Egalitarian silting up, democratic filling in, so that there will be no exceeding, so that nothing will exceed in anyone, and thus pain, thus the ordeal, thus salvation, and thus God are not able to enter into play.

Such are the impieties of all this patience. Such are the impieties of all this prudence. Or rather, such is the central impiety; and I do not believe there is a greater. Such is their "wisdom": poor and dismal, flat and sly wisdom. This is the patience of not being patient. For to be patient is to suffer, and to be patient all the same. To be patient is *to endure*. Not to suffer, to refuse all purchase to suffering, to refuse to suffering all the points of infallible alignment it brings to bear on us, this is not only to cheat, this is not only to denature, this is not only to dis-grace: this is not to be patient.—"Do you think I'm going to put up with that?" said the women when I was little. "That," it did not matter just what: all that was not going well; all that displeased them; the neighbor saying something contrary; their offspring (they had them) lacking respect (that was seen). They were within the healthy French tradition, and I will say in the healthy tradition of the French parish.

They did not wish to endure. As good Frenchwomen, they imagined quite well what it is to endure. *Tolerare, pati, tolerare tamen.*[20]

---

20. "To endure, to suffer, nonetheless to bear."

In Latin, in Greek, and even in German, to tolerate is to bear, to put up with, to raise, to sustain, to lift up, a burden of pain. *Tolerare, tollere, tulisse; tuli, (t)latum;* and there are, says Bréal "numerous traces of a verb **tulo*.[21] The corresponding root in Greek is ταλ or τλη, from which τάλας 'that which puts up with,' τλῆναι 'to put up with,' τέτληκα 'I have put up with,' πολύ-τας 'that which puts up with much.' . . .—*Tolero* does not come directly from *tollo*, but from a lost substantive, **tolus*, **toleris*.—Germanic *thulan* 'to put up with,' from which the German *Ge-dul-d* 'patience.'"[22]

Τάλαινα is that which puts up with. Τάλαινα, *wretched one*, the ancient chorus repeats tirelessly. In French, to endure is to find that it is very hard.[23] But in French it is above all not to endure. (I mean it is to endure because one cannot do otherwise, and as the good women used to say interiorly, *it's unbearable* and again as they used to say: *it's eating me up*.)

To endure is not to have no teeth. It is to have them and to endure their being extracted. And it follows, it is not never to have had them. It is to have had them and to have endured their being extracted. The martyr in the arena is not the one who had no limbs. It was the one who had them and who endured their being ripped away. And we who have nothing to give, or rather have been left with only miserable days to be taken away, to endure is not to not have these miserable days, it is to endure, all the same, their being ripped away.

Thus similar, thus different; thus enemies, but thus friends; thus strangers, thus intimates; thus entangled; thus allied and thus faithful; thus contrary and thus conjoined, our two philosophers, these two accomplices descend that street. Another difference, profound, walks between them but does not disjoin them. It is a difference between them going far back, another difference of ancestry, more subtle, a fissure perhaps yet more disjoining. The Jew knows how to read. The Christian, the Catholic, does not know how to read.

In the social category to which he belongs the Jew can go back from generation to generation and can go back centuries: he will always find someone who knows how to read. Even if he were to go back to

---

21. The asterisk indicates that the proposed etymology is hypothetical.

22. Péguy is here consulting Bréal et Bailly, *Leçons de mots,* an etymological dictionary of Latin (1906).

23. In this paragraph Péguy plays on the close connection in French between *endurer* ("to endure"), *dur* ("hard"), and *durer* ("to last").

some cattle merchant of the plains of the *pulta*, or horse merchant of the immense *tchernosioum*,[24] even if he were to go back to some match merchant of the late Roman Empire or Alexandria or Byzantium, or to some desert wanderer, the Jew belongs to a people where one will always find someone who knows how to read. And not only that, but reading for them is not merely reading a book. It is reading the Book. It is reading the Book and the Law. To read is to read the word of God. The very inscriptions of God on the Tables and in the Book. In all this sacred apparatus, the most ancient of all, reading is a sacred operation as it is an ancient operation. All the Jews are interpreters, readers, reciters. It is for this reason that they are visual, and visionary. And that they see everything. Instantaneously, so to speak; and with only one glance, run over, cover surfaces instantaneously.

Perhaps a more profound and, so to speak, mellow penetration is reserved for the one who does not know how to read (one should understand me well), and perhaps a third dimension is granted to the one who is not visual. Whatever the case—and the introduction of this variation, or rather the consideration of this variation, is of almost infinite consequence in the social category that is our reference and that is perhaps of sole importance—the Catholic, or to begin at the other end, the Jew is a man who has been reading since forever, the Protestant is a man who has been reading since Calvin, the Catholic is a man who has been reading since Ferry.[25]

Some other day, and when I am not so keen on our discussing Descartes particularly, it would be necessary to try to hold in mind and examine some of the implications of this classification. They appear to me infinite. Perhaps no one feels it as much as I. When I am in the presence of Pécault,[26] I am in the presence of a man who has been reading since Calvin, since the sixteenth century. When I am in the presence of Benda (and perhaps of Bergson), I am in the presence of a man who has been reading since forever, for centuries and centuries. When I am in my own

---

24. A reference to the Russian steppe; and *pulta* (Péguy's incorrect rendering of *puszta*) refers to the grazing plains of Hungary.

25. Jules Ferry was a prominent republican politician, a strong proponent of laicism and educational reform, and Minister of Public Instruction and Fine Arts in successive governments of the Third Republic. He was assassinated in 1893.

26. Pierre-Félix Pécault became Minister of Public Instruction and Fine Arts in 1911; he was a subscriber to the *Cahiers*, and a frequent visitor to Péguy's publishing office.

presence, I am in the presence of a man who has been reading since my mother and myself, since 1880.

Or if you like, the Jew has been well read since forever, the Protestant since Calvin, the Catholic since Ferry.

Or if you like, the Jew has been *alphabet*[27] since forever, the Protestant since Calvin, the Catholic since Ferry.

Considering this, the Catholic reflects on himself. On whatever side he goes back, he is *inalphabet* in the generation of the grandparents. Neither those from the Bourbonnais, nor perhaps those from the Marche, nor those from the Val de Loire and the first fringes of the Orléans forest, none of his grandfathers, none of his grandmothers knew how to read or write. And they counted in their heads (which is to say they counted better than you and I). The Catholic, the Frenchman, the peasant turns back towards his people and on whatever side he goes back, he collides, right after his father, right after his mother, with this quadruple front of unlettered people. Neither his paternal grandfather nor grandmother; neither his maternal grandfather nor grandmother. He comes at it from another direction: neither his two grandfathers nor his two grandmothers. He comes at it from another direction: neither the lineage of his father, nor the lineage of his mother. And he would be quite embarrassed to go back further. Being poor and French, Catholic and peasant, he has no family records. His family records are the parish registers. Not one family clearly discernible in this vast ancestry. Not one landholder in this long-lasting race. Nothing that leaves a trace in notarial documents. They never possessed anything. Poor and common, they left to the Jews, the Protestants, the bourgeois Catholics the possession of an inscribed genealogy.

The man lingers, he considers for a long time this classification of the world and this classification of the world appears to him new. On one side together all the Jews, all the Protestants, all the Catholic nobility and bourgeoisie (soldiers of the aristocracy, members of the legal profession, holders of public office, country squires, farmers, all possessors, possessors of battles, possessors of office, possessors of land), who have their family records and so to speak their titles to property—and then he who has never had anything, he Catholic and poor, he who has never been anything, being in his place, he whose family records are parish registers, he whose property titles are parish registers, and he who until judgment day will only be inscribed in parish registers.

27. This wording is equally unusual in the original French, where *alphabet* is also italicized.

He stops for a little here. He perceives a great division within the world. On one side, the notary (in all his forms), on the other, those poor parish registers. On one side, the notary, that is the official of the civil order, the mayor, the town councilor, also the court clerk—that is to say also, the agent of change; and the trading floor and stock exchange; and the ledger-book of the public debt (and the inscriptions of the bank). On the other side, those poor parish registers.

On one side, all historical inscription. On the other side, those poor parish registers.

On one side, all temporal inscription. On the other side, those poor parish registers. That is to say, the book of baptisms.

The man turns back toward his people, and immediately after his father and his mother he sees advancing that front of four, and immediately after that, immediately behind, he sees nothing more than a vast mass and an innumerable people, he no longer distinguishes anything. Why not say it: he plunges with pride into this anonymity. Anonymity is his family name. Anonymity is his vast family name. The more the earth is common, the more he wants to have sprouted from this earth. The more the night is opaque, the more he wants to have come out from this darkness. The more the people is common, the more he has a secret joy and, we must say, a secret pride in being a man of this people. He is the same man in the taste for his people as in his taste for everything else. He is the same man who has never dressed except in common fabric, who has never written except on common paper, who has never sat except at a common table. And this taste for the common and the poor, which among the rich is the most dreadful crime and ignominious indecency, being the most monstrous affectation, the most criminal and monstrous derision, the most fraudulent simulation and exactly that for which there will be no forgiveness—this is for the poor only the most unadorned decency. That which among the rich is the most obscene and perverse invention of pride and perversity, (Tolstoy), is among the poor only the poorest decency.[28] Thus our man wants only to be a tree in this vast forest, a common ear of wheat in this vast harvest.

28. It is not entirely clear whether the parenthetical reference to Tolstoy is Péguy's way of including him among the rich who "simulate" poverty, or, rather, that as he writes this, his thinking is influenced by Tolstoy. The placing of the parenthesis between two commas would likely point to the latter. Tolstoy was the subject of a piece in the 1911 *Cahiers* by André Suarès.

A citizen of the common sort, a Christian of the common sort.
The citizen in the city; the Christian in the parish.
And a sinner of the most common sort.

He looks toward his people, and as in the passage through the Red Sea a great wall of wave concealed the enormous ocean suspended behind, so this wall of four, his two grandfathers, his two grandmothers, conceals from him the silence of an innumerable people. It is like a partition of the ocean itself. And as one knows nothing of that enormous mass that is behind the partition, except that it is of water, so he knows nothing of that vast people that is behind this wall of four, except that it is of Christendom.

And he plunges with joy into this enormous anonymity.

He looks toward his people. That very wall, that wall of four, that wall of illiterates, that rank of four, presents itself as a wall of silence. And he goes back and he plunges not only with joy into this enormous anonymity; he immerses himself in it with a secret joy. But he also immerses himself in it with a kind of fulfillment, a crowning, a plenitude of humility. And it might be possible that he immerses himself in it with a crowning and a plenitude of pride. And more yet, perhaps with a certain *je ne sais quoi* of achievement, plenitude of annihilation.

When he is tired, and he always is, he tells himself that the peasant also is always aching with fatigue; and he does not work less for that; he only works better. This is not only a consolation, it is a theory. He has invented this theory, that one works better when one is at least a little tired. Since he is always very tired, he lacks some competence in this matter of being a little tired. And he quite lacks the other term of the comparison, which is to know what someone who is not tired at all would be and would do. He has developed his theory at length. He claims that the fatigue of the morning is the passing on of the work of the day before to the work of the next day, that this residue of fatigue in the morning is the legacy of the fatigue and work of the day before to the fatigue and work of the next day, that it is like a bitter fermenting agent, like the leaven of the day before that will cause today's bread to rise. It is a lovely theory for tired people. He claims that the peasant, the carter always wakes up with a sore back, stiff legs, aches and pains, which make him swear the name of God, but gets up all the same and by noon is no longer thinking about it.

(What detracts a little from the reasoning behind the comparison is that he himself, at noon, is still thinking about it.) Such is his theory of fatigue and work. He has many theories. What is amazing is that with so many theories he works all the same, and a great deal. And he produces all the same, and a great deal. And when he works, and when he produces, one does not perceive that he has theories. He has this theory that the leftover fatigue from the day before is what sustains from one day to the other the continuity of the work.

When he is really tired his mental equipment refuses him all service. (As with everybody, but he still has this pride in wanting it to be much more, and so to speak more eminently, the case with him than with the others.) His writing equipment, his writing machine, is the first to fail him, to fail him straight away, his machine for written form, his visual images and fine motor apparatus, all that we learn from Janet.[29] He wants to see in this the just price for his grandparents not knowing how to read or write. His people did not yet have the time to make it habitual; the visual images did not have the time to enter into his memory; the fine motor apparatus did not have the time to enter into his hand. He is the first of his people who writes. Why be surprised that his ancestry within him does not yet know how to write, or at any rate does not know well; that it has so many failures in writing; so many faults; so many defects. These are the failings of a machine that has not been made supple, not been habituated, not been trained, and has been set in motion only for one or two generations. But the more frightful this defect, the more frightful this price, then without doubt the more precious the good for which it is the price, and this good is precisely to come out of, to stand directly in a people still immersed in the secret of not knowing how to read, in the silence and darkness of never having taken a pen in hand.

Taking pen in hand, this solemn phrase of the legendary trooper seems to him filled with a mysterious sense. *My dear parents, I take pen in hand, it is to tell you that the captain* . . . . In these words he makes out a formidable meaning. So, excepting his father, whom he never even knew, excepting his mother, no one of his people ever took pen in hand; and his mother has a handwriting so gauche, so maladroit, so working class, so little "writerly." He is the first and as if alone. Himself so maladroit. And

---

29. Pierre Janet was the author of *Névroses et idées fixes* (1898), as well as a doctoral thesis on "psychological automatism" (1889).

truly so little habituated. With his large maladroit fingers where all the chilblains of his childhood have left their deformities.

This pen, his proper instrument, seems to him a dangerous instrument. He discovers in it a dangerous instrument. There are, however, some compensations. When it goes well, when the machinery is in synch, when he writes, he does not find that it is a dangerous instrument. When it no longer goes well, when the machinery is out of synch, when he is unnerved before his ordinary paper, he is able to say to himself that it is very good that he does not know how to write, that the machinery is out of synch, because this is a warrant of non-habitude. (Habit being, in this line of thought, the most dangerous, the only dangerous enemy.) A warrant of being new.

There is in writing a particular hardening. There is in the printed form a particular ageing. During the days when he cannot work, the man tells himself this is the proof that by the newness of his intellectual race he escapes this hardening, this ageing; this is the proof that he is not a habituated being.

Whatever one writes (and this would be another question), there is in writing itself a hardening. Whatever one publishes (and this would be another question), there is in the printed word an ageing and a vulgarity. (The vulgar, in this line of thought, being the contrary of the common; the vulgar is of the crowd, the common, on the contrary, is of the people.) The days when it goes well, our man does like everybody. He writes and publishes. The days when it goes badly, he reminds himself that writing and publishing are the first hardenings and ageings of death.

Whatever one writes, there is in writing a hardening that will no more be made supple. Whatever one publishes, there is in the printed word a staleness of memory that no abrogation will ever efface. One has trodden too much on that path (even when there are beautiful traces). One has marched that route too often (even when the armies have been victorious). When the man was ashes and powder, his nothingness itself was great. His nothingness itself was beautiful. He was still earth. And even when he was mud, his lowliness itself was great. This mud was still alluvial earth. The hollow itself of the road was still of the earth and the rut of the road was like a ploughed furrow. Our wretched modern memories are no more than tarmac roads. And always the entanglements of these baggage trains.

There is a rigidifying of inscription, there is a hardening of writing; and there is not only a stiffness of the printed word: there are innumerable stiffenings superimposed on innumerable printings. Every modern person is a wretched newspaper. And not even a wretched newspaper of one day, of one day only; but like a wretched old newspaper of one day on which, on the very same paper, they have every morning printed the paper of the day. Our modern memories are only ever miserable memories, crumpled and worn-out memories.

The unlettered of ancient times read from the book of nature. Or rather, he was from the book itself, he was the book itself of creation. The lettered of ancient times was a person of the book(s) and was himself one or more books. The modern person is a newspaper, and not only *one* newspaper, but our miserable modern memory is like so many miserable, worn-out newspapers on which, without changing the paper, have been printed every day the newspaper of the day. And we are no more than this frightful staleness of letters.

Our ancestors were blank paper and the linen itself from which the paper is made. The lettered were books. We moderns, we are no more than the ink traces of newspapers.

Seized by a kind of profound dread before his own craft and before what this craft has become and before the human situation of his time, the man turns back toward his people, no more with that secret joy, no more with that secret pride, but with a fearful, timid recognition of having escaped at least a little from the debasement, by having for so long completely escaped from it in the past of his people. He has the impression that what he takes from that is nothing less than this: to have recently come out of the hands of his creator.

In the silence and the darkness of the unlettered soul what then is this profound virtue; what above all is this profound grace? Is it not the virtue and the grace of the disarming power of darkness? Is it not the grace of the release of night? Are not letters all letters of illuminated signs? Are not letters always lighted ramps? Are not letters always alternating? Are not letters neon signs and instruments of illuminated advertising, and are not letters all and always intermittent? Are not letters always what break up and pierce and split apart the night?

Are not letters always those letters linked together that carve out in the night hideous advertising? The man turns back toward his people, towards that long untroubled night. That silence and that darkness are so much closer to the creation; they alone are so noble; they alone are so close to the creation. All the rest is industriousness. All the rest is jumble. All the rest is alphabet.

The man turns back toward the innumerable, the tacit, the vast ocean of his silent people. What a reserve! (What has he made of it?) What a secret treasure! (Has he not squandered it?) But above all, what a mysterious prolongation! Like those oceans that stretch out from latitude to latitude, so the first silence, broken from all sides elsewhere, is prolonged from age to age in the silence of the soul's ignorance. And this silent people is the only echo we can perceive of the first silence of the creation.

Silence of prayer and silence of vow, silence of repose and silence even of work, silence of the seventh day, but silence even of the six days; the voice alone of God; silence of pain and silence of death; silence of the orison; silence of contemplation and of offertory; silence of meditation and of mourning; silence of solitude; silence of poverty; silence of elevation and falling again; within the immense parliament[30] of the modern world the man listens to the immense silence of his people. Why does everyone talk, and what are they saying? Why does everyone write, and what are they publicizing? The man remains silent. The man plunges back into the silence of his people, and going back, back, discovers there the last prolongation we are able to grasp of the eternal silence of the first creation.

Like every man of this time who is worthy of the name, like every man of this time ashamed of this time, proud of his ancestry, turning his back on an entire world, the man turns toward his people. What remains of it in the world? What remains of it outside of him and within him? He turns toward it, he wants at least to re-immerse himself in the memory he has of it. Behind his mother, behind his father, whom he did not even know, that wall, that silent partition, that rank of four illiterates. And a word rises up to the man from the depths of time: *the letter kills.*

Littera occidit. Littera necat.[31] Like so many others, he knew that saying about murder and didn't know it was a saying that murders. He repeated that saying about murder and didn't see it was a saying that

---

30. It is worth noting here that the French word *parlement*, the origin of the English "parliament," has literally to do with "speaking, debating, arguing things out." See also footnote 6.

31. "The letter kills." See 1 Corinthians 3:6.

murders. He didn't take literally that indictment of the letter. He didn't take to the letter that indictment of the letter.

That word that the letter was an instrument of murder and perhaps the only instrument of murder.

And that in the letter was the very apparatus of death.

And as if having escaped an immense danger, he considers his ancestors who did not know the letter. Words of his grandmother, forgotten for forty years, suddenly come back to him: *I don't know my letters,* or: *I've never known my letters,* or: *They never taught me my letters,* she would say, a little ashamed (or animated by some secret pride); for she considered herself a little (and even a lot) as a curiosity, as a rarity, as a being from another time. (She was indeed right. She was very much from another time.) She was very intelligent. She saw clearly what she was witnessing. She saw clearly the whole rise of primary education. She saw clearly that everyone was going to school.

I've never been to school, she used to say; or in preference:
They never sent me to school. Sometimes she explained:
At that age I was working. Or in preference:
At that age everybody worked.

I would like to know if there is now an age when "everybody works"; and at what age "everybody works."

She had not been to school, but she had been to catechism class.

She used to say also:
We didn't even know what a school was.

She used to say also:
I don't even know how to read street names.

And she used to say also:
I don't know how to read the newspaper.[32]

The newspaper, the greatest invention since the creation of the world and certainly since the creation of the soul, for it touches, it reaches into the very constitution of the soul. The newspaper, second creation. Spiritual. Or rather, the beginning, the origin-point of de-creation. Spiritual.

---

32. The italics in this passage are Péguy's.

Origin-point of a second creation. Or rather, origin-point of a degradation, a deformation, an alteration which really constitutes the beginning of de-creation. At least the de-creation of the eminent creation, the essential creation, the central creation, the profound creation, which is the spiritual creation. And in this, through this, some others. And here it is necessary to understand one another well.

I am convinced that there are good and bad newspapers. Above all I am convinced there are bad ones. And there are also those that are good and bad; in varying proportions. I acknowledge there is an entire hierarchy, according to a table of values we can make. Very well, what I am saying is that it is not this table of values that interests me.

What interests me is the very register that makes it a table of values.

I am convinced that there are good and bad publications. And maybe many in-between. I am convinced that there is a good and a bad press; and maybe many in-between. The good thing is that the good press is sometimes bad and perhaps often; while the bad press is never good. It is always the same process of irreversibility and continual degradation. We always lose. We never win. What I am saying is that the bad newspapers do infinitely more evil as newspapers than as bad, the bad press does infinitely more evil as press than as bad. And here it is that we finally rejoin our Bergson: a bad ready-made idea is infinitely more pernicious as ready-made than as bad; a false ready-made idea is infinitely more false as ready-made than as false.

It is in this sense that the invention of the newspaper is without doubt epoch-making, marking the date since the creation of the world that is the very date of the beginning of the de-creation. There is something worse than having a bad thought. It is having a ready-made thought. There is something worse than having a bad soul and even making oneself a bad soul. It is having a ready-made soul. There is something worse even than having a perverse soul. It is having an habituated soul.

We have seen the unbelievable play of grace and the unbelievable graces of grace penetrate a bad and even perverse soul, and we have seen saved what appeared lost. But we have not seen penetrated by moisture what is varnished, permeated what is impermeable, soaked through what is habituated.

The cures and the successes and the rescues of grace are marvelous and we have seen won and we have seen saved what was (as if) lost. The worst distress, the worst baseness, turpitude and crime, sin itself are often cracks in the person's armor, cracks in the breastplate through which grace can penetrate human hardness. But on the inorganic breastplate of habit everything slides off, and every sword is blunted.

Or to put it thus, in the spiritual mechanism the worst distress, baseness, crime, turpitude, sin itself are precisely the points of articulation for the levers of grace. It works through these. Through these it finds the point in every human sinner. Through these it leans on the point of pain. We have seen the greatest criminals saved. Through their very crime; through the mechanism, through the articulation of their crime. We have not seen the most thoroughly habituated saved through the articulation of habit, precisely because habit is that which has no [points of] articulation.

We can do many things. We cannot moisten a material that is made not to be moistened. We can put as much water on it as we wish, for it is not a matter of quantity, it is a matter of contact. It is not a matter of putting water on it. It is a matter of whether it takes or does not take. It is a matter of whether it enters or not into a certain contact. It is the mysterious phenomenon called moistening. Here the quantity is of little importance. We have left behind the physics of hydrostatics. We have entered the physics of moistening, a molecular, globular physics, which rules on the meniscus and the formation of the globule, of the drop. When a surface is greasy, water does not take. It does not take any the more if we put on a lot of water. It does not take, absolutely. The moistening does not get established; a certain contact called moistening does not get established. And it is not a question of quantity because, the moistening not getting underway, this entry into contact not getting underway, every second drop that presents itself is like a first drop. It is just like the first. It is (for the purposes of moistening) the first. It is no more advanced than the first. In order for the physics of quantity, weight, volume, for hydrostatics to come into play, it is necessary that the first drop has already accomplished something, to which the second drop adds. In order to make a weight of one kilogram on the scale of a balance you can raid all the pharmacies and amuse yourself successively placing on it a million weights in tiny flakes of one milligram, which you have swiped from all the glass containers of all the precision balances. You will arrive at a weight. What am I saying? You will arrive at a weight from the beginning, from the first milligram. You are in the physics of weight, because the second milligram does not find an empty situation, an intact situation. Something has begun with the first milligram. The second has only to join it. And the others and the others, as many as there are. As many as it takes.

While in the phenomenon of moistening, in the physics of moistening, nothing has ever begun. You can pass over a greased surface a million drops of water, successively or together. Every second drop that presents itself finds an empty situation. Every second drop that presents itself finds an intact situation. Every second drop that presents itself finds an uninitiated situation. Every second drop that presents itself is (like) a first, presents itself (like) a first. Every second drop that presents itself finds that it must begin. And that it cannot begin.

Every second drop that presents itself finds that it must create.

A comparable phenomenon, a phenomenon of the same order makes itself apparent in the administration of grace. Or rather I will say: this difference, this profound division that registers itself between ordinary physics and the physics of moistening, and that makes it so that one can always add weight but cannot always moisten, this gulf not only persists, but becomes yet deeper when we pass from physical nature to spiritual nature, to what I shall call spiritual matter and spiritual physics. There are spiritual phenomena that behave according to the physics of weight and there are spiritual phenomena that behave according to the physics of moistening.

We have seen many things. But there are fruits that have a down covering made not to be moistened. And now the heavens can rain down. *Rorate, coeli, desuper.*[33]

So long as we are in the physics of weight, of quantity, the abundance of grace flows as an abundance. It even flows, we might say, as a hydrostatic abundance, as an abundance of the hydrostatic order. It soaks, it bathes, it penetrates. Every person who has some experience of grace, in himself, in the neighbor, knows those irresistible infusions, those impenetrable penetrations, those invincible victories. But when we enter the physics of moistening, the physics of humidity, nothing is anything, nothing does anything, the laws of causality do not come into play, notably the laws of physical causality, because the little bit of coupling necessary for the cause to have its effect, for the effect to hold on to the cause, for the cause to hold the effect, for the cause, in a word, to have an effect on the effect, because this little bit of coupling, this little bit of clutch action, which is nothing but which is everything, which is nothing

---

33. "Rain down, heavens, from above" (Isaiah 45:8).

but which is the indispensable nothing, does not take place, does not operate, does not come into play, does not present itself. Whatever all the theories of causality, including the most determinist of them, say, for the passage from the cause to the effect a certain uncoupling, or if you wish a certain kind of coupling, a getting underway, a placing of weight on the pulley is necessary before it turns. The metaphysics of the most hermetically sealed determinism, the metaphysics of the most totally exhaustive causality and efficacy, lack, in order to exhaust, this inevitable little coupling action (which they cannot evade and which reality cannot evade), precisely the same lack that the atomist materialist metaphysics lacked, of a hook for the coupling-together of the atoms, a *clinamen*.[34]

In ordinary or, if you wish, first physics, in the physics of weight and hydrostatics, the coupling and through this the causation is always in play. In the physics of moistening, on the contrary, in the physics of humidity (and it is the same as the physics of the meniscus, of the equilibrium of liquid surfaces, of the formation of drops and droplets, of atmospheres, of diffusions, and of colloidal solutions, and perhaps other solutions), the coupling and through this the causation is not always in play. Everything has a weight, but not everything is subject to moistening. One can always be weighed, one cannot always be dampened. One can always be counterbalanced. One cannot always be penetrated.

From this come so many gaps (for gaps themselves are caused and "come"), from this come so many gaps that we witness in the efficacy of grace, which winning unhoped-for victories in the soul of the greatest sinners, often remains inoperative in the most decent people. It is precisely because the most decent people, or respectable people, or those we call such and who like to call themselves such, have no defects at all in their armor. They are not wounded. Their constantly intact covering of morality makes for a faultlessly armor-plated skin. They do not present that opening made by a terrible wound, an unforgettable distress, an invincible regret, an eternally badly stitched suture, a mortal worry, an invisible anxiety, a secret bitterness, a perpetually masked inner collapse, an eternally unhealed scar. They do not present that entry to grace that sin essentially is. Because they have not been wounded, they are no longer vulnerable. Because they lack nothing they are brought nothing. Because they lack nothing they are not brought that which is everything.

34. In the system of the ancient Greek philosopher Epicurus, the *clinamen* designates the capacity for declination of the atoms, which allows them to come together to form the universe.

Even the charity of God cannot bandage where there are no wounds. It is because the man was on the ground that the Samaritan lifted him up. It is because the face of Jesus was dirty that Veronica wiped it with a kerchief. The person who has not fallen will never be lifted up; and the person who is not dirty will not be wiped clean.

The "decent people" are not moistened by grace.

It is a question of molecular, globular physics. What we call morality is a coating that renders human beings impermeable to grace. So it comes to be that grace acts on the greatest criminals and raises up the most wretched sinners; it has begun by penetrating them, by being able to penetrate them. And from this it comes to be that the beings most dear to us, if they are unhappily coated with morality, are closed to attack by grace, cannot be broached by it. It begins by not being able to penetrate them. Through their skin.

They are impenetrable, in everything, absolutely, because they are coated, because they cannot be moistened through the skin, because they are impenetrable to the moistening, which is also penetration.

A moistening liquid, a moistening body moistens or it does not moisten. It does not moisten more or less. It moistens or it does not moisten. It is not a question of more or less. It is a question of all or nothing. It is a question of beginning or not beginning. And then of having begun or not having begun.

An acid eats into or does not eat into; attacks or does not attack. A lot of sulfuric acid will not do what a little sulfuric acid has failed to do.

No more is it a question of quantity. It is a question of entering or not entering.

It is for this reason that nothing is so contrary to what is called (by a rather ashamed name) religion as what is called morality. Morality coats the person against grace.

And nothing is so foolish (since nothing is so Louis-Philippe and Monsieur Thiers)[35] as putting morality and religion together like this.

---

35. Louis Philippe was the King of France from 1830 to 1848, whose reign was marked by the ascendancy of a wealthy, conservative bourgeoisie. Adolphe Thiers, an historian of the French Revolution and politician, served as Prime Minister of France at various times during the reign of Louis Philippe, and as President of the Third

Nothing is so inane. One might almost say, on the contrary, that everything that is taken by grace is taken away from morality. And all that is won by so-called morality, all that is recovered by so-called morality, is re-covered by that coating we have said is impenetrable to grace.

(It is the same malady as putting the family and private property together. As if it was not principally the regime of modern property and the modern taste for this regime and this private property that is causing the family and the race to perish, to be destroyed in the modern world. And it is really, moreover, the same confusion, the same false ligature and conjunction. Morality is a proprietorship, a regime, and certainly a taste for private property. Morality makes us proprietors of our poor virtues. Grace makes us a family and a race. Grace makes us children of God and brothers and sisters of Jesus Christ.)[36]

It is really what they were saying in the centuries of French grandeur, it is really what our elders and fathers were saying (when one knew how to speak French) when they said that grace touches the heart. This implies also that when it does not invade, when it does not penetrate, then it does not touch. It does not establish a contact. This is the formula itself of *Polyeucte*.[37] It is therefore the definitive formula. It would be vain to want to look for another. And it would be vain to want to look for a better. I have said often that *Polyeucte* is the greatest and most perfect work we will ever see. For it is not only perfect: it is perfect in every part, it is fecund with everything, it gives with both hands. It is filled with all plenitude. It is without fear and *nevertheless* without reproach. And it is without reproach and *nevertheless* without fear. It realizes without a shadow of trouble and so without a shadow of effort, without the appearance of effort, the most rare liaison, the most rare conjunction that it can be given a work to effect. It is a work of nature and at the same time a work of grace. It is a work of the interior life and at the same time public life. It is a work of the spiritual life and at the same time civic life. It is war and peace. And it is one and the other kind of war and one and the other kind of peace; the Scythians and sin; the enemies and the

---

Republic in the aftermath of the Franco-Prussian war of 1870–71.

36. See Romans 8:14–17.

37. *Polyeucte* was the last great play written by Pierre Corneille (in 1642); its subject is the martyrdom of Polyeuctus, an Armenian nobleman converted to Christianity in the ancient Roman Empire during the persecutions of the Emperor Valerian in the third century.

Enemy. It is the whole of humanity and it is the whole City; humanity and Rome; the world and the city; *orbis* and *urbs*;[38] all the distress and all the triumph. And it is also all ancient philosophy; all wisdom grappling with grace (and how well he has shown, of all that there is in the world, it is wisdom that is most impenetrable to grace). And also the whole secret of the legacy of the ancient world. For though he lacks any respect for false gods, he does not lack respect for those who respect the false gods, he does not lack respect for those who adore the false gods and who have been nourished on the ancient wisdom. In this way the Christian world was going to reject Jupiter but not Virgil; the Christian world was going to reject Zeus but not Plato, nor Homer; nor, and perhaps not enough, Aristotle—and yet more, in this Polyeucte, not [reject] Rome and the province, naively and I will say almost charmingly: "Son-in-law of the governor of the whole province."[39] And the work is as perfect, as irreproachable, as unimpeachable, as impeccable theologically as it is poetically. It is a work without sin.

"This God *touches* hearts when they least think about it": such is the formula of Polyeucte. It is the very formula of the bite, the attack, the invasion, the penetration of grace. It implies that the one who thinks about it, who has the habit of thinking about it, who is covered with that coating of habit, is also the one who offers the least purchase, and so to speak the least risk of purchase [for grace].

I do not want to force the meaning of this verse of Corneille's. It is not a theological proposition. There are many propositions of theology in *Polyeucte*, all impeccably expressed. This verse is not one. It is markedly something else, which demands particular attention. It is a proposition of the history, or rather the chronicle of grace. It is a proposition of memory, of recollection, a proposition both memorable and monumental of that which occurs, that which happens in the reality of the usage of grace. I mean in the double sense of its usage, of the use we make of it and above all of the use it makes of us. I find these propositions of memory, of recollection of what happens in reality infinitely more pertinent than a purely theoretical proposition. Such a proposition of history and of memory, of recollection, such a proposition of reality gathered up, reality attained, is to a theoretical proposition what a campaign of Napoleon is to a course at the École de Guerre.

---

38. "world" and "city."
39. *Polyeucte*, Act IV, scene 3.

But let us get back into the text, this text filled with poetic, dramatic, theological inspiration. We are going to see how much it is in complete agreement with our direction.

[POLYEUCTE]

Seigneur, de vos bontés il faut que je l'obtienne;
Elle a trop de vertus pour n'être pas chrétienne:
Avec trop de mérite il vous plut la former,
Pour ne vous pas connaître et ne vous pas aimer,
Pour vivre des enfers esclave infortunée,
Et sous leur triste joug mourir comme elle est née.

PAULINE

Que dis-tu, malheureux? Qu'oses-tu souhaiter?

POLYEUCTE

Ce que de tout mon sang je voudrais acheter.

PAULINE

Que plutôt . . . !

POLYEUCTE

C'est en vain qu'on se met en défense:
Ce dieu touche les coeurs lorsque moins on y pense.
Ce bienheureux moment n'est pas encor venu;
Il viendra, mais le temps ne m'en est pas connu.[40]

40.
[POLYEUCTE]

Lord, through your goodness, I must win her;
She has too many virtues not to be a Christian:
It pleased you to form her with too much merit
Not to know you and not to love you,
To live as the wretched slave of hell,
And under this dismal yoke, to die as she was born.

I do not want to analyze these verses. And above all, I do not want to put them into prose. And I do not want to comment on them. As much as anyone I know that verse and prose are two different, non-communicating beings, and to say the same thing in prose and in verse is not to say the same thing. I know that there is in verse a virtue of its own, a destination of its own. All that I want to hold on to from this admirable poetry is that God takes human beings, so to speak, through their lack of attention. But what will become of those who do not even have lapses of attention?

God takes human beings through their defenses. But what will become of those who do not even put themselves in a posture of defense?

Let us note that Corneille's subject here is the contrary of ours. Or rather, it is our subject that is the contrary and complement of Corneille's. Corneille's subject is the story of Polyeucte. It is the story of a martyr and saint; the flowering of grace and the fructification of blood. Our poor subject, on the contrary and complementarily, is the story of those who are not Polyeucte. It is the story of those who are not saints and who are not martyrs. And I will say above all, it is the story of those who are not even sinners.

PAULINE:

What are you saying, poor wretch? For what are you daring to hope?

POLYEUCTE:

For what with all my blood I would like to buy.

PAULINE:

What...!

POLYEUCTE:

It's vain to defend oneself:
This God touches hearts when they least think about it.
That blessed moment has not yet come;
It will come, but the time is not known to me.

Polyeucte, Act IV, scene 3. My translation above is a close literal rendering; for a more poetic English version of this and other major plays by Corneille, see *The Chief Plays of Corneille*.

Corneille shows us how grace acts, how it surprises, how it seizes, how it penetrates. Our poor subject today is to note how it does not act, how it does not penetrate.

And so Corneille triumphs. But we do not triumph.

Corneille triumphs. If it is a question of considering the ravages of grace, all is marvelous. And all will happen marvelously. It carries away those who are for it. Perhaps more it carries away those who are against it. But those who are neither for it nor against it; the immeasurable herd of the neutral; the immeasurable neutrality of the lukewarm?

It carries away those who have put themselves on guard. But those who have not even put themselves on guard?

It carries away those who have put themselves in a posture of defense. But those who have not even put themselves in a posture of defense?

> And to the angel of the church in Laodicea write: The words of the Amen, the Faithful and True Witness, the Origin of God's creation:
>
> I know your works: you are neither cold not hot. I wish that you were either cold or hot.
>
> So, because you are lukewarm, and neither cold nor hot, I am about to spit you out of my mouth.

> *Et angelo Laodiciae ecclesia scribe: Haec dicit: Amen, testis fidelis et verus, qui est principium creaturae Dei:*
>
> *Scio opera tua: quia neque frigidus es, neque calidus: utinam frigidus esses, aut calidus.*
>
> *Sed quia tepidus es, et nec frigidus nec calidus, incipiam te emovere ex ore meo.*[41]

Corneille's subject is itself gracious. It is a question of showing how grace operates. Our poor subject, on the contrary and complementarily, is ungracious. It is dis-graceful. It is a question, unhappily, of showing how grace does not operate.

So long as we are on the side of grace, there are only marvels and dazzling sights. It remains, unhappily, to ask ourselves why all is not on the side of grace.

I am well aware of the sort of baseness there is both in analyzing and commenting on a work like *Polyeucte*, and in attempting to draw up some inadequate complementary table, some inadequate inventory of

---

41. Revelation 3:14–16. Péguy quotes the passage in both French and Latin in the original text.

complementarity. However, things are so bad at this point that we must go through this baseness. The problem we are posing to ourselves is the very problem of the historian. And it is less that of the theologian than, if I may say so, of the historian of theological material. (The theologian being, in this system of language, the theoretician of theological material.)

May I be forgiven, then, and may I forgive myself for analyzing, commenting on, complementing this incomparable work. At the point where we now are this baseness has become inevitable.

Corneille chose the better part. I do not speak only of his genius, which was a unique gift and itself a unique grace in the history of the world. I speak of the material on which he was going to apply his genius.

Corneille chose the better part. He took an entire world prior to the first explosion of grace. Or rather, he gave himself *the* world, for it is always the same. It is always the same that serves, the same material, time (even, in this sense, duration) having only one dimension, so that there is no second dimension where properly historical action would be able to break out. So that it is necessary that the spirit always work on the same material, operate always on the same world.

Corneille gave himself the springtime of grace. And even that first dawning of the spring, which surpasses in hopefulness the spring itself and which is like an advance of eternal life. Like an anticipation of beatitude. He has left us not even the melancholies of autumn and the fallen leaves, but the ingratitudes of dead wood.

He gave himself that first explosion of the budding of grace in the world. He gave himself the world before the first explosion of grace and had to do no more than represent for us that marvelous bursting forth. He had to do no more than represent for us those extraordinary advances. But as for us, our baseness and our unhappy fate constrains us to examine the limitations, the lapses of grace.

Corneille was taking the world, if I may say so, before the beginning of grace. So he had everything to win. And nothing to lose. He could only win. However, from a certain moment, which it remains to situate precisely, as well as the time and the place, begins an unhappy second era, where we can win or lose.

A wretched, paltry era, which is ours, and which is the era itself of militation.

And of limitation.

And which is now forever.

Which comes back to saying, and very simply, that grace itself, in entering the world, introducing itself, operating in the world, was not at all removed, not at all shielding itself from the general conditions of humanity and the world, and that for grace too and for the Christian revolution, it is the beginning that was most beautiful. For the Christian revolution too there was a dawning.

Et le premier soleil sur le premier matin.[42]

Which comes back to saying that it is another face of the mystery of the incarnation. *Et homo factus est.*[43] In the same way that Jesus was truly and literally made man, made man faithfully and without cheating, so truly and literally, through a movement parallel and conjoined, and perhaps included, through an incarnation, might one say parallel and conjoined and perhaps and probably included, faithfully and without cheating, grace was made temporal and historical; it entered faithfully into the general conditions of humanity and the world, and among all of them, the dominant conditions that perhaps gather up all the others, which are the conditions of memory, and within those the conditions of the hardening of habit, the clogging-up of habit.

Now if the Bergsonian philosophy was the first in the history of the world that came to memory (and within it, history) as the heart of the difficulty, if the Bergsonian philosophy was the first in the history of the world that went directly and centrally and by a way that has all the character of the direct and immediate way of genius, if it was the first that went axially to matter and memory as the two terms, the two poles to be rapidly extricated from the most profound problem, who does not see through this new aspect, who does not begin again to see what an enormous command, for the first time in the history of the world, the Bergsonian philosophy has given us over the profound difficulties, the central and axial difficulties of this problem of grace, which is probably the most profound Christian problem?

Within this problem of grace Corneille reserved for himself, gave himself grace itself, and he left us, unhappily, only dis-grace. He gave himself the part of grace, and he left us, unhappily, only the complementary

---

42. "And the first sun on the first morning." This is from Péguy's "Ève," verse 4.
43. "And was made man."

part, which finds itself by definition the part of dis-grace. He assigned himself the marvelous way of grace, leaving us only the dis-graces and ingratitudes of the counter-way and the limitations of the way. He gave himself sufficiency, leaving us only deficiency. He gave himself efficacy, leaving us only the failings.

He gave himself the life and the flower and the budding, leaving us only the thankless care of knowing how all this ended in nothing more than dead wood.

Now dead wood is wood that is extremely habituated, it is wood brought to the limit of habitude. It is wood entirely full of its own memory and the residue of its vegetal memory.

In a Bergsonian system (I do not say in the Bergsonian system; I do not wish to implicate our *maître* in the progression I am seeing), the death of a being is its complete saturation by habit, its complete saturation by memory, that is its complete saturation by ageing. And thus its complete saturation by sclerosis and hardening.

(I mean material, temporal death; and within that material death, non-accidental death—not death through disease, which is mechanical in this sense, that it is always the result of a fault in the mechanism—I mean death that is so to speak essential, normal, by ageing.)

Well then, in a Bergsonian system (I do not say in the Bergsonian system) that material death, temporal, normal and not irregular, essential so to say and not accidental, regular and not abnormal, physiological and not mechanical, that usual death of the being, that death-as-user is attained when the material being is filled up with its habitude, filled up with its memory, filled up with the hardening of its habitude and its memory, when all the material being is occupied by habit, memory, hardening, when all the matter of the being is *busy* with habit, memory, hardening, when there no longer remains one atom of matter for the new which is life.

In this sense and in this system the so-to-speak essential death of the being is obtained, attained, when the being reaches the limit of its habitude, the limit of its memory, the limit of the hardening of its habitude and its memory. In other terms, as we could expect, death is the limit of the amortization period.

Or what amounts to the same thing, it is the limit of ageing.

That then is the dead wood. Death is the limit of the filling up by memory, the limit of the filling up by habit, the limit of the filling up by hardening, ageing, amortization.

When all the matter is consecrated to memory, there is death.

When all the matter of a being, all the matter at its disposal, is allotted to memory (to ageing, hardening, amortization, habit), when there is no longer one atom of *free* matter, then one attains that limit that is death. (Material, physiological death.)

And by this again one perceives the profound triple liaison of freedom, grace, and life; and that there is a gratuity common to the three; and that determinism (to the extent it is thinkable; but I do not charge myself with thinking it: that A yields B without ceasing to be A and without becoming B, which itself is not A, *is no longer A*), physical and metaphysical determinism, is perhaps merely the law of residues, of what unceasingly falls by the way.

Determinism (to the extent it is thinkable) would be the law of a vast refuse.

And if it is not thinkable by a living, thinking being, this is perhaps precisely because it is the law of that which is no longer within the living, no longer within being, of refuse.

A being that is dying is a being that has arrived at this point, at this limit, of being completely invaded, completely occupied by its refuse, by the immense refuse of its memory.

Dust and debris, the immense debris of its habitude.

Dead wood is wood habituated to the extreme. And a dead soul is also a soul habituated to the extreme.

Dead wood is wood habituated to its limit. And a dead soul is also a soul habituated to its limit.

It is highly noteworthy that spiritual death, the death of the soul, is represented in the traditional language of the Church as the result (and we could say as the limit) of a hardening. We must refrain from seeing this as a metaphor. Moreover, it is never a matter of metaphor. When one speaks of the final hardening and final impenitence,[44] it is necessary to understand this as a real phenomenon of induration that renders the soul like dead wood. It is really a spiritual incrustation, a cladding of habit, which henceforth prevents the soul from being moistened by grace.

All the spiritual matter, all the matter of the soul, is thus allotted to the cladding of habit, consecrated to the cladding of habit, devoured by habit in order to be, to become that cladding.

---

44. See Romans 2:5.

It is strictly a degeneration and even a physiological degeneration. The cladding does not only clad. Not only is it a cladding. But in descending the cladding reaches into the heart. All is nothing more than cladding. It is strictly a degeneration of the tissue. The heart itself becomes cladding.

The cladding is all and there is no longer anything to be clad.

We know those words of the old man, which for my part I find admirable: "What a shame," he said, "that one must die." (He was thinking only of his physical death, for someone capable of such sweet and profoundly innocent words is evidently not bearing any trace of that hardening of the soul which ends in spiritual death.) "What a shame," he said, "that one must give up life. *I was finally getting used to it.*"

He didn't realize how well he spoke. It is precisely because he *achieved* that habituation[45] that he ended up also as one of death's achievements.

Let others look for quarrels about literalism. The letter kills. For me, how not already to see, and while expecting perhaps so many other features, how not to see a profound kinship, a mysterious accord in the depths of thought, how not to see a parallel approach and deepening between that old traditional formula of the Church's teaching that spiritual death is the result of a hardening, and those profound theories about memory and habit that are one of the irrevocable conquests of Bergsonian thought?

Let others look here for petty quarrels. Perhaps we will address them one day. Today, I want only to see what I see. I see that Christian thought, expressed in one of the oldest and most traditional formulas of the teaching of the Church, and Bergsonian thought, expressed throughout the work of our *maître*, and notably in *Matière et mémoire (essai sur la relation du corps à l'esprit)* and in the *Essai sur les données immédiates de la conscience*,[46] proceed in such parallel ways, penetrate into spiritual realities through such a parallel and kindred deepening, that we only entered fully into the intelligence of this old formula of the teaching of the Church when armed with the fullness of the meaning and intelligence of the Bergsonian illumination.

Yes, the Church and the Church's teaching have always said that spiritual death was the result of a hardening, and that final impenitence was a final hardening. But who does not see that the fullness of meaning

---

45. Péguy's point is even clearer in the original French, where "to get used to" is *s'habituer*.

46. Published in English as *Matter and Memory* and *Time and Free Will*.

of this formula, and not only the fullness but also the extreme rigor and exactitude, who does not see that the fullness of the content of this formula only appears (and consequently only appears in world history) in the light of Bergsonian thought?

Yes, the Church and the Church's teaching have always said that spiritual death, the death of the soul, was the result of a final hardening. But what now, in its entire depth, is the hardening? What is the sclerosis, metaphysically? And thus what is a final hardening? In what does it actually consist? In what way is it essentially and also exactly mortal? In what way is it an infallible progression towards death and the only road to death and the only death itself? That is what we have only been able to fathom armed with the results of the Bergsonian deepenings, that is what we have only been able to see armed with the results of the Bergsonian illumination.

Yes, the Church and the Church's teaching have always said that spiritual death was the result of a hardening. But what this hardening was in itself, what this hardening was in being itself—it is Bergsonian thought that has deepened this for us, that has actually illuminated this for us.

For it was necessary for Bergsonian thought to come into time, into world history, that finally the metaphysical reality of matter, memory, habit, ageing, hardening be penetrated to the depths, so that this profound connection of memory, habit, ageing, hardening unto death also be illuminated and penetrated.

Thanks to Bergson and Bergsonian thought, when we speak of matter and memory, and of the connection between matter and memory, when we speak of habit, of ageing, of hardening we finally know what we are talking about, we know it exactly, we know it in depth; and by this, and in this, we know the mechanism of the progression to spiritual death; and by this, and in this, we know the mechanism of that hebetude, that blunting effect of habit, that finishes by rendering a soul impenetrable to the infusions of grace.

Which is to say that by this, and in this, we know the mechanism of that limitation of grace, or finally, of the action of grace, which has become, which is presently, the object of our poor study.

For dead wood is wood entirely invaded by the *ready-made*, entirely occupied, entirely dedicated to the ready-made, entirely devoured by the ready-made, entirely consumed by the invasion of the ready-made. Entirely shriveled up, entirely mummified; filled by its habit and its memory. It is wood that has arrived at the limit of its amortization.[47] It is wood all of whose matter has been conquered little by little through this ageing. It is wood all of whose suppleness has been eaten away little by little through this stiffening, all of whose being has become sclerotic little by little through this hardening. It is wood that no longer has an atom of room, an atom of matter, for the *being-made*. For the making of the being-made. So no more of it is formed, no more of it is made.

Similarly a dead soul is a soul entirely invaded by the *ready-made*, entirely occupied, entirely dedicated to the ready-made, entirely devoured by the ready-made, entirely consumed by the invasion of the ready-made. Entirely shriveled up, entirely mummified; filled by its residue, filled by its debris; filled by its habit and its memory. It is a soul that has arrived at the limit of its amortization. It is a soul all of whose matter, so to speak, all of whose spiritual matter has been conquered little by little through this ageing. It is a soul all of whose suppleness has been eaten away little by little through this stiffening, all of whose being has become sclerotic little by little through this hardening. It is a soul entirely invaded by the crusting over of its habitude, by the incrustation of its memory. It is a soul that no longer has an atom of room, an atom of spiritual matter, for the *being-made*. For the making of the being-made. So it no longer forms with it; no longer makes with it. It no longer has an atom of freedom. And here we find again, we rejoin that profound connection between grace and freedom, the gracious and gratuitous, that mutual irrevocable requirement of grace and freedom.

Dead wood is wood residual in the extreme; a dead soul is a soul residual in the extreme.

Dead wood is wood habituated to the extreme. A dead soul is a soul habituated to the extreme.

Dead wood is wood that remembers too much organically. A dead soul is a soul that remembers too much organically and psychologically.

Dead wood is wood habituated to the limit. A dead soul is a soul habituated to the limit.

Dead wood is wood too stuffed with its past. A dead soul is a soul too stuffed with its past.

Dead wood is residual to the limit. A dead soul is a soul residual to the limit.

---

47. *amortissement*; my translation as "amortization" attempts to convey Péguy's wordplay on *mort* ("death") and *amortissement* throughout this section.

In this line of thought, the seed, on the contrary, is at the limit at the other end. The seed is what is residual to the minimum; what is *ready-made* to the minimum; what is of habit and memory to the minimum.

And so of ageing, stiffening, hardening, amortization to the minimum.

And so, to the contrary, of freedom, play, suppleness and grace to the maximum and to the limit.

The seed is what is least habituated. It is where there is the least of matter monopolized, fixed by memory and habit.

The seed is where there is the least of matter dedicated to memory.

It is where there is the least of *dossiers*, the least of *memoranda*.

The least of paperwork, the least of bureaucracy.

Or again, it is what is the nearest to the creation; what is the most *recent*, in the sense of the Latin word *recens*.[48] It is what is the most fresh; the most recently come from the hands of God.

Dead wood is where there is the most matter dedicated to memory.

And memory and habit are the harbingers of death.

For they introduce the ageing, the stiffening, the hardening that are the very expressions of the amortization of death.

Dead wood is that which has been completely overcome by its *dossiers*, by the accumulation of its *memoranda*.

Dead wood is wood that has been organically overcome, and to the limit, by the invasion of its organic memory.

Dead wood is wood that has succumbed to the accumulation of its paperwork; of its bureaucracy.

Or again, it is what is farthest from the creation; the least recent; the least fresh. The least, the most remote from coming from the hands of God.

A dead soul is a soul where the most matter (spiritual) is dedicated to memory.

And memory and habit are also the harbingers of that death.

A dead soul is a soul that has been totally overcome by its *dossiers*, by the accumulation of its *memoranda*.

It is a soul that has been organically and psychologically overcome, and to the limit, by the invasion of its organic and psychological memory.

It is a soul where there is no longer an atom of room; for freedom and conjointly for grace.

---

48. The Latin *recens* has the meaning of "recent," and also "fresh," "young," "vigorous."

It is a soul where there is no longer a vacant atom.

It is a soul where there is no longer an atom of matter (spiritual) which is free for freedom and conjointly for grace.

A dead soul is a soul that has succumbed to the accumulation of its paperwork; of its bureaucracy.

Or finally, it is a soul that is the farthest from the creation; the least recent; the least fresh; the most de-created. The most remote from coming from the hands of God.

And when they say that the Church has received eternal promises, which are gathered together in one eternal promise, it is necessary to understand rigorously by this that she has received the promise that she will never succumb to her own ageing, to her own hardening, to her habitude and her memory.

That she will never become dead wood and a dead soul; that she will never go to the end of an amortization ending in death.

That she will never succumb to her *dossiers* and to her history.

That her *memoranda* will never crush her totally.

That she will never succumb to the accumulation of her paperwork, to the stiffening of her bureaucracy.

And that the saints will always splash back up.

Here appears in a new light, here shines forth, here at this juncture splashes up in its fullness the sense and force and central purpose of that virtue that we have named the young child Hope.[49] She is essentially counter-habit. And so she is diametrically and axially and centrally counter-death. She is the source and the seed. She is the splashing up and the grace. She is the heart of freedom. She is the virtue of the new and the virtue of youth. And it is not in vain that she is a theological virtue and even the princess of the theological virtues, and it is not in vain that she is at the center of the theological virtues, since without her Faith would slide over the cladding of habit; and without her Charity would slide over the cladding of habit.

It is notably she who guarantees to the Church that she will not succumb to her own mechanism.

Thus shines forth in its full light the sense and force and vocation and, so to speak, virtue of what we have named the young child Hope. She

---

49. In *The Portal of the Mystery of Hope*.

is the source of life, for she is that which constantly dis-habituates. She is the seed. Of every spiritual birth. She is the source and the splashing up of grace, for she is that which constantly unclads that mortal cladding of habit. And it is not in vain that she is a theological virtue. For she is the child-princess of the theological virtues. And she is the *dauphine* and daughter of France. And it is not in vain that she walks in the center between her two big sisters and that her two big sisters give her their hand. But they do not give her their hand in the sense one might believe. Because she is little one believes she needs the others. In order to walk. But it is the others, on the contrary, who need her. And who are glad to give her their hand. In order to walk. For without her Faith would have taken on the habit of the world, and without her Charity would have taken on the habit of the poor. And so Faith without her and Charity without her would each in its own way have taken on the habit even of God.

It is she who is charged with beginning again, as habit is charged with the ending of beings. Both material beings and spiritual beings. She is essentially and diametrically counter-habit, and so counter-amortization and counter-death. She is charged with constantly dis-habituating. She is charged with always beginning again. She is charged with constantly dismantling the mechanism of habit. She is charged with introducing everywhere beginnings, as habit introduces everywhere endings and deaths. She is charged with introducing everywhere organisms, as habit introduces everywhere mechanisms. She is charged with introducing everywhere beginnings of beginnings, beginnings of beings, as habit introduces everywhere beginnings, or rather the unnumbered and always the same beginning of the end.

She is the principle, this child is the principle of re-creation, as habit is the principle of de-creation.

She makes, as habit unmakes.

She introduces everywhere and always unnumbered creations.

She is the always young agent of creation and of grace. She is thus the most direct, the most present agent of God.

She introduces everywhere entries and gains, entries of creation, as habit introduces everywhere exits by amortization and burials.

She is charged in a word, and here we find again our Descartes, she is charged with the service of continued creation.[50]

---

50. See the preceding chapter, footnote 14.

The two others [i.e., Faith and Charity] have their proper object, but without her, who has no proper object, the proper objects of the two others would gradually sink into the amortizations of habit.

She has no proper object precisely because her object is all. It is the whole creation and the Creator; it is the world together with God. She is charged with applying to all (not, probably, to God, but to everything that comes to us from God and the little that we render to God) a certain treatment of which she has the secret, and which is the treatment of renovation, of perpetual renewal and the constant re-introduction of the virtue of creation.

So she is not defined by her object (by an object), but by a certain treatment that she applies, and she only, to every object.

Faith has a proper object, which is belief. Charity has a proper object, which is love. But without the child Hope, Faith would habituate itself to belief, to the world, to God. And without the child Hope, Charity would habituate itself to love, to the poor, to God.

It is by Hope that all the rest remain ready to begin again. From there comes its unique place among the virtues. At the world's baptism the angels and human beings received their names and their portions, and the cardinal and the theological virtues shared out the world. Only one received nothing, except to be the one that would watch over all the others.

Only one received nothing, except to be the one without which the others would be nothing.

Only one received nothing, except to be the one without which the others would grow moldy.

Only one received nothing, except to be the one without which grace would *grow old* in the world.

And one can almost say that this child who has no domain at all, no portion at all, and who provides for the domains of all the others, and who alone provides, one must say, for the needs, for the one profound and veritable need of all the others, which is not to perish and not to grow sluggish in the amortizations of habit, it must be said that this child-virtue, this *Innocent*,[51] this Hope offers hereby an example and a model of absolute charity.

---

51. An allusion to his poem, "Le Mystère des saints Innocents."

(Here I open a parenthesis; and be reassured: I will close it. I will even close it not far from here. That the battle that has arisen around Bergson and the Bergsonian revolution is at this point furious, is in the order of things. But that it has arisen in such a backwards manner, is in the disorder of things.

That it is at this point fierce and unrelenting: it is generally thus that the world welcomes thought. That it is generally malicious, I yet consent to: it is generally thus that the world welcomes the good.

But that it has arisen in such a backwards manner, I confess that continues to seem to me to defy belief.

Here again it is necessary to distinguish. Bergson has enemies who are in order and enemies who are in disorder. He has enemies who are the right way round and enemies who are the wrong way round.

That the positivists combat the man who has forever undone positivism—that is a straightforward battle, a clean battle, and the right way round.

That the materialists combat, and even to the end, the man who has forever undone materialism—I declare this to be their office. They deliver a straightforward battle, a clean battle, and the right way round.

That the determinists combat, and implacably, the man who has forever undone determinism—I will go so far as to say that in a sense they are only doing their duty. Since they are charged with being determinists and defending this thesis and occupying this position. They deliver a straightforward battle, a clean battle, and the right way round.

But that the man who has reintroduced freedom into the world has so strongly against him the politicians of liberty;[52] that the man who has snatched France away from German intellectual servitudes has so strongly against him the politicians of an action called "*française*";[53] that the man who has reintroduced the spiritual life into the world has so strongly against him the politicians of the spiritual life[54]—this is what I call a reversal and something defying belief and a deliberate scandal and

52. Péguy is likely thinking here of the Socialist party, and particularly the most prominent among them, Jean Jaurès.

53. A reference to the conservative, nationalist movement known as the Action Française, whose most prominent figure was Charles Maurras.

54. Péguy has in mind here the Catholic critics of Bergson, especially the leading proponent of neo-Thomist rationalism, Jacques Maritain (another friend-opponent of Péguy's), whose criticisms of Bergson helped to precipitate the placing of the philosopher's works on the *Index*. For more on the debates swirling around Bergson, and Péguy's own position, see the Introduction.

a battle the wrong way round; or rather a battle threefold the wrong way round. This could not be comprehended if we did not know that we are living precisely in the diametrical reversal of parties; and if we did not know that generally the political parties are diametrically opposed to the mystiques that they pretend to be continuing. Nothing is opposed to the mystiques of freedom like the politicians of freedom. Nothing is opposed to the mystiques of France like the politicians of the Action Française. Nothing is opposed to the mystiques of the spiritual life like the politicians of the spiritual life.[55]

I will confess, however, that I am not surprised the French politicians of the spiritual life have so hastily succeeded in getting the thought of Bergson condemned by the Roman [Catholic] bureaucracy. It was entirely natural that a bureaucracy, of whatever sort, be warned against the philosophy that has set itself the most diametrically, in the way we have just seen, against habit, ageing, mummification, bureaucracy, death.

I don't want to enter in passing into such a serious debate. I don't want to enter it slantwise. Angled bridges make for admirable artifacts, especially for railways, under the name of viaducts, and especially when they are made of stone and so have the form of a Roman arch. However, we will not make one today. In another *cahier*, if I am able, beginning with the beginning, I myself will open up that great debate. Bergson has today two races of enemies, or (how to put it?) two classes of enemies; or rather two continents of enemies. He has against him the enemies of the Old World; I mean belonging to the Old World. And he has against him the enemies of the New World; I mean coming out of the New World, belonging to the New World. He has against him the enemies of the Old Continent. And he has against him the enemies of the New Continent. He has against him the enemies he deserves. And he has those he counter-deserves. He has those he made for himself. And he has those he counter-made. He has his direct enemies. And he has his counter-direct enemies; or perverse.

He has against him his enemies and the friends of his enemies. That's good. But there is this.

---

55. Péguy's distinction between *la mystique* and *la politique,* and his analysis of how the former is deformed in the latter, is central to his thought about history. For his fullest account of these concepts, see his essay about the Dreyfus affair, and his own participation in it, "Notre jeunesse," adapted and translated into English by Alexander Dru as "Memories of Youth," in *Temporal and Eternal.*

He has against him his enemies and the enemies of his enemies. But he does not have for him the friends of his enemies. The old irreversibility still operates. In this system also one always loses and never wins.

In sum, today he has everyone against him. It is a sign of his greatness.

He does not even have for him all the friends of his friends. For enmity always eats into friendship. And friendship never eats into enmity. And hatred, envy, and pride always win.

He has against him those he has lost. And he has against him those he has saved. It would be to know the world badly not to be convinced that the latter are the more relentless; the more filled with venom; the more filled with malice and complacency; the more filled with assurance and condemnation.

He has against him all those he has ruined. He has against him those who owe him everything. It would be to know humanity badly not to be convinced that the latter will never forgive him.

The man who undid materialism has against him the materialist party. That's good. It's right.

The man who undid determinism has against him the determinist party. That's good. It's right.

The man who therefore undid atheism has against him the atheist party. That's good. It's right.

In a word, the man who undid a false intellectualism has against him the scientistic party. That's good. It's right.

But the man who reintroduced freedom has against him the radical party.

The man who snatched French thought away from German servitudes has against him the party called *action française*.

The man who reintroduced the spiritual life has against him the devout party.

This is the threefold defying of belief it would be necessary to counter. This is the threefold scandal it would be necessary to elucidate; and perhaps to clean up. This is at least the threefold interior contrariety, the threefold reversal (the threefold ingratitude) that it would be necessary to analyze a little, to clarify, classify, establish, perhaps to dismantle.

I am not a polemicist. Today I have preferred to follow a thought. And it has led us far. Bergson is not charged with being a Catholic. He is not charged with drafting the Apostle's Creed. He is not charged with formulating a theory of grace. And he is not responsible for having discovered the second Hope.[56] But I have just shown, and really without doing so expressly, that the theory of grace and its splashing up, hermetically articulated within the theory of human freedom and of desuetude, and the theory of hope and of ageing only provide their exactitude and fullness for a humanity that has passed through Bergsonian thought. And I go further. I will say my entire thought, for I will say: If God were served fully in his Church (he is served in it with exactitude, but with such a meager exactitude), he would perhaps not need to remind himself, when wishing to give a great grace of thought, that always there, and always in his hand, is the people of his first servants.)[57]

It is precisely that youth of the world and that people of hope and that vast newness and universal non-habitude that Corneille undertook to represent to us, that he devoted himself to represent to us. How well he succeeded we perhaps know. But I don't know whether we know this well enough. I see so much beauty in *Polyeucte*, and of such perfection, and so much plenitude, that I don't know whether everyone sees all of it. I would like to become old enough one day to be able to give myself the space to enumerate some of the features I see there. I would like to engage in that childishness of placing commentaries around a text that does not need them (and because it is a text, and because, among all, it is *Polyeucte*). I would like to demonstrate such innocence as to place explications around a text that, having the most plenitude, has the least need of explication. (They say these contradictions, this *gaucherie*, this making a point of speaking at the moment one should keep silent belong to love.) I only wanted today to note his subject and perhaps in this way to distinguish it from ours, separate it from the unhappy subject remaining to us.

Corneille gave himself that world, that people of hope, that invention of the new, that innovation of newness. He gave himself that childhood and youth. And that reflection as if of the climate of the first garden. He gave himself that dawn and that first light and that beginning of all beginnings. He left us the morning and the noontime and the evening and the long day. He left us the evening and the ageings of the evening. And the ageings of middle age, perhaps worse yet than the ageings of old age. And we can now say, we who have been formed by the Bergsonian

56. Perhaps a reference to Christian hope, associated with the incarnation, as distinct from the "first" hope, associated with Jewish messianism.

57. An allusion to the fact that Bergson—who, in Péguy's view, had done so much to give meaning and clarity to Christian hope and grace—was Jewish.

discipline, and now that humanity has passed through Bergsonian thought and possesses the resources of Bergsonian language: Corneille gave himself grace. And he left us only habit. He gave himself the world of grace. And he left us only the world of habit.

He gave himself the Roman world non-habituated to God; and the immense and unbelievable ravages of grace in a non-habituated world. He left us a world habituated to God, and the unbelievable lack of purchase for grace in a habituated world.

When one knows grace a little, when one has some experience of it, even historical or so to say literary, the problem is not the action of grace. It is its inaction. It is in the limitations that it meets. One does not naturally wonder that it acts. One does not even wonder why and how and where it acts. One only wonders one thing: why it does not act always and everywhere.

That kind of false shame that unhappily holds sway among Catholics, that human respect, that bad respect, that narrow shame makes them think ever only of bringing forward their proofs. (What they call their proofs, it's generally just excuses. They always plead guilty.) It is the proofs of the others that they should demand. I would really like to see them, the proofs of the others.

For someone who has some idea of what grace is, the real problem is not grace. The real problem is dis-grace and ingratitude.

That is to say the limitations and inactions and failures of grace to take hold.

It is like the celebrated proofs for the existence of God. For a mind a little truly philosophical, the real problem is not fullness but the void, or rather the voids. The real problem is not God but, if I may say so, the limitations and even the lapses of God.

There are in the world and in humanity two limitations and, so to speak, two lapses in regard to God. Two limitations on the action of God. Two limitations, two lapses (in the action) of grace. Or rather, the will of God has created, has created for itself, two limitations and, so to speak, two lapses: one is human freedom, in the order of life; the other is the force of habit, in the order of amortization and death.

Habit is not simply a stranger, which supplants reason within us; or a clever domestic, which installs itself in the house. It is one of the two essential components of human mechanism and articulation. As long as the human being is non-habituated, new and spiritually young, human freedom articulates itself hermetically with grace for the sake of eternal life and salvation. The outcome of this free and exact game is salvation and eternal life. Habit is what clogs up this articulation. All that it takes from newness, from human freedom, is thus taken from grace and prepares for amortization and death. All that coating with which it covers human freedom, all that coating of age prevents the play of the free articulation of freedom with grace, and thus prevents, in proportion, grace from *taking* through freedom.

(In all thought, in all philosophy the real problem is the deficiencies or rather the one deficiency. Accordingly, there is the problem of evil and there is not the problem of good. It is not the problem of good, it is the problem of evil that gradually strolls across all the philosophies and would almost allow, like a universal reagent, their classification according to the positions they have taken, according to the graduated places they occupy, in the presence of this problem.)

(It is not in regard to what is that there is a problem. It is in regard to what is absent.)

Corneille placed himself prior to the failings themselves, prior to the beginning of the gaps. He gave himself the budding and the seed, that life-full branching-out, that immense germination of God in the Roman world. He left for us what had to come afterwards. He left for us what was going to come later. He left for us the dead wood and the dead soul.

He gave himself that immense wave. He left for us the silt and the mud, which is the memory of the wave.

He gave himself the influx of that immense flood. He left for us the reflux, the deposits, the silting up of the estuary.

Let's go the end of our thought. He took the simplicities. (One understands well in what sense I say this.) He took, he gave himself, he represented exactly what didn't need explanations. He left us what did need explanations. Let's say it: He took the *simplicities* of the martyr.

It is not necessary, however, to believe that he did not see that there was a problem; and where this problem was. Or rather, where it was going to be. He saw very well that there would be limits, that there were limitations. He even saw that there were two, and he posed them as two terms to the outcome of his work. He posed these two terms at the boundaries of his work. He saw very well, he knew, he set it down that there would be a limit, that there was the limitation of Severus; and he set it down that there was the limitation of Felix.[58]

Let's recognize this and salute the great fidelity, the great purity of the genius. Let's recognize this and salute above all the great fidelity of Corneille. This great advocate who pleaded so many times, and who pleaded so many causes, retained a certain fidelity of the young man and of grace, a certain native naiveté that was unbelievable. And it seems he himself did not think about vanquishing. It is the very mark of genius, this strength. And it is the very mark of strength, this consent to the rules of honor.

Not that he wasn't sometimes, how shall I say, a little cunning in some of the pleas of his plays. But that is still through a sort of honesty, of the innocence of the advocate who wants each of the opposing theses to be pleaded thoroughly and with all the resources of the bar. When he is not pleading anymore, an immense honesty catches him up again, his native honesty, and it must not be said it is the honesty of a child but of a young man, and yet more a man of youthfulness, the very honesty of the work and of genius, and of fecundity, which are the same, moreover, and which will not allow each of the theses that are in opposition, in human beings and in the world, not to be presented thoroughly and with all the resources of being. He knows that in these great debates the nobility of the field of battle has more importance than the sense of victory, and that the noble person who is wrong is more right than the base person who is right. He knows that in these great disputes the nobility of the debate has more importance than the pronouncement of victory. He knows that it is a contest of God. And before all, that its conditions must be pure, and that its conditions must be respected. And it is up to us that the conditions be pure, and it is up to us that the conditions be respected. But what is not up to us is the event of victory; and the verdict is up to God.

Let's repeat it: this infinite concern for equity, this profound concern for justice and, so to speak, for rendering what is due is the very token of genius. It belongs to a man who knows well that he will do what he

---

58. Two leading characters in *Polyeucte*: Severus was a pagan Roman soldier-aristocrat, close to the court of the Emperor, and Felix was the pagan Roman governor of Armenia and Polyeucte's father-in-law. Felix's daughter, Pauline, also a pagan, had been in love with Severus, before becoming betrothed to Polyeucte, according to her father's wish. Polyeucte's very public opposition to Roman paganism, following his conversion to Christianity, required that he be judged and punished by Felix and Severus. What concerns Péguy is the nature of the confrontation between Polyeucte and his judges, especially the noble pagan, Severus.

wants to do, and that his genius will never refuse him anything. It is the small, the base, the feeble who mark the cards. A noble sentiment of the nobility of the game guards strength and genius from these weaknesses. Weakness wants to win against God. Strength and genius do not even want to win. They want to present before God in their strength and in their plenitude, they want to present in their beauty (a beauty that is honest and, so to speak, naked) those two or three great theses of human thought that are still (even should they be opposed) two or three of the greatest pieces of creation. After that, the judgment is not up to human beings. *Nolite judicare.*[59] The verdict is God's.

Such is the profound thought of genius. And here we rejoin what I was writing about in my first *Note on Bergson and the Bergsonian Philosophy.*[60] In such matters, it is not a question of vanquishing. It is a question of having fought well. Fighting well is up to us. Victory is not up to us. The weak one who fights another weak one, and a little more weak, has accomplished nothing. But a great thought that confronts another great thought, that is what rejoices God's heart.

In such matters (and perhaps in such matters only), a base victory is nothing compared with a noble defeat, a weak victory is nothing compared with a strong victory.

The weak one who takes on a weaker, that really helps! But a great thought that confronts another great thought, what a magnificent offering.

It is the grandeur, it is the beauty, it is the nobility of the combat that is everything in the eyes of the one to whom alone the combat is devoted; in the view of the one to whom alone the combat is devoted. And altogether this is the purity of it. And altogether this is the honesty. The fidelity to the rules of the game.

Fidelity to the rules of the game is not merely a fidelity of form. It is a characteristic of fidelity that every type of fidelity is connected, and that every type of fidelity comes from the depths.

Fidelity to the rules of the game is the supreme decency; and the first and indispensable and most simple decency, when one thinks for whom, before whom, one is playing.

---

59. "Do not judge" (Matthew 7:1).

60. See, for instance, 48–49.

Here we rejoin what I was writing about in my [first] *Note*.⁶¹ It is not a matter of the seasons of the earth being interchanged or even being interchangeable. It is not a matter of the spring being the autumn and the summer setting out to mix itself into the winter. It is a matter of the spring being fully young and fully new and fully the spring. And it is a matter of the autumn being fully the melancholy autumn. And it is a matter of the summer being fully hard and beating down and fully the summer. And it is a matter of the winter being the hard and frank one and fully the winter.

And it is not a matter of wheat coming from vines and grapes coming from wheat fields. It is not a matter of grains of wheat being found in the heart of clusters of grapes and grapes being found in the heart of ears of wheat. It is not a matter of reaping the vines and picking the wheat. What we have to do is operate straightforwardly and, I will say, separately. What we have to do is work straightforwardly and, I will say, separately.

In such matters confusion is the worst impiety. For it is the most base infidelity. It is a matter of the wheat-harvesting being real wheat-harvesting and the grape-picking being real grape-picking. We must—my God but it's simple, if there were no commentators and *messieurs* the annotators—we must harvest the wheat well, and we must pick the vines well.

All harvesting must be pure; and separate. The wheat (not the grapes) must go to the mill, and the grapes (not the wheat) must go to the press. The fruits of the earth must not be contaminated. They must be carried back honestly and separately to the feet of the Creator.

This is the profound piety and the unwavering fidelity of the genius—who also is a fruit of the earth. Or perhaps better, the one who is charged with bringing back the fruits of the earth. So what are you telling me? That there is a wheat-harvester who vanquished a grape-picker? What can that really mean? And what is a wheat-harvest that has vanquished a grape-harvest? What is this confusion? What is this impiety? Let each one make their harvest, those who are charged with it. There aren't so many who are truly charged with it. Let each bring back what they are charged with bringing back. I don't even want to know about a wheat-harvester who vanquishes another wheat-harvester, a grape-picker who vanquishes another grape-picker.

---

61. See, for instance, 27.

Those great thoughts like Platonic thought, Cartesian thought, Bergsonian thought, what are they other than fruits of the earth, and certainly not the least savory for anyone with a thinking soul, I will say for anyone who *is* a thinking soul. Those great philosophies, what are they other than harvests of thought?

Those great systems, what are they other than our wine cellars and our barns? And when we say that the world is shared out in them, what do we mean except that they are the cellars and the barns in which our harvests are shared out? And before everything, let each actually bring back what he is charged with bringing back. Let each actually be what it is his to be. Let us not put the wheat-harvest away in the wine cellars. And let us not bring the grape-harvest into the barns. Let each type be realized in its exactitude and fullness. Let each type of thought be realized in its most beautiful form. Let each type of thought be harvested in its perfection, ἐν ἀκμῇ,[62] in its highest and most perfect maturity. And let the one who found the sickle be charged with bringing back the wheat. And let the one who found dialectic be charged with bringing back the idea. And let the one who found the pruning knife be charged with bringing back the grapes. And let the one who found intuition be charged with bringing back duration.[63] We do not harvest wheat with the pruning knife. And we do not harvest grapes with the sickle and the scythe. The greatest wheat-harvester in the world will find nothing to harvest in the vines. The greatest grape-harvester in the world will find nothing to harvest in the wheat. Now what are you saying to me about knowing if it's the sickle or if it's the pruning knife which is the better instrument, βέλτιον ὄργανον?[64] That depends for what. Speak to me rather of the eternal storehouses.

And Christian thought and Christian philosophy (if it is permissible to call it this) and the Christian system and Christianity and Christendom, what is all this other than, in a sense, a fruit of the earth? *Fructus ventris.*[65] The most beautiful, naturally, and the most eminent. But of the earth. For if it was not of the earth, then the incarnation was not both honest and total. But it was the one and the other.

---

62. "in its prime."

63. "Dialectic" and "the idea" are allusions to Plato, and "intuition" and "duration" to Bergson.

64. "the better tool."

65. "Fruit of the womb" (Luke 1:42).

Such is the great exactitude and justice and fidelity of the poetic genius. Such should be the great exactitude and justice and fidelity of the philosophic genius. And isn't the latter, in a sense, a poetic genius of thought? Those great theses that share out the world, aren't there several because they share out several things in reality? And don't they appear opposed when they are simply extrinsic? Hence the extreme care of a Corneille always to present the theses in the fullness of their exactitude and in the fullness of their force. What an irreducible abyss between the patriotism of the Horatii and the patriotism of the Curiatii. A whole humanity separates them. But each of the two is presented in the fullness of their exactitude and in the fullness of their type. Even the sumptuous deliberation of Cinna presents the respective advantages and inconveniences of popular government and monarchy in a double procession that is symmetrically honest and symmetrically complete.[66]

In this system of thought the battle takes precedence over the victory, and death itself is as nothing compared to the correctness of the combat. It is a very well-known system, the most ancient, the most foreign there is to the modern world. It is not only the system of honesty. It is the system of heroism. And it is the system of honor. It is all gathered together in the code of the duel (on the condition that one take it seriously), and it is not an accident that a duel is the arch-stone, the key-stone of the arcature of *Le Cid*. As it is no accident—by an application of that general threefold advance from *Le Cid*, *Les Horaces*, and *Cinna* to *Polyeucte*—that a prodigious spiritual duel and several admirable chivalric duels are the key-stones of the immense and pure architecture of *Polyeucte*. In this system of thought and of action, the duel is a clash, a perpetual confrontation of values. In the duel of arms each of the two adversaries presents himself in his exactitude and his fullness. In the duel of thought, which is also a duel of arms, each of the theses presents itself in its exactitude and its fullness. Honor and the beauty of the world do not require, do not consist in Rodrigue killing don Gormas.[67] They consist precisely in their fighting each other. Whoever is, or should be, the victor, provided they fight each other, to the extent they fight each other, there is no derogation. God is able to look at the world and not find it too disgusting. What matters to each of the two adversaries, and to the world, and to God, is solely (and

---

66. In this paragraph, Péguy refers to two of Corneille's plays set in ancient Rome, *Les Horaces* and *Cinna*.

67. This duel is found in Corneille's *Le Cid*, based on the legend of El Cid in medieval Castile.

not as one would be tempted to say it at first), is solely that the duel take place, and naturally that it take place according to the proper form. That in the aftermath there is a victor and a vanquished no longer has any importance. It is no longer a matter of derogation. It is in the order of event.

Gormas dead is as convinced of this as Rodrigue alive. A fine combat, and in the order of thought, a fine debate, that is what matters. God is served. God can look. God can know of it. God can look at the world and at humanity. And the rest belongs to the order of event.

Life and death (temporal) are only what comes. And what goes.

It is the system of thought of chivalry, and notably of French chivalry. War is often spoken of as an immense duel, a duel between peoples, and reciprocally, the duel is often spoken of as a war that is, so to say, reduced and schematized, a war between individuals. War is spoken of as a duel on a grand scale, and the duel as a war on a small scale. This is really a great confusion. Many historical obscurities, and considerable ones, would perhaps be clarified, many difficulties would disappear, if we would be willing to distinguish between two types of war that have perhaps nothing in common with each other. I will not even say that the old struggle for life is divided into two types, one the struggle for honor and the other the struggle for power. I will not even go so far as to attribute a common origin to these two types of war. I will say: There are two types of war that have perhaps nothing in common with each other, and that are constantly entangled and disentangled in history. One proceeds in effect from the duel and the other does not proceed from it at all. One is an extension of the duel, literally a duel between peoples, or as in *Les Horaces* (but this comes to the same thing), between individuals delegated by peoples. There is a type of war that is a struggle for honor and there is a whole other type of war that is a struggle for domination. The first proceeds from the duel. It is the duel. The second is not and does not proceed from the duel. It is even all that is most foreign to the duel, to the code, to honor. But it is not at all foreign to heroism.

There is a type of war that, being for the sake of honor, is all the same for the sake of the eternal. And there is a type of war that, being for the sake of domination, is exclusively for the sake of the temporal.

There is a type of war where it is the battle that matters, and there is a type of war where it is the victory.

There is a type of war where a dishonorable victory (for instance, a victory through treason) is infinitely worse (and even the idea of it is intolerable) than an honorable defeat (that is, a defeat suffered, and I would say obtained, in an honest combat).

And there is a type of war, on the contrary, in which success justifies everything, a type of war where the idea does not even arise that one could have a war that is dishonorable, provided one wins, a type of war where the idea does not even arise that one could have a victory that is dishonorable.

There is a type of war where everything aims at the beauty of the combat and a type of war where everything aims at the pronouncing of the victory.

There is one where everything aims at expressing and one where everything aims at pronouncing.

There is one where everything aims at the posing of the problem and another where everything aims at the solution.

There is one that aims at the position and another that aims at the decision.

There is one that aims at chivalry and one that aims at empire.

These two types of war have been more or less connected and disconnected, entangled and disentangled, woven together and twisted apart in military history and in political history. They have been more or less allied, misallied, dis-allied, through the entire history of humanity and the world. Many obscurities would be clarified, many difficulties would disappear, if we did not always confuse them (and here again how right Bergson is, how language is everything, and should not be anything, how difficult it is to distinguish two types, even though they are strangers to each other, as soon as they are mixed up under the same name throughout history), if from one end of history to the other we had applied ourselves only to distinguishing these two types, to separating what is separated in reality. In Homer the battle, and consequently the war, is an indefinite series of duels. The general combat is the ensemble of singular combats. And on either side they wait for a general victory as the outcome of so many singular combats. This is when Ulysses intervenes, and with one stroke falsifies the entire system; for he contrives not only to introduce into the city a wooden horse: in this very act he contrives to replace the system of the battle with the system of victory, he contrives to substitute in one stroke the system of winning for the system of fighting, the system of empire for the system of the singular combat. In this sense, and with one stroke, and with the first stroke, Ulysses is already a Roman among the Greeks. He is already no longer the man who boasts and the man who does battle. He is already the man who keeps quiet and the man who wins.

He is already no longer the man who expresses himself and who offers himself. He is the man who imposes himself and who governs himself and who is going to govern the world.

He is already a consul. He is no longer a knight, a cavalier, the charioteer who depends on an axle and who is made to roll in the dust by a broken axle.[68] He is already the man on foot, the foot soldier, *pedes,* and of that race for whom the cavalry has never been more than mounted infantry.

For us moderns, to place us exclusively at that stage of the world's age that is the modern age, in looking from these days where we are towards past days, in looking from this viewpoint we occupy towards the ascent of these two types of war tirelessly climbing from century to century across the world's history, one might say without much distortion of reality that one type of war, the chivalric, is for us of Celtic origin and the second is of Roman origin. And at a second degree, we could perhaps say that the first is of Christian origin and the second would perhaps be of imperial origin.

Duellum, bellum,[69] it's the same word. *Duellum* is the *du-*form, which is that of *duo,* and *bellum* is the *b-*form, which has yielded *bi-*. And the *du-*form itself is the same as the *b-*form, because *b* is the *v* in *dv,* which is the same as *du.* And this isn't a charade. *Duellum, dvellum, bellum.* "*Duellum,*" says Bréal and Bailly,[70] "is still used, beside *bellum,* by the writers of the classical era. Horace, *Ep.* I, II, 7. *Græcia barbariæ lento collisa duello.* Id. *Od.* III, XIV, 18. *Et cadum Marsi memorem duelli.*[71] The change from *duellum* to *bellum* (the *v* being changed to *b* and the *d* being dropped) is similar to that from *duonus* to *bonus.* The proper name *Duilius* became in the same way *Bilius.* In *perduellio,* on the contrary, the *d* remained: notice the particular meaning of this word, which is applied to the crime of *lèse-majesté; per* is probably the pejorative prefix we have in *perjurium, perdere, perire.*[72]—*Bis* is for **dvis;*[73] in Greek, it is the *v* which has disap-

---

68. An allusion to *Ben-Hur,* the novel written by the American, Lewis Wallace, and translated into French in 1902.

69. *Duellum* and *bellum* both mean "war" in Latin.

70. See footnote 22.

71. "Greece was pulled into a difficult war in a foreign place," "And a wine-jug mindful of the Marsian war."

72. "to forswear, destroy, perish."

73. See footnote 21.

peared (δίς for δυίς)." And it said in the article about derivatives: "They divide into two series, those with *du (dualis, duellum),* those with *b* by the change from *du* to *dv-, b-, (b-is, b-ellum).*" And it adds: "An ancient derivative of the name of the number 'two' [*deux*] is the prefix *dis*, (see this word)." So that when we say "discern," "dissolve," "distinguish," "dissect," we are actually saying resolve into two, cut into two. And "dissection" is the same word as "dichotomy."

Duellum, duo; bellum, bis. War is what we do when we are two. But when we are two, in a system [of chivalry] we measure each other.[74] When we are two, thinks the Roman, I dominate.

Everything is proposition in the system of chivalry. Everything is domination in the Roman system. Everything is request in the chivalric system. And everything is conquest in the Roman system. Everything is conquest for the empire.

In the chivalric system it is a matter of measuring values. In the imperial system it is a matter of obtaining and fixing results.

For us moderns, where we are, one is Celtic and the other is Roman. One is feudal and the other is imperial. One is Christian and the other is Roman. The French have excelled in one and the Germans have sometimes succeeded in the other and the Japanese appear to have excelled in one and succeeded in the other.

One can say that in the modern world the French are still the eminent representatives, and perhaps the only ones, of the chivalric type (rigorously defined in this way), and the Germans are the imminent representatives, and perhaps the only ones, of the dominating type. And for this reason we are not deceiving ourselves when we believe that an entire world is interested in the resistance of France to German encroachments. And that an entire world would perish with us. And that this would be the world itself of freedom. And thus it would be the world itself of grace.

Germany would never remake a France. It is a question of race. Never would it remake freedom, grace. It would only ever remake empire and domination.

---

74. *on se mesure. Se mesurer* can mean "measure each other," as I have translated it here; it can also mean "enter into confrontation with" or even "fight with." *Mesure* can also, in contrast with *démesure* ("excess"), convey the ancient Greek idea of "measure" in the sense of "limit." Péguy seems to have all three inter-related ideas in mind as he uses the term throughout the ensuing discussion, though the particular emphasis might vary with the context. In translating that discussion, I will sometimes translate *se mesurer* as "fight with measure" in order to make his emphasis clear.

When the French say they are carving out a colonial empire, one must not believe it. They are propagating liberties. When Napoleon imagined that he had established an immense empire, one must not believe it. He was propagating liberties. *Veillons au salut de l'empire.*[75] This "empire" was a system of liberties. This was apparent afterwards. All the peoples that repulsed the "empire" have put one hundred and fifty years into not even succeeding in reconquering a few of the liberties that the "empire" brought without even noticing it, in the iron of its lancers, in the canteens of its *vivandières*.[76]

What is amazing is that with all the apparatus of empire the Germans have not done more than we did, in the wretched disorder of our liberty. There must be in this unhappy liberty a great secret. A virtue. A grace. A marvelous strength. An (other) order.

I'm not saying that we are worth more than others. We are a people. And they are a certain other people. We are human beings (we are sinners). We are not always good rulers. We are always bad dominators.

We who suffer every despot, especially when they are popular, we are by tradition people of liberty. It is a unique good, uniquely precious. The Germans, who went for centuries without establishing their empire, and who only re-established it on the ruins of ours, and forty-four years ago, are by tradition, and have always been, people of empire. The Germanic Holy Roman Empire.

And it is for this reason again that Germany has not been able to give birth to any genuine philosophy of liberty, or even any genuine thought of liberty. What they call liberty is what we call a decent servitude. What they call socialist is what we call a pale center-left.

And what they call revolutionary is what we call around here good conservatism.

And it is for this reason again that a philosophy like the Bergsonian philosophy, essentially liberal and liberating, and not merely in its system but in its heart and ancestry, could only have been born *en français* and in French soil and culture. Only French liberty could eventuate in Bergsonian freedom. And it is for this reason also that it (I mean Bergsonian thought and Bergsonian freedom) is all that is most opposed to German thought.

    75. A line from a patriotic marching song of the French Revolutionary wars, "Let us be vigilant for the salvation of the Empire."
    76. A female victualler providing extra food and drink to soldiers of the French armies in the early nineteenth century.

When one sees the immense apparatus of empire, one believes the universe will be crushed by it. What foolishness to fight other than to win. And how much the one who fights with measure must be the prey of the one who thinks only of dominating.

When one sees arrayed the immense apparatus of empire, when one compares these two types of war, that which compares and that which dominates, that which fights and that which vanquishes; when one measures these two systems, that which measures up the other and itself and that which dominates, and on the one side that immense bureaucracy of command and on the other side so much disorder, one is convinced that domination long ago exterminated freedom. And that the one who dominates long ago dominated the one who measures (himself). And that the one who vanquishes long ago vanquished the one who fights. How would it not be thus? It's mathematics. The forces that the other employs in fighting with measure, he no longer has for dominating. The forces he employs for fighting, he no longer has for vanquishing. The forces he employs for being just, he no longer has for being strong. He is mathematically diminished by that much. And he who engages in the struggle for honor in a world where everyone else engages in the struggle for survival, how would he not long ago and since forever have disappeared from the face of the earth?

Obviously this is a problem. And I will say it is a mystery. In fact, the one who fights with measure has sometimes been found greater; and he has sometimes dominated. The one who fights has sometimes vanquished the one who vanquishes. The one who wanted to be just has sometimes been found stronger. Empire has sometimes crushed freedom. By the means belonging to it, freedom has constantly worked upon empire.

How could the one who loses his time, his forces to shaping himself have been able to hold out against the one who thinks only of striking? The fact is simply that he did hold out and the first type of war has never been exterminated by the second, and the first system of the world, which is the system of comparison, has never been exterminated by the second system, which is the system of extermination. There must be in freedom, in justice (and perhaps in truth) a secret strength, a peculiar vigor, a splashing-up, a hope and, to say it all, a grace and a secret destiny. Since the beginning of time the two types of war have been entangled and disentangled, since the beginning of time they have been connected and disconnected, since the beginning of time the two systems have meshed and unmeshed, without our being able to say that one has ever eliminated the other. And even in modern times....

In modern times the murky political and parliamentary demagogy concerning freedom, justice, truth must not confuse us in ourselves and make us underrate these noble virtues. The murky eloquence must not break us down. If we had to renounce all the values of humanity and the world to the degree that the politicians grab hold of them and undertake to exploit them, there would long have been nothing left. There is a freedom, a justice, and a truth that are on the parliamentary political programs. However, there is a freedom, a justice, and a truth that I will call theological and that walk with the theological virtues. There is the truth. ... But let's begin with the first. There is that freedom of the human being that is an essential part of the operation of salvation and that articulates itself hermetically with the gratuity of grace. (God wishes to be loved freely.) There is that justice of which it is written: *Beati qui esuriunt et sitiunt justitiam: quoniam ipsi saturabunter.* Happy are those who hunger and thirst for justice: because they will be filled. There is that justice of which it is written: *Beati qui persecutionem patiunter propter justitiam: quoniam ipsorum est regnum cælorum.* Happy are those who suffer persecution for justice: because the kingdom of heaven belongs to them. And there is that truth of which it is written: *Ego sum via, veritas, et vita.* I am the way, the truth, and the life.[77] So when I see for ten years professional "Christians" not having sarcasms enough for their most essential virtues because these virtues have been fraudulently stolen by their adversaries and copied and pasted onto modern parliamentary political programs, I am entitled, I am forced to note that these unhappy, so-called Christians are the first dupes and probably the most base and maybe the most miserable victims of their modern adversaries. For they deny their own virtues, and the most cherished daughters of Jesus Christ, and they forget the three Gospels[78] and they forget the seven Beatitudes and they forget the very teachings of Jesus Christ, and they underrate and they despise and they deny all this under the pretext that these three Gospel-virtues have been plagiarized and, as it were, monopolized by frauds and forgers. In that case nothing remains.

---

77. Matthew 5:6, 10; John 14:6.
78. The *three* Gospels Péguy has in mind would be those directly pertinent to his biblical quotations in this paragraph: that is, Matthew and John, as well as Luke (which also contains a version of the Beatitudes, in 6:20–26).

For in this system of thought[79] it is not a question only of vanquishing. It is not even at all a question of vanquishing. It is a question of replacing. It is not a question of an empire crushing an empire. It is a question of a certain lamp not being extinguished, and as the same one[80] said, of a certain light not being hidden under a bushel basket.[81] It is not a question of whether Berlin crushes Paris; it is a question of whether Berlin can stand in place of Paris. And they are not even close, and not only are they not close but these unhappy, ponderous, ungrateful, disgraced ones do not appear even to have entered on the path and they do not appear to be designated, to be marked out in the secret of the world, for such a great grace.

In the eternal debate of those who are vanquishers and those who are shaped, we do not know if they are destined to vanquish. But we certainly know they are not destined to be shaped.

"The passage of peoples," says Halévy magnificently (*Quelques nouveaux maîtres*),[82] "is not like that of herds, monotonous, blind, determined by a single play of forces and causes; another influence presses upon them, animates them, chooses certain among them and obliges them to work on its behalf. Who does not know these elect peoples? From Jerusalem to Paris (Athens, Rome, Florence mark off this route) one spiritual gesture traverses humanity, a long sacred uplifting that touches from a distance slower or lesser races, astonishes them, irritates them, and willy-nilly raises them up. France is the last of these elect peoples. It is thus that a Michelet, a Hugo, understand the history and mission of France. Their patriotism is no less absolute . . . ."[83] If it appears less harsh and less exclusive in its forms, less tense, less armed against the foreigner, it is because it matured in times that were more glorious, or more simply, happier.

Let us try to see how it is today, our country under attack and threatened. A grave movement, entirely contrary to her genius, has happened beside her and even within her. This material movement advantages

---

79. That is, the chivalric system of thought.

80. That is, Christ.

81. Matthew 5:15.

82. "Some New Masters" was a piece by Daniel Halévy about Romain Rolland, André Suarès, Paul Claudel, and Péguy himself. Halévy was Péguy's friend and close collaborator on the *Cahiers*.

83. Here Péguy omits from Halévy's text the words *que celui de* Péguy ("than that of Péguy").

brutal and disciplined peoples, bent under machines and regulations, advantages a dismal and lowly multitude, massively opposed to the human aspirations of the ancient world, of humanist and Christian Europe, of the old Europe that France led. And this France is there, weakened by lost blood, checked by regret for reckless mistakes, disarmed by the destruction of the order wherein she flourished. She has sunk; however, she retains a prestige for those new peoples who have the numbers and the strength; she still stands with all the *hauteur* of her failed endeavors. She still carries the sacred charge, she remains the most devout, the most inventive, and if any nation would be her heir, the least one can say is that we are still waiting for this nation."

"The Christian," he says again, "follows a master who carried a heavy burden; he does not pretend to vain domination, to temporal greatness; he is creation's man of toil. Providence put him in this place, this charge fell to him: he assumes it as best he can and does not boast of any merit. So, when on the morning of battle the brigades awaken and arm themselves in the mist, each one occupies its post and awaits the day. They have only to wait and hold themselves ready. Then chance chooses one among them all, and places it at the center of the combat. It did not deserve this: the honor is chosen for it. And the other brigades, its comrades, while they fight, feel obscurely that elsewhere the combat is more real, death more exacting, sacrifice more useful, and the outcome decisive. For them, the effort has some respites; there are none for those at the center; and those there are quite certain that they are in the battle; they are aware of the looks, the cries pressing towards them, and above them the thought of the leader. Under these looks, these cries, this thought, their bloodied troop, decimated, struggles with a courage greater than its own courage, resists with a strength greater than its own strength. In the morning it was similar to the others, neither more brave nor less brave; and in the evening it is different. It has gone through the trial, it comes out of the fire. It is, it remains different, marked in the eyes of all by the august grace of combat. Mere chance is the cause of it: heroism has entered into it. Such is the Christian: a being among others, and similar to the most humble. But he fights for the whole of nature, the powers on high place hope in his effort, he has been chosen and from this comes his extra strength."

It is the same debate that unfolded for such a long time about knowing what the king is. It is the whole debate of the *ancien régime,* and it is the whole story of the history of France. That of knowing which man is the king. If it is the first among the barons; or the first among the masters. The whole history of France, the whole history of the *ancien régime,* is also the history of a long connection and disconnection, which is only a particular case, an eminent case, of the other.[84] Everywhere, and for a long time, if not always, these two ideas have fought and struggled against each other, these two ideas have been connected and disconnected, entangled and disentangled, joined and disjoined, distinguished and confused—the one that the king is first among the barons, the other that the king is first among the masters. The one that the king is first in the order of measure, in the order of baronage and chivalry. The other that the king is first in the order of victory, in the order of the regime and domination. One understands nothing of the admirable histories of Joinville[85] if one doesn't take into account first that the saintly king is a French baron, Louis de Poissy, and we today can perhaps say Louis de Paris, baron of the Île-de-France and the country of *Parisis,* prince of barons, prince of knights. And one understands nothing of the trial of Joan of Arc if one doesn't always have in mind that the king she thought she would find at Chinon, and the king she thought she would have consecrated at Reims, the king of France finally, was and would be a king of the baronage and of chivalry, a king of the crusade and of Christianity. And in that life of Joan of Arc, which is the most beautiful of all and the greatest and the highest and the most absolutely pure and notably so in at least six or seven orders and according to six or seven levels of perspective and starting from six or seven points of view, it might perhaps be said that the greatest secret distress of that life and its point of sadness and its tragic catastrophe was that she thought she would find one king and she found another. She thought she would have one king consecrated and she had another consecrated. She thought she would find a king of the baronage and of courtesy, a king of grace and of chivalry, a king of the crusade and of Christianity. She found a king of business and of brokerage.[86]

84. That is, the other "connection and disconnection" between the two types of war discussed earlier.

85. Péguy is referring here to the chronicles of the medieval French baron, Jean de Joinville (1224–1317), and especially to his *Saint Louis,* an account of the life of Louis IX (1214–70).

86. Charles VII, whom Joan had crowned at Reims in 1429.

Much has been said about the ingratitude of her king towards her. This was not only the profound and, as it were, essential ingratitude of human beings towards their rescuers and saviors; not only that profound ingratitude, so to say, of nature; not only, moreover, a profound ingratitude of character; not only the profound and prideful ingratitude and inexpiable resentment of the rich towards the poor and the powerful towards the wretched to whom they owe something and even everything; not only, moreover, the profound genetic ingratitude of that family that furnished the most notorious ingratitudes of history, and to say it all in a word, not only the beginning of the famous (Bourbon and) Orléanist ingratitude. This was not only, lest I forget, the compendium of mortal, of ordinary ingratitudes. A still more serious misunderstanding separated and divided the king of France from the greatest saint of France and of the world. She had come for a king of chivalry. And she found a commercial king. She had come for a king of justice. And she found a king of miserable calculation. She had come for a king of war. And she found a trembling king. She had come for a king of grace. And she found a paltry negotiator.

She had come for the very Christian king. And she found merely a king of hesitation.

She had come for the greatest of kings, that is for a king of the order of measure, of the tradition of measure. And she found merely a king who kept paltry accounts.

She had come for the king of France. And she found only a little bursar.

She had come for a mystical king and she found merely a political king and a politician. And immersed in what a despicable bog of Church-politicians and State-politicians.

People for whom Reims itself and the consecration and the ampoule[87] and the Holy Spirit were components of politics.

She had come for a royal court and an army and she found paperwork (on parchment, but it was paperwork all the same). She found paperwork and bureaucracy.

She had come for an ancient house and she found a king already modern. Such was the bottomless depth of misunderstanding, the bottomless depth of disillusionment, the bottomless depth of distress, that

---

87. The *Sainte Ampoule* at Reims contained the anointing oil for the coronation of the kings of France; its first recorded use was by Pope Innocent II in 1131 at the coronation of Louis VII.

just so much was the bottomless depth of forgiveness she measured out instantly, with her profound and clear political intelligence, of which she had elsewhere given so many proofs. She had come for the house of France and she found merely little offices, the offices of State. She had come for men of arms and she found merely a miserable band of legalists. She had come for a second Saint Louis. She found merely a second Philippe le Bel.[88]

What more striking example could we choose of that long war conducted between the two races of war, the connection, the disconnection, and of that long debate conducted between the two races of king (if this word *race* doesn't here make for a double meaning),[89] than to consider that the hideous Philippe le Bel was the grandson of Saint Louis. It required only the space and interval of a generation for the stock of Saint Louis to produce this modern offshoot and for the race of Saint Louis to become the race of Philippe le Bel and for the sons of Saint Louis, as that chaplain said,[90] to become the sons of Philippe le Bel.

Let's compare a war of Saint Louis, his war against the English, with a war of Philippe le Bel: all the distance is there. It's incredible to think that, for Philippe le Bel, Saint Louis was his grandfather; and that one was almost touching the other. And that when Saint Louis was dying in Tunis,[91] Philippe le Bel (if I can call him that)[92] was in his second year. And to go to the culminating point, it's incredible to think that when the elderly Joinville was writing, Philippe le Bel had already been ruling for twenty years. And that this was the same time when Guillaume de Nogaret, the chancellor of France, was making the voyage to Anagni; and the sinister affair of the Templars was breaking out.[93]

88. Philip the Fair (1268–1314) was, as Péguy goes on to note, the grandson of Saint Louis, generally recognized by historians as a key early figure in the transformation of France from a feudal kingdom into a centralized state.

89. See the preceding chapter, footnote 24.

90. Perhaps a reference to Jean Desnouelles, a nineteenth-century chronicler, whose history of medieval France, the *Chronicon*, might have been one of Péguy's sources. Desnouelles, however, was an abbot.

91. This happened in the course of the Seventh Crusade, which Louis led.

92. For Péguy, Philippe is better described as "hideous" (*hideux*) than "beautiful" (*bel*), or "fair," as the usual English translation of the name has it.

93. In 1303 Guillaume de Nogaret, a member of the King's Council, was sent by Philippe le Bel to capture and imprison Pope Boniface VIII at Anagni, Italy. A few years later, in 1307, at his instigation, the Knights Templar of France were accused of

Let's compare a war of Saint Louis, his war with the English in the Charente, and a war of Philippe le Bel. A war of Saint Louis is a just war. A treaty of Saint Louis is a just treaty. Such is a Christian war, seeing it is unavoidable that these two words go together. A just war, for lack of a just peace, and in order to prepare a just peace. And the crusade itself is a just war.[94]

A war of Philippe le Bel, a modern war, is a profitable war, or supposed to be profitable, or desired to be profitable. And this division goes very far and has lasted a long time, and he was inspired in way that was indeed unfortunate, but in fact he was continuing (badly) an ancient and obscure tradition, this king who wished that peace be made (and consequently who wished war to have been made) not as a merchant, but as a king.[95]

If royalty had remained in the *ancien régime,* if it had remained Saint Louis's royalty, it would have been invincible; and it would have been eternal. If it had remained within the order of measure, it would have been the greatest. If it had remained within the order of its strength, it would have been imperishable. But from the moment it entered into the modern, it was bound inevitably to come up against what was more modern than itself. And this is the punishment of the one who betrays his order: in the new order for which he has betrayed his own he always comes up against someone who is more of this new order than he is. In the new order he enters, or at least in the new order he wishes to enter, he always comes up against someone who belongs there in himself and essentially, someone who consequently is master there and will vanquish him there. Whereas he, the renegade and traitor, can neither be at home there nor be himself there, nor be master there nor vanquish there. And likewise, he who betrays his order for disorder, does not know himself in the disorder into which he enters and always comes up against his

---

heresy and the order was viciously suppressed.

94. It is worth noting here that, given the context, Péguy is not making a general pronouncement about the Christian crusades, but about the crusade undertaken by Louis IX, which most historians would agree was, at least in his case, motivated entirely by religious concerns—what he saw as the need to defend and protect Christ and Christian pilgrims by liberating the important sites of Christ's historical life from Islamic rule—rather than self-interested economic, political, and territorial concerns.

95. Péguy's point here seems to be that Philippe waged war within the "indeed unfortunate" tradition of war as domination (rather than comparison), but deceived himself into thinking he was doing it as a great king like his forebears, rather than the calculating "merchant" he actually was.

master there. When the French Revolution decapitated royalty, it did not decapitate royalty. It only decapitated something modern.

What was modern decapitated another modern.

From the moment royalty made itself businesslike it was bound to come up against what was more businesslike than itself. And from the moment it made itself "philosophical" it was bound inevitably to come up against what was philosophical than itself. And this was just. One must be what one is, and here we again encounter that thought that underlies this entire essay and that we haven't left. It is better to be who you actually are in the lowest order than to be who you are not in an order supposedly more elevated. It is even better to be who you are in disorder than to be who you are not in any order or other. When the revolution decapitated royalty, it was not a new regime that decapitated the old regime. It was some new regime that decapitated some new regime. It was some self-declared new regime that decapitated some self-ashamed new regime. It was some more successful modernity that decapitated some less successful modernity. It was some modernity truly itself and at home with itself that decapitated some modernity strange to itself, some modernity newly arrived and *parvenu*. It was some more competent modernity that decapitated some less competent modernity.

It was not the sons of commoners who decapitated a son of Saint Louis. The sons of commoners would no more have decapitated a son of Saint Louis than the commoners themselves would have decapitated Saint Louis. It was the sons of Philippe le Bel who decapitated a son of Philippe le Bel. It was jurists who decapitated a jurist. It was legalists who decapitated a legalist. And it may be said and must be said: It was sons better sprung from Philippe le Bel who decapitated a son less well sprung from Philippe le Bel.

When you go to the wolves you must expect to be bitten. And when you go to the fools you must expect to be fooled. If royalty had remained faithful to itself, everybody would have remained faithful to it. But how to remain faithful to the one who betrays himself and who isn't faithful to himself and his own institution?

Joan of Arc had come for a leader and she found merely a cabal. She had come for a king and she found merely courtiers. There's what was paid for on the day of January 21.[96]

---

96. January 21, 1793 was the date of the execution of Louis XVI.

He who betrays his race, his being, his own institution, where does he want respect to take hold? Where does he want faithfulness to attach itself?

And today if we were presented with a king of the caliber of Saint Louis, everybody would be loyal. If we were presented with a good king of the baronage, everybody would be loyal. If we were presented with a king who was a king of chivalry, all the people with hearts would be loyal. If we were presented with a king who was a king of politics, all the people with heads would be loyal. But we are presented with a king who will be the plaything of parliamentarians.

And who will always be beaten in an order that is not his own.

And where they will always play better than him.

Saint Louis, Philippe le Bel, a tragic bringing-together. And was there ever a more pointed confrontation? Thus, when the saintly king was dying before Tunis, from that bleeding of the stomach that carried him away, it was this infant of two years, the son of his son, born at Fontainebleau, a man of his race, who was going in his turn to mount the throne of France, who was going, as the old histories say, to be the house of France. The flower of sanctity, the most modern of kings. The flower of probity, the king of false coinage.[97] And when the elderly Joinville, seneschal of Champagne, was writing that book that is like the gospel of the royalty of France, they had already been in the modern world for twenty years, at least in the sense that they had already for twenty years been under the rule of the most terribly modern of kings.

What a lesson for us who always moan about having come into the world in modern times and who find the service is hard. And that it goes badly. It has always gone very badly. And service has never been a convenience. Twenty years after the death of Saint Louis it was going very badly in France. And while Saint Louis was in the Holy Land it was not going very well in France (Joinville says it often enough). And when Joan of Arc came to Chinon, do we believe she found all was going well? A few months later she was going to have consecrated at Reims a king who was not of the order of the sacred.

She thought she would find a king of the parishes of France. And she found merely the king of the diplomats.

---

97. In response to grave financial difficulties, Philippe le Bel resorted to various expedients, including the alteration of the coinage of the realm.

By one point in tennis, or rather by one hit, one can lose a game, and the outcome of twenty games, and the championship of the world. That being the case, which is best: to win by one point in a game and in a championship where all the players are strong, or to win by twenty games in a championship where all the other players are weak? Such are the two systems of thought, the two types of war, such are the two systems of measure—measure itself and victory, and one might say, right and fact. Let's go further and pass on to the other side. Let's get past the decision of fact. Let's get past the bar of the event. Which is best: to win in a game where all the other players are weak, or to lose in a game where all the players are strong; to win in a weak game or lose in a strong game? Win in a base game or lose in a noble game? This is to say: Are we charged with winning at any price; or are we charged with maintaining a certain standard of the game; and of the game of war; and thus a certain standard of the world? And not only with maintaining it, but elevating it or re-elevating it, base though we are? This is to say: Are we charged with being conquerors or being noble? And with maintaining in the world a certain standard of nobility? Every person who is of a certain race will opt for the theory, the system of thought, of the noble game.

Or rather, he will not opt for it. He will already be of this system and this race.

So long as the French language is spoken, Corneille will remain the poet of the noble game. Of the system and the race for whom all of life itself and all action and all behavior is an exercise and application of this noble game. So long as French is spoken, and later, perhaps as long as French is read and is the third classical language, Corneille will be the theoretician and philosopher as much as the poet of the noble game. I say the theoretician and philosopher because no poet as much as he has been fortunate on this point, no poet as much as he has succeeded in including in the poetic, without doing damage to the forms of the poetic, the unfoldings and the formulas of thought. No one has been so constrained, so exact, so fortunate in the deepenings and perspectives and gradations of thought, all the while remaining a poet, both resolute and fortunate in the forms of the poetic. And not only in tragedy where one believes it is easier and where it might seem more called-for, but just as much in comedy itself, which means more, being without any ceremonious air. The same secret tenderness and the same nobility and the same ardent and assured youthfulness that animates and informs and inhabits *Le Cid* also animates and informs and inhabits *Le Menteur*.[98] It is the same poet and it is the same being and the same greatness on two parallel planes. It is the same play and the same poetics on two linked planes. And the comedy even proves more, precisely because it is comedy. It is the same play that plays itself out two times, one time on the plane of tragedy and one time on the plane of comedy, and never has it been so obvious that the tragic and the comic are two parallel linked planes of the same art (classical), the same being, the same people, the same time. And it is marvelous to consider how *Le Menteur* is not the comedy of the Liar, nor of a liar, nor of lying. And how it is so uniquely the comedy of honor and of love (and also a little, of chance).

Le Menteur is the comedy of honor and love, as *Le Cid* is the tragedy and as *Horace* is the tragedy of honor and love, and as *Cinna* is the tragedy of power, and as *Polyeucte* is the tragedy of faith (and secondly, of love).

For we must know what we really mean when we say, with Corneille's contemporaries and with Corneille himself (but he was in his own regard quite a bad contemporary), that all Corneille's tragedy presents a conflict between passion and duty, a conflict that always ends with the triumph of duty. He himself spoke in this way and agreed with it, but this was a being who essentially lacked pride, the most just pride, and defended his own work badly before the critics, and defended his own genius badly before his contemporaries, and surrendered his arms, and voluntarily condescended to speak like them. When he declared, like the others and perhaps before the others, that his tragedy was or represented a conflict between duty and passion, and when he implied and even said that duty triumphs and should always triumph over passion, and when he implied and even said that duty is greatness and nobility and passion is weakness and certainly baseness, he was making an effort to be of his time and to speak everyone's language. He was making an effort to speak the language of his age, and of his entire century. In a word, he was making an effort to speak in a Cartesian way.

And even very sincerely, because he lacked pride, in this effort to be Cartesian.

Yet it is really a bad understanding, at once inexact and false, to represent his genius and his work solely as the theatre of a conflict between duty and passion, a conflict where great and noble duty finally triumphs

---

98. Corneille's comedy of 1644 about a "liar."

over weak and base passion. I will say it is somewhat a conception *à la* Hugo,[99] antithetical. This is to say how arbitrary it is, artificial, mechanical, and rigid. And it is still a worse understanding, really much worse, if one gives to this word "duty" and this word "weakness" the meaning of the moralists.

Reality, here still, here always, is much more gripping and much more profound. One will have difficulty making us believe that the love of Chimène and the love of Rodrigue is weakness (and the love of Pauline), and one will have yet more difficulty in making us believe that it is baseness. In reality the conflict in Corneille is not a conflict between high duty and base passion. It is a tragic debate (and one time comic, but we have seen that it's of the same family) between one greatness and another greatness, between one nobility and another nobility, between honor and love.

On one hand, it is not morality, this invention. It is infinitely more and infinitely other: it is honor. And on the other hand, it is not passion, this weakness. It is infinitely more and infinitely other: it is love.

Let's go further, let's enter, penetrate, further ahead. This tragic debate[100] (and one time comic debate) is not a disparate debate and an unequal debate. It is not a lame debate. It is not an uneven debate. It does not take place, it does not occur between greatnesses out of touch with each other, between greatnesses not of the same order, for this nobility is of the same order as that nobility, and this greatness is of the same order as that greatness.

The uneven, that would be the "Preface" to *Cromwell*.[101] Tragic and one time comic (but it's the same), the poetic of Corneille is essentially even. It is essentially at equality. And in this sense it is essentially a poetics of the noble game.

The uneven, the disparate, the out of plumb, this is romanticism itself, the secret of romanticism. And it is not a cunning secret. It is a poor secret. It is a secret of mechanics and a secret of rigidity. The fine secret, the profound secret of the classical (and never and nowhere else is this so fine and so profoundly achieved as in Corneille), the secret of

---

99. Victor Hugo (1802–85), the French novelist and poet, leading representative of French romanticism, was the subject of a long essay by Péguy, "Victor-Marie, comte Hugo," in the *Cahiers* (1910).

100. That is, the debate between honor and love.

101. A play written in 1827 by Hugo, who, as a romantic, drew inspiration from Shakespeare rather than the French classicists, such as Corneille and Jean Racine.

the classical and preeminently of the Corneilleian is the even and the comparable; it is honesty, and that all worlds and all beings are at equality.

It is doubtless a debate (tragic, one time comic, always equally poetic) between honor and love. But it is an essentially even debate, and more than even, it is a profoundly intense and co-intensifying debate. Mutually connected. Mutually intensifying. For, and here we reach the secret itself, the secret point of the poetics and the genius of Corneille: honor is truly loved, and love is truly honored.

Honor is still a loving and love is still an honoring.

We understand nothing of the tragic and the comic and the poetic of Corneille if we want to see in it only a conflict, intellectual and bookish so to speak, between duty taken in the sense of the moralists and passion taken also in the sense of the moralists. The debate and at the same time the disconnection and the connection is infinitely other, infinitely more serious and more real. There can be no doubt that in Corneille honor is truly loved, particularly in *Le Cid*, where this shines forth, and love is truly honored, particularly in *Le Cid*, where this shines forth. Neither is honor esteemed or loved with a meager esteem and a meager moralistic love (if there are moralistic loves), nor is love honored or condemned with a meager and bookish sentiment of moralism or immoralism. This shines forth in *Le Cid*, where all that youthfulness, the most beautiful and the most youthful youthfulness we have ever seen put into poetry, loves honor truly and as a love, and honors love truly and as an honor. It is thus that honor and love are always present, the one to the other and the other to the one. It is thus that honor and love are continually co-intensifying, mutually intensifying. It is thus that they are able continually to confront one another and together play the noble game.

Poets must never be believed according to what they say, and Corneille less than any other; due to that great lack of pride, which he lacked more than any other, and consequently due to that great and admirable naiveté. For him more than for any other, attention must be given to what he did, and not to what he said he did. He said he represented the conflict between duty and passion. But he represented the immense debate, the immense connection and disconnection, between honor and love.

Love is a pleasure, honor is a duty.[102] Let's not believe him. Love (I'm saying in his system of thought, in his system of feeling, and in his poetics, and in his system of life), love is an honor, and honor is loved. I'll

---

102. Words of Don Diègue in *Le Cid*, Act III, scene 6. Péguy clearly thinks the old Don Diègue does *not* represent what Corneille has actually expressed in the play.

say more. For these admirable young people, in whose presence everything else is old, everything else is shriveled, love is a pleasure and honor too and at the same time is a pleasure. Or rather love is a pleasure and honor at the same time is the same love and the same pleasure. They love everything, in their youthfulness, they love everything with a true love, and honor more than anything. And they honor everything with a true honor, and love more than anything. The long and slow elegiac balancing of what I will call the demi-stanzas of *Le Cid,* of that admirable dialogue, that admirable alternating verse between Chimène and Rodrigue, perhaps the sole piece in all of modern poetics that yields to us an echo of the ancient purity, that gives back to us, that has transferred all the way into the modern world, the alternations of certain demi-choruses of ancient tragedy and certain demi-dialogues between the character and the choryphaeus and the chorus and one or two of the demi-choruses; that admirable and perfect balancing of demi-stanzas (and it would maybe be better to say double stanzas), more profound still and more pure and perhaps less lined up than that of [full] stanzas, is not at all the balancing, inevitably a little mechanical and a little exterior, of duty to passion. It is not at all an articulated balancing of the same to the other, or rather of the other to the other, inevitably a little brutal and a little obvious. It is a secret balancing, painful, blessed, unhappy, happy, a return and a return, a silent balancing of the same to the same, of that honor and love called honor to that love and honor called love.

We have only one honor. Ladies are so many, says the old don Diègue. But Rodrigue's idea, and the Corneilleian idea, their system of being and their system of thought, is firstly that we have one honor, secondly that we have one lady, thirdly that it's the same uniqueness.

Their idea, their system of thought, is that the destiny of love is the same as the destiny of honor; unique as well.

We must reread *Le Cid*. Or rather, we must read it for the first time, ourselves, with dis-habituated eyes. The love of Chimène and Rodrigue for honor is one of the most profound nourishments for their own love. And their love is a profound nourishment and a perpetual offering that they make to honor. And the honor they render to love is again a nourishment for their love.

We must reread *Le Cid*. We must see to what point honor is surrounded by, is an object of love and tenderness. And we must see to what point love is an object of honor.

It is in this sense, and not in the sense of the critics and historians, and not in the sense of Corneille the critic, analyzer, and historian, that it must be said that *Le Cid* is the tragedy of honor and of love, and that *Le Menteur* is the parallel and conjoined comedy of honor and of love. It is in this sense that it must be said, and only in this sense that it can be said, that *Le Cid* is a heroic tragedy, and that in parallel and conjointly *Le Menteur* is a heroic comedy. In comparison with *Le Menteur* all the comedies of Molière (and yet he is the greatest comic genius who has ever appeared in the world) are bourgeois comedies. I don't speak of *Les Plaideurs*,[103] which in comparison with the one and the other is no more than a sour, dry and bad little comedy of the seminary, made to be performed on the day of the distribution of prizes.

It is in this sense, in the sense of an honor and a love that nourish each other mutually, that are of the same race, the same nobility, the same family, and that are the object of combined cults. It is in this sense that *Le Cid* is the tragedy of the noble game, as *Le Menteur* is in parallel and conjointly the comedy of the noble game.

All is honor and all is love in Corneille, all is honest and noble confrontation and fine and just contest. Above all, that nothing be false. That this great, continual combat be fought out in full equality. That no chances be favored. Also that no chances be fraudulently reduced. The opposite of Corneille and what he combats and targets and hits at diametrically is not weakness, but fraud. There is the only enemy and the shameful object of the only banishment. So a total banishment.

Thus transpires in the great Corneilleian *oeuvre* the perpetual confrontation, the continual comparison, the continual clash of beings and of lives, of characters and theses. God himself is gentlemanly and before God even the thesis of God will not be advantaged. What is formidable in *Polyeucte* is certainly the total absence of pious fraud, and that execrable fraudulent devotion.

It is the poetics of comparison, and of perfect comparison. God will be compared, like the others; honestly, like the others; he will be compared to the false gods. And he will be found better to a just degree, which is infinity, but by no more. And in the composition of this infinity (if I may say this) there will not enter an atom of the fraudulent.

Such is the poetics of Corneille. An immense and continual honest comparison. An immense and continual comparison of beauty. An

---

103. A comedy of 1668 by Jean Racine about "litigants."

immense and continual comparison of grace and strength. The combat between Rodrigue and the count extended to the entire world. And even to God. The combat of God extended even to God. And God will not be in the least advantaged there. This is to say he will not receive any supplementary advantage, any fraudulent advantage, any advantage in excess (if I may say) of those natural advantages that are the advantages of his nature and his grace. It is not God who is afraid that God will not be strong enough. In the combats. In the comparisons. It is not God who would add proofs of God's existence.

Who would pile on too much, like our theologians.

It is not God who is afraid that God is not good enough as he is.

This is the shattering and unique beauty of *Polyeucte*. It is not only that the thought springs forth complete and intact in the poetics, that the proposition remains complete and intact in the verse. It is that the saint and the martyr and even God do not receive any fraudulent increase. He does not give them too much.

There is the shattering and unique beauty of *Polyeucte*. It is this magnificent divesting of the saint, of the martyr, and of God. It is this magnificent disarming. No cloak of virtue, of our meager virtues. Only the theological virtues. No cloak of our false virtues. No magical cloak. The upholders of the good cause do not receive any fraudulent arms, any fraudulent armament. It is so rare that the upholders of the good cause do not receive a miraculous armor, that is, a fraudulent armor. That is, it is so rare that the upholders of the good cause are not afraid.

It would be necessary to analyze, to show still more this shattering and unique beauty of *Polyeucte*. No piling up of proofs. He doesn't stack up the furniture. He doesn't block up the leaks. He knows that the vessel of Saint Peter has no leaks.

He doesn't plug the gaps. He knows there are no gaps.

It is the complete divesting and disarming of grace. He doesn't put some there just in case. Maybe he isn't in the tradition of the theologians. He is, however, in the line and the race and the tradition of the saints and martyrs. And he is in the line and the race of Jesus Christ. *Misereor super turbam.*[104] He doesn't despise the world. As for himself, he is governed only by compassion. He doesn't debase the world in order to elevate himself. And in this regard he is markedly different from a certain tendency in Pascal. He renders to the temporal its due. And to say it all, he renders

---

104. "I have compassion for the crowd" (Mark 8:2).

to Caesar what is Caesar's. Here again he is not fraudulent. He takes on in its fullness this teaching of Jesus.

Those who take their distance from the world, those who take on height by leaving the world, leaving the world while debasing the world, don't elevate themselves. They remain at the same height. And the height they believe they have taken on is a counter-height, is the debasement of the world, the debasement they have given the world. It is a height under the common point of departure. That is what they are measuring.

They are measuring the height to which they have debased the world and not the height to which they have been raised.

Those who are really raised, those who really take on height, are those who leave the world at the height where it is, and who climb from there, from there take on height.

It is the question of relative movement and absolute movement. There is an absolute ascent, which is an ascent, and a relative ascent, which might not be an ascent, and which might even be a descent. The world and human beings are at a certain height, are granted a certain common height, which I will call the initial height, the height of the point or level of departure. It is a matter of knowing who is climbing and who is descending. The man who debases the world and who takes on height by leaving this world that he debases can have the illusion of climbing absolutely, of taking on absolute height. Yet it might not be the case at all, if he does not himself climb absolutely. If he does not himself climb absolutely, he can climb relatively and at the same time remain at the same level absolutely and even descend absolutely. But the man who leaves the world where it is and from that level raises himself, that man is sure of climbing.

Here we come upon, here we catch the most frequent and naturally the most serious error of calculation. It is not enough to debase the temporal in order to raise oneself into the category of the eternal. It is not enough to debase nature in order to raise oneself into the category of grace. It is not enough to debase the world in order to climb to the category of God. And perhaps the operation doesn't consist in this at all and is infinitely other.

This error of calculation, the most frequent maybe because it is the most convenient, and the most serious since it is almost an error in the meaning of signs, in the usage of the plus and minus signs, and thus bears on the very bases and givens and conditions of calculation and on the very foundation of the operation, this error of initial and even preliminary calculation is the condensation and schema of that global error of calculation that constitutes the devout party.[105] Because they do not have the strength (and the grace) to be of nature they believe they are of grace. Because they do not have temporal courage, they believe they have begun to penetrate the eternal. Because they do not have the courage to be of the world, they believe they are of God. Because they do not have the courage to belong to one of the parties of humanity, they believe they belong to the party of God. Because they are not with humanity, they believe they are with God. Because they love no one, they believe they love God.

But Jesus Christ himself was with humanity.

From this devout party, from falling into this devout party, Corneille was marvelously and entirely guarded by a unique grace throughout *Polyeucte*. Nowhere and in no sense is this incomparable work a devout work, nowhere does it carry a trace or hint of a trace of the coldnesses and impurities of the devout style. And nowhere does it carry a trace of that error of calculation that is at the center of the paragenesis of the devout party.

As he was guarded from the devout language, so Corneille was guarded particularly from that error of calculation that is at the center of the devout system. He was guarded particularly by the system of thought of the honest combat and the comparison at equality.

In that advance that I've noted elsewhere, that triple advance and culmination of *Le Cid*, *Horace*, and *Cinna* (and we must almost say *Le Menteur*) up to and in *Polyeucte* (*Polyeucte* and *Le Menteur* are from the same year), what has been carried through, what has been advanced fully among so many advances, is the system of thought of the honest combat and the confrontation at equality. In this continual debate, in this universal presentation and confrontation at equality, no one will be advantaged. No being. No thesis. Nor God.

Nor the saint; nor the martyr; nor God.

Nor the human being.

Nor faith; nor grace; nor God.

No one will be diminished so that others appear greater. Everyone will be present in their full greatness and those who have it to be greater will be greater yet.

No one will be diminished in order to allow others to surpass. And God will surpass all the same. In the way God should surpass.

---

105. Péguy is referring here to the Roman Catholic opponents of modernism, the heirs of a conservative Roman Catholic politics that had its origins in the early seventeenth century as a movement to combat Protestantism.

This is perhaps the greatest beauty of *Polyeucte*. It is essentially a Christianity of the parish. Healthiness itself. Nothing of a fanatical asceticism. Nothing monstrous. Nothing that is not French and chivalric. Grace will be raised to all its height above nature, without nature having been fraudulently debased. The high temperature will not come from having debased the zero. It is the climate that will have changed and not the meteorological lab, not the climatic or climacteric *station*. It is the temperature that will have climbed and not the thermometer that will have fallen. The eternal will rise in all its height above the temporal and it is not the temporal that will have fallen. The saint, the martyr will rise in all their height above the human and it is not the human that will have fallen. God will rise in all God's height above the world and it is not the world that will have fallen. No one will be served fraudulently, no one (and it is shameful to have to say it), no one and not even God.

No one will be fraudulent. And I'm ashamed to say it, no one and not even God.

Hence the great and profound humanity of *Polyeucte*, that immense goodness and deepening of tenderness. He does not love God at the expense of the neighbor; he does not obtain his salvation at the expense of the neighbor. Hence that great and surpassing tragedy is double, a sacred tragedy, a profane tragedy, and the surpassing of the profane tragedy by the sacred tragedy is not obtained fraudulently.

The very grandeur and flowering and brilliance of the sacred tragedy in *Polyeucte* conceals from us not only the grandeur and flowering and humanity, but almost the existence itself, of the profane tragedy, which is underneath. We are all like that princess who wanted to compare Racine and Corneille, and who in order to balance *Bérénice* found *Tite et Bérénice*.[106] We are all crushed by literary history. We are all obliterated. And we are also habituated. We do not see that the great profane tragedy of Corneille (putting *Le Cid* to one side, for to speak truly, it is not a profane tragedy; it is a kind of sacred tragedy of honor and love, and of youth, more precisely a sacred tragedy of what honor and love possess of the sacred in the age of youth), historians and *habitués*, we do not see that the great profane tragedy of Corneille, comparable (and incomparable), the profane tragedy of the age of Titus and Berenice, is still *Polyeucte*, is the profane tragedy that runs underneath the sacred tragedy in *Polyeucte*,

---

106. Henrietta of England, sister-in-law of the King of France, Louis XIV. *Bérénice* was Racine's play (1670), and *Tite et Bérénice* (also 1670) was Corneille's version of the same story from ancient Rome.

or rather, the profane tragedy on which rests and from which arises the sacred tragedy of *Polyeucte*. The response to Titus and Berenice (and to Antiochus) is not Tite and not Bérénice. It is Pauline and Severus (and again, it is Polyeucte). There is the pure tragedy of a love that is profane and completely, purely antique and melancholy and incurable, or rather, there is the pure, complete, antique, melancholy, and incurable profane tragedy of love.

It is one of the greatest errors we can commit to believe that Severus is a character on the secondary plane. There is no secondary plane in *Polyeucte*. There is a first plane, which is the plane of humanity. And above it there is a plane, which is the plane of the sacred. The grandeur of the sacred is not obtained by the subsidence of the plane of humanity and the world. There is no first plane, which would be the plane of the sacred, and behind it a secondary plane, a subsidiary plane, which would be the plane of the profane. There is a first plane, which is the plane of the human and profane. And there is above it a plane, which is the plane of the sacred.

If there were not in *Polyeucte* this incomparable and moreover unique sacred tragedy, then it would seem to us that the profane tragedy we have in *Polyeucte* is the most complete, the most pure, the most antique, the most profound, and if I may say at the same time, the most gracious, the most serious, and the most sacred profane tragedy of love and of honor that we have. But what must be the greatness of a sacred tragedy that conceals all this other from us so completely? And what to say about a poetics, which in the space of five acts can in this way superimpose on one world another world?

Hence Severus is not at all sacrificed, not even in any way diminished. He is one of the finest Romans we have. He also is presented in his exactitude and fullness. Serious, honest, a gentleman, grave, and as if finished, cultivated, discrete, human and consummately so, good, undeceived, noble, brave, and incurably melancholy, he is there to remind us of what only imbeciles ignore: that pagan antiquity, ancient pagan humanity, was itself a temple of purity.

And that it did not have the gods it deserved.

That is to say, it did not have *its* gods.

It is the opposite with us, who have the God we do not deserve.

One might say the ancient world did not have the gods it deserved.

The Christian world had exactly the God it deserved; its God.

The modern world still has the God it does not deserve at all anymore.

Like the ancient world, we do not have our God, but in the inverse sense.

The world is out of synch with God in the other sense.

And the Christian world alone was in true, resting on God; in equilibrium with God.

Hence, again, that fine attitude and behavior of Polyeucte towards Severus. There is no doubt that he has for him a particular esteem. He does not treat him only as the honorable man, the gentleman, the chivalrous man, and the man of good company. He has for him a particular affection and respect, a kind of fidelity, the emotional origins of which would be highly obscure and extremely profound, while the avowed origins are more apparent and clear. A combat of honor is engaged in between these two men, and Polyeucte considers himself committed in honor not to yield in the matter of honor to this great Stoic.

It is not in vain, it is not by accident that Pascal fixed on Stoicism and a certain Epicurean skepticism as the two poles of thought and system in the ancient world from the Christian standpoint (and particularly from the standpoint of the absence of the Christian); as the two poles of philosophy and ancient wisdom responding to each other; of pagan thought and profane thought. As the two poles of thought and system of humanity itself, that is a humanity not yet clothed in Christianity, purely profane and (if I may say) secular, a humanity as though reduced to its own proper strength, and considered independently of the introduction and superimposition of Christianity. And that he considered Stoicism as the pole of thought and system of heroism and the sacred in a profane world, and skepticism, or at least a certain Epicurean skepticism, as the pole of feebleness and the profane in a profane world. He saw very well that in the whole ancient world, it was Stoicism that was comparable and capable of dealing a blow to the Christian. Which could present itself at the confrontation. He saw very well that in the whole ancient world, Stoicism alone was worthy. That it alone could present its stuff in comparison. That it alone had been able to provide, that from it alone had come what in the ancient register corresponds to the saints and martyrs in the Christian register: the heroes and, perhaps we must also say, the martyrs.

If we can consider, as I believe, the ancient city to be a figure, a temporal pre-figuration of the city of God, it is certain that within this figuration and parallelism, it is Stoicism that has provided, and that alone could provide, in the register of the ancient world, what alone corresponds to the saints and martyrs: the heroes and, perhaps we must also say, the martyrs.

I have very little liking for that expression, "lay saints." It is a major source of confusion and error. But confined to the figure, and to the meaning of the figure, it is profound and real and true. There really was in the ancient world a certain enclave, in philosophy and ancient wisdom a certain citadel, there really was in the lay world and in the profane world a certain sacred, and Pascal saw very well that it was Stoicism that had been charged with furnishing this sacred, with providing what alone could respond to the saint and martyr, what alone could foreshadow laically, figure temporally, the saint and martyr: the hero and already perhaps the martyr.

Like all the truly great Christians, Pascal kept himself from scorning antiquity. He knew too well there had been Rome and Greece. And ancient philosophy and wisdom. And a lay thought and a profane thought. And even an ancient science. And a veritable temporal figuration. He knew too well there had been the ancient city. And going, as he always did, to the very heart of the debate, and going immediately, like a geometer, to the *maxima*, he saw very well that Stoicism provided, was charged with providing, the maximum of antique greatness, *sub specie*,[107] from the viewpoint of Christian greatness, the maximum of nature from the viewpoint of receiving grace, the maximum of the hero (and the martyr) from the viewpoint of the saint and martyr, the maximum of the human without God from the viewpoint of God, the maximum of the world without God from the viewpoint of God.

It is in this same sense that Severus is a Stoic and it is also in this same sense that Polyeucte esteems, honors, and, it must be said, admires Severus. He does not love him only, he is not attached to him only for the most obscure and profound sentimental reasons, by an obscure sentimentality, an obscure and profound faithfulness of confidence, of trust. He does not love him only out of Christian charity. He does not love him only out of a benevolence and *philia* that is ancient and pagan and Greek and philanthropic. And philosophical. He loves him as a noble partner and he sees in him his own figure.

---

107. "from the viewpoint."

It is a tender inclination and it is an admiration of competence. Which is to say it is nearly a predilection. What a temptation for the one who is great in a given order to esteem, admire, perhaps to love amongst all the one who is the greatest in another order, and most of all perhaps the one who is greatest in the contrary order. It is as an expert that Polyeucte admires Severus; for his Christian greatness is based on the surpassing and not on the ignoring of pagan greatness and antique severity. He knows the false gods are nothing. But he also knows that the adorers of the false gods are not nothing. He knows the false gods are of wood and stone. *De bois, de marbre ou d'or comme vous les voulez.*[108] But he also knows that the adorers of the false gods are of the human and the world; and of the soul. And he knocks over, and a little brusquely, the false gods. But he treats Severus with infinite consideration.

A consideration itself enveloped in infinite regret and incalculable melancholy. Severus is at the same time the limit. He is the one who will not be had.

Polyeucte measures Severus. For his own sanctity is based on the surpassing and not the ignoring of antique heroism. And his own martyrdom is based on the surpassing and not the ignoring of antique martyrdom. And his God is based on the surpassing and not the ignoring, and a certain despising, of the world.

Polyeucte's system of thought doesn't require that God underrate and ignore and despise his own creation, the world come from his hands. (In this again, he is all that is most opposed to the devout system.)

Hence that humanity of Polyeucte, that tenderness both pliable and firm, which increases the more he approaches martyrdom. He doesn't only admire Severus, he doesn't only love him. It is more:

He regrets Severus.

And far from his humanity being opposed to his sanctity (as in the atheist system, and in parallel and conjointly in the devout system), on the contrary, we have the impression, we see that his sanctity is so great that departing from the humanity, founded on the humanity, it returns there and still nourishes the humanity. Such are the true forms of sanctity, and it is by this that one recognizes them. They are happy, they overflow,

---

108. "Of wood, of marble, or of gold, as you wish them" (*Polyeucte*, Act IV, scene 3).

they always have too much. The more he is a saint, the more and by this very thing, he is good. The more he is a martyr, the more and by this very thing, he is human. The goodness, the humanity, the security, the smile, and the relinquishment of those who know well they are winning for the others.[109]

A kind of *bonhomie*, familiar. And a kind of *on ne sait quoi* in heroism that would almost rejoin the comic; that is, the true French military heroism.

So here they are, Severus and he. Not like two rivals, in the crude sense of the word. Not even like two emulators in the modern sense of competition. But like two fine combatants. It is always the combat of God. It is even the combat of God between the one who upholds God and the one who does not uphold God. And Polyeucte's thought is that the one who upholds God should conduct himself at least as well as the one who does not uphold God.

Each will defend his cause in its exactitude and its fullness. Each will present himself in his exactitude and his fullness. And Polyeucte's thought is that the one who presents himself on God's side should at the least not present himself more badly than the one who does not present himself on God's side.

Polyeucte sees Severus before him as a fine combatant and as a fine partner worthy of him. And as for himself, at the very least he should be worthy of the other.

Polyeucte sees Severus before him in contest, in a comparison with him. At the very least each of the two terms of the comparison should be worthy of the other. And this is necessary for the contest itself, for the comparison itself to be worthy of God who is watching it. And of that crown of other saints and preceding martyrs who, circled about God, are watching it.

Before such witnesses, before such a judge of the contest, how offer a false contest, how deliver up a fraudulent contest?

Before such experts, how deliver up an inept contest?

To such spectators, how offer a false spectacle, a tricked-up spectacle, present a fraudulent spectacle?

To such assessors, before such a judge of the contest, before the one who sees everything, before the one who weighs even the imponderables,

---

109. In regard to "for the others," Péguy's point here will become clearer in his subsequent analysis of the confrontation between Polyeucte and Severus.

before a *juge du camp*, a *maître-du-camp*,[110] who is just, how not offer a just contest, how not present a just comparison?

It is necessary for Polyeucte, it is necessary that before God, that is, in the most secret hidden recesses of the soul and being, the contest be fully honest, the comparison fully at equality.

It would not do for the upholder of God to present any shadow of fraudulent thought in the face of the one who does not uphold God.

For Polyeucte, Severus is a Roman knight, and he, Polyeucte, is a Christian knight. The law of chivalry, the honesty of chivalry, will thus govern the entire contest, will regulate the entire comparison. It would not do in a contest of chivalry, in a comparison of chivalry between one who upholds chivalry and one who does not, that it would be the upholder of chivalry who fails in the laws of chivalry, in the honesty of chivalry.

Polyeucte thus declares in the third century,[111] and in Corneille brings together and sums up and presents magnificently the system of thought, the always reliable rule that through all the centuries of Christianity has governed for the Christian the relationship of the Christian to the non-Christian. It is the rule, it is the system of thought of the just war, of the honest combat, of the comparison at equality.

This rule shines through, as must be expected, in the crusades. In Polyeucte's time it was necessary that the Christian not be inferior to the pagan even in regard to pagan honor. In the time of crusade, it was necessary that the Christian not be inferior to the infidel, that the Christian knight not be vanquished by the Arab "knight" even in regard to infidel honor. Hence that comparison in honor, that continual courtly jousting that was rapidly established in the crusade between every Frankish knight and every Muslim "knight."

And all this comes back to the immense general rule of not scandalizing. *Nolite scandalizare*.[112] For the same reason that one must not

---

110. *Maître-du-camp* was a high rank or function in the French army prior to the French Revolution, which might have still been in effect in Péguy's time. *Juge du camp* appears to be an equivalent rank or function.

111. A reference to Saint Polyeuctus, who was executed by the Roman authorities in 259 CE, in Melitine (in Armenia), under the Emperor Valerian. The character, Polyeucte, in Corneille's play, who "brings together and sums up" is based on the historical figure.

112. "Do not scandalize" or more literally "do not put up a stumbling block." See Matthew 18:6–7; Mark 9:42.

scandalize the children, one also must not scandalize the pagans and infidels. They also are ignorant; and consequently in a certain sense innocents and in a certain sense children, for they do not know the true God and consequently cannot offend him, and consequently they cannot sin like us. They do not have that terrible privilege of (being able) to sin like us. It is the whole system of a Polyeucte, to say nothing of a Godfrey of Bouillon;[113] it is the whole system of a Saint Louis.

It is the whole system of measure, of thought, of a Polyeucte. When the Christian is in the presence of the pagan, when the Christian enters into comparison with the pagan (and he is always in the presence of the pagan, he is always entering into comparison with the pagan), it is not enough that the Christian win within himself and for himself and in his own system of measure and thought. It is not even enough, if I may say, that he wins for God. And before God. It is still necessary as well that he win for the other. It is still necessary that he win in the system of the other. Polyeucte will not be content with less. It is necessary that he win also according to the honor that is in the system of the other. And as he himself *regrets* Severus, he must want Severus also to regret him. As he himself regrets that Severus is not a Christian, he must want Severus also to regret that Polyeucte did not remain a pagan. This regret for Polyeucte in Severus's heart, this is the only vulnerable point there may be in Severus's heart; let's not forget this, for it's the only point of recourse we have there against habit (and here we find again the irrevocable acquisitions of Bergsonian language, of Bergsonian thought). (And we would not be able to push these analyses of the Christian heart to the depths if a Bergson had not intervened.) Severus is a man habituated to everything; and who consequently is not moistened by grace; and upon whom grace has no point of leverage. Severus is a man habituated to everything and particularly to everything pagan, and upon whom consequently the Christian has no point of leverage—except he is not habituated to this, he is not used to this and we see that he will never be used to this: that a man like Polyeucte could have become a Christian.

There is the point of non-habitude, and it is the only one we have. He is content that all the world be Christian. He is habituated to all the world being Christian. He is not habituated to Polyeucte being Christian.

It is for him a kind of scandal (in his system), and this point of scandal is also the only point of non-habitude, and thus the only vulnerable

113. A Frankish knight and one of the leaders of the First Crusade from 1096 until his death in 1100.

point we have. It is the only point of opening and entry and penetration. It is the only point through which we can hope that grace could ever pass.

It is thus also our only point of hope.

And here we find again that diametrical opposition of hope to habit.

It is, strictly, a scandal in reverse, a scandal in the good sense. The scandal being precisely this, consisting precisely in this: a rupturing of habit, a point, a rupturing through the intercalation of non-habitude.

A scandal thus in reverse, a scandal in the good sense, is one of the very forms, and one of the most frequent, and one of the essential, of the explosion of grace.

If habit is what introduces the amortization of grace, the scandal in reverse, the scandal in the good sense, is what puts an end to this amortization, being what breaks apart the habit.

Thus, the scandal in reverse, the scandal in the good sense, is sometimes the point of the explosion itself of grace, sometimes the point of penetration it has reserved for itself for one does not know what later introduction.

It is not enough for Polyeucte that he vanquish Severus in reality. It is not enough that he vanquish Severus in regard to honor in spiritual reality and in himself and before himself and before the other saints and preceding martyrs and before Nearchus[114] and before God. He still wants, it is still necessary, to vanquish (in regard to honor) Severus before Severus himself and in the system of Severus. It is still necessary that Severus retain in his side that point of wounding, that he carry away that point of anxiety and of memory, that point of non-habitude and of scandal, that Polyeucte is a Christian and that he has been vanquished in regard to honor by a Christian.

For if every point of anxiety coincides with a point of non-habitude, it is because the surfaces themselves of tranquility come into coincidence with the surfaces of habit.

Every point of non-habitude is a point of anxiety. Every plane of habit is a plane of tranquility.

Now Severus can only reckon within the system of reckoning of Severus. Severus can only measure within the system of measuring of Severus. Otherwise he would be converted himself, he would be a

---

114. A Christian friend of Polyeucte, who first encourages him to convert.

Christian, he would be with Polyeucte and not opposed to Polyeucte, and the problem would no longer be posed.

He would no longer be in comparison with Polyeucte. He would be in communion with Polyeucte, and the problem would not be posed.

Now we do well to suppose that Corneille is not one to conjure away a problem, or gloss over its givens; or suppress it. Everything saves him from this: that genius to which we have referred, that intelligence, and that same system of complete honesty of which we are speaking.

So that there is no cheating in the comparison, so that the difficulty is not fraudulently eluded, so that the problem remains and is presented in its exactitude and in its fullness, Severus must be entirely himself and naturally must not come out of the system of Severus. Neither out of the system of thought nor the system of measure.

That being the case, so that Severus carries away that point of anxiety and that point of memory, that point of non-habitude and that point of scandal, so that he suffers at least from that breach, so that he is touched at least in that point, it is not enough that Polyeucte vanquish Severus before God; he must vanquish him before Severus.

Let's say it rigorously: The measures of God, the reckonings of God, do not count for Severus. Otherwise he would be a Christian.

The system of God does not count for Severus. It is the system of Severus and only the system of Severus that counts for Severus.

So it is not enough that Polyeucte win (in honor, in greatness) in the accounting of God; he must win in the accounting of Severus.

If one wants Severus to carry away that point of insecurity.

It is not enough that Polyeucte win in the system of God; he must win in the system of Severus.

It's what I said, I believe, in *Le Porche du mystère de la deuxième vertu* or in *Le Mystère des saints Innocents:* that the one who loves enters into dependence on the one who is loved, and so even God enters into dependence on the one he wants to win.

When the good shepherd goes in search of the lost sheep, he enters into dependence on the lost sheep, and one can say that in order to find it he guides himself by it and by its erring ways.

The one who searches enters into dependence on the one who is sought.

The one who wants to win enters into dependence on the one he wants to win.

Thus not only does Polyeucte enter into dependence on Severus, but God himself enters into dependence on Severus. For it is necessary that Severus not leave unscathed.

It is necessary that Severus not leave without a certain wounding. And in a word, it is necessary that Severus not leave as he came.

And not only them, but all the Christian world, it is necessary that all the Christian world enter in this way into dependence on the pagan world, for it must not be that the pagan world leave unscathed and without a certain wounding. It must not be that the pagan world leave as it came.

It is not enough that the being of Polyeucte vanquish within itself and before itself and before God. The *image* of Polyeucte must vanquish in the spirit of Severus. Severus cannot know Polyeucte in himself. He cannot know the being of Polyeucte. Otherwise he would be a Christian. For to know here is to know in communion. He can only know a certain image of Polyeucte. That which he has. And it is a pagan image. Polyeucte cares extremely that this image (pagan) of himself be a high image and an image of greatness and an image of honor, and for Severus and in Severus the image of one who has vanquished him even in regard to pagan honor. It is in the contest itself of Severus that Polyeucte must win. For Severus doesn't understand the other contest. And in order for him to realize that Polyeucte wins and vanquishes, it must be in his system of contestation that Polyeucte wins and vanquishes.

It is the system and the theory itself of the image. No assurance of conscience, even integral, is enough for Polyeucte. It is not enough that he is sure of himself, *conscius sui*,[115] and that he is integrally right with himself. It is not even enough that he is sure of God, that is of the judgment that God brings to bear on him and the knowledge God has of him. He must still be sure of an infirm judgment because it is all the same a judgment of honor. And he must still be sure of an inexact knowledge, imperfect, transposed, because it is all the same a knowledge of honor. It is not enough for him that he is integrally right with himself. It is not even enough for him that he is integrally right with God. He must still be right before the one who doesn't have knowledge here, because this one is all the same a man of honor.

---

115. "self-aware."

It is not enough that in adoration and martyrdom he gives his entire being to God. It is still necessary that in the conversation (and also in the adoration and martyrdom), he present a certain image of himself to this great pagan.

It is not enough that in what is Christian he gives everything. It is still necessary that in what is pagan he gives something else, an image.

A singular situation. The more does not suffice. The less must be added to it.

It is not enough that he vanquish for God, who knows it well. He must add to this that he vanquishes also for the other, who is only a man of honor.

To an absolute knowledge, he must add; to a perfect knowledge, he must add. What? The imperfect knowledge, the inexact knowledge, the infirm knowledge, the noble knowledge that this man of honor, this pagan, will have of him.

It is not enough that the Christian world reveal its being and offer the fullness of its love and its being before God. It must also offer a certain high image of itself to the pagan world.

It is the system and it is the politics of Saint Louis. What is perhaps the more beautiful in Joinville (but does one ever know what is the more beautiful?) is that infinite care that Saint Louis takes so that this sultan of Egypt[116] has a high idea of what the king of France is. It is not enough to be the king of France for the ordinary people of France and for the French barons. And it is not enough for him to be Saint Louis before God. It is necessary still that he be the king of France before this sultan of Egypt and that he be Saint Louis before these infidels.

And above all that these Muslims not believe that French barons serve their God less well than they serve theirs.

It is not enough that the true God be served in exactitude and in fullness of adoration, of sacrifice, and of martyrdom. It is necessary still that the sectarians of the false God (they adore Mohammed)[117] have at no moment the idea that Mohammed is better served.

---

116. Baibars, Louis IX's primary Muslim opponent in the Seventh and Eighth Crusades.

117. Péguy's view here appears to be not that the God of Islam is false, but that the tendency to "adore" Mohammed as a god is false. If and insofar as such a tendency indeed existed among the Muslim opponents of the Christian crusaders, this would, of course, be a violation of the teaching of Islam itself.

It is always the system of the idea one offers of oneself. It is always the theory of the image. It is necessary that these infidels have a certain image of what a French baron is and of what the word of a French baron is. It is necessary that this sultan of Egypt have a certain image of the king of France and it is even necessary that he have a certain image of Saint Louis.

In a word, a French baron must not scandalize the infidels. The king of France must not scandalize the sultan of Egypt.

(I say adoration and martyrdom in relation to Saint Louis because I don't believe the martyrdom can be disputed. He died on crusade and he died there in illness and toil, and Joinville defends him strongly on this point.)

It is not enough that Saint Louis be Saint Louis for the sire of Joinville. It is necessary still that he be so even for a Muslim chronicler and witness.

It is the system, it is the politics of Joan of Arc. Just as Polyeucte understood that the combat he was offering against Severus and before Severus was both a martyrdom and a combat of honor, just as Saint Louis understood that the crusade was both a crusade and a combat of honor, so Joan of Arc understood that the just war she was going to offer was a combat of honor and a combat of God and a combat of chivalry (and certainly the preliminary to a crusade, the return to the crusade). It wasn't enough for her that she was sent by God and accountable only to God, alone, directly. It wasn't enough for her that she was integrally right with God and before God. She wished, it was also necessary, that she be right with the enemy and before the enemy.

Hence that summation to the English, an act of extreme importance, which must not be considered a declaration of war but a declaration of the honor of war. It isn't enough that she present herself armed with a mandate from God, invested with an imperative mandate. It is necessary that this mandate be presented according to the rules, and these rules are the rules of honor and of courteous combat. Even while sent by God, she solicits something like a judgment of God. If war is to be engaged, it is necessary that this war she will conduct be a just war. If tomorrow morning battle is to be offered, this battle must be a battle of honor, the battle of a chivalrous combat, the battle of a combat of God, the battle of a judgment of God. Therefore, this summation is not at all an ultimatum, or rather not an ultimatum like those of diplomacy or even of the law of war. It is a formal notice of courtesy prior to engagement in honorable combat.

If it were up to her only, all warfare would present itself as an immense combat of God, and the outcome of all warfare would be an immense judgment of God. The old French proverb: *Chacun pour soi, Dieu pour tous*[118] isn't only a proverb, it's an adage. And one grasps it poorly and in a counter-sense when one makes of it a kind of justification and shorthand for egoism. On the contrary, it is the very formula of the courteous combat. It is the rule of the game in the honest comparison. It is the very formula of the judgment of God. Each one defends his cause in its exactitude and its fullness, each one pushes his chance as much as he can, without reproach, because God presides over the entire contest.

What is perhaps most fine in the *Trials* is this summation to the king of England: "[You] King of England, and you, duke of Bedford . . . ."

[You] King of England, and you, duke of Bedford, who call yourself regent of the kingdom of France; you, Guillaume de la Poule, count of Sulford; John, sire of Talbot; and you, Thomas, sire of Escales, who call yourselves lieutenants of the duke of Bedford, give your reasons to the King of heaven . . . ."[119]

Even sanctity is temporal, and it is subject to the seasons and times. It is subject to the ages of life. If nothing is as beautiful as youthful genius, and if nothing in all the *oeuvre* and all the career of the genius is worth as much as the first resolves of youth, nothing and not even the most profound experiences; and not even the plenitudes of maturity; and not even the remote detachments of old age, what will be the parallel for the young saint, what will be the parallel sanctity? I don't believe anything is so beautiful in the *Trials* as this first summation to the king of England, and to "you who call yourself regent, and you who call yourselves lieutenants." Nothing but what is youthful and firm. An unparalleled assurance.

118. "Each for himself, God for all."

119. The summation is from a letter written by Joan on March 22, 1429. Péguy is quoting it from a book of original sources concerning Joan compiled by Jules Quischerat, *Procès de condamnation et de réhabilitation de Jeanne d'Arc*, published in 1841. The italics are his.

It is the assurance of God himself. A line of thought that is perfectly pure. A line of vocation in its full and firm and complete purity. The invention of life itself and of war and of honor and of God. A newness without limit. Nothing faded, nothing worked at, nothing willed. The source itself of honor. An admirable ease and liberty under arms. No effort and to go so far as to say this, no merit. The rising of the sun of greatness and of force. The dawn of sanctity. The simple utterance of the enterprise. The first advancement of the vocation. The first movement of the *cortège*. The first step of the procession.

Nothing withered. Not even that withering that marks the greatest saints and that is to have lived and to have been a human being and to have felt the ingratitude of human beings and, who knows, to have known one's own ingratitude (a few excepted). None of that withering that is the mark itself of time and that scores the greatest lives, according to the sole condition that they pass, they advance. That with regularity they go towards the culmination of the last rendezvous. None of that withering that is the mark itself, the inscription, of the accumulations of memory, the mark and the inscription of the memory itself even without its accumulations. Nothing withered, nothing residual, nothing recalled. None of that residual withering that is the continual product of the most simple exercise of memory.

None of those wrinkles on the soul that are the continual product of the most wise, the most poor, the most noble, the most simple exercise of the inseparable memory.

None of that withering left by everything that passes on, so long as and according to the sole condition that it does pass on. None of that withering that sanctity itself leaves as it passes on (for it also cannot not be an experience). And that ordeal leaves by definition. And that even martyrdom leaves.

None of that residue that is the trace of memory.

Nothing withered, and since we must always return to this: *nothing of habit*.

Youthfulness itself, that is the zero of memory, the zero of withering, the zero of habit.

A total grace. A new grace. And if I may say so, a young grace. For eternity itself is in the temporal. And there are new graces and there are graces that seem to be aged. Or if you prefer, there is an integral hope.

None of that withering that makes people of a certain age resemble each other more than they resemble themselves at different ages. And makes the forty-year-old executioner and martyr more brothers to each other than either is to the man he was at twenty.

None of that withering that makes it so that a man never returns to his father's house the same as he left it. And so that even Jesus was not the same man at the end of his third year of ministry as he was at the beginning of the first. And that he was not the same man the night of Gethsemani as he was that first day he left his father's house.

"*Give your reasons to the King of heaven . . . .*" It is the very formula of the single combat. So she is an upholder of God in a combat of God, that is in a combat fought before God according to rules in order to provoke a judgment of God. This sheet of paper (yes, yes, monsieur the scholar, it's on parchment), this sheet of paper that she dictates to the clerks and has brought is not an ultimatum of war, is not even a summation. It is a summons.

Or rather, it is a mandate even. It is the particular mandate that she has received and that she is only sending on, that she is only transmitting. This child is running an errand for God. As God has only a very small staff, in this combat she must be at once the upholder and the herald.

We know how she was received. She found the English (and the Burgundians) and, we must say, the French and the Sorbonne and the king of England and, we must say, the king of France and the Church of England and, we must say, the Church of France more deaf and closed to God's voice, more rebellious against God, than Saint Louis found the infidels of Egypt. And this is one of the reasons why she was the greatest saint and martyr. We would perhaps have to say that she was a saint to the second degree and that she was a martyr to the second degree. For it was within Christianity itself that she found her points of application, her points of resistance, her points of war, her points of honor, her points of sanctity, her points of martyrdom. She was like a soldier who fought not only at the frontiers, but for whom her own home would prove an immense, universal frontier. A more fortunate Saint Louis had only to deal with the infidels.

We can say that Saint Louis had around him a people of the faithful and that he fought against a people of infidels who were, rather, a people of the counter-faithful. Joan of Arc, on the contrary, had to respond to her vocation and to pursue its purpose, had to accomplish her mission within a people of unfaithfulness, in the midst of a people inveterately unfaithful, in the midst of a people *habitually* fallen into a state of unfaithfulness.

No one was faithful to her up to the end. She was abandoned and denied like Christ. And among those who were faithful some of the time (if these words "to be faithful some of the time" can have the least sense), it was only ever the ordinary people. The ordinary people of the soldiery, the ordinary people of the Church, the ordinary people of the people. Monks, soldiers, bourgeois. Not prelates nor, we might as well say, barons. Nor king. She had to be a Christian and martyr and saint against the French and against the Christians. She found unfaithfulness installed in the very heart of France, in the heart of Christendom. She had to break that long habitude. She had to climb back up that long memory. That's what I call being a saint and martyr twice. That's what I call an ordeal to the second degree, a sanctity, a martyrdom to the second degree. Non-habituated, she had to break that long habitude. Un-memoried, she had to climb back up that long memory.

To make war against the enemy, to fall prey to the enemy, I'm not saying that would be nothing, but finally it would be the first degree. To make war against one's brother, to fall prey to those of one's spiritual race, there is the second degree of the ordeal, the ordeal redoubled.

To leave, to battle at the frontiers, is fine. But to battle at the heart of your house, to devour yourself in your own heart, what a doubling.

This difference and this doubling, this distance is so important that we can say it cuts war into two, it divides victory itself into two categories: the category of wars undertaken and battles fought and victories won on the frontier, and the category of wars undertaken and battles fought and unhappy victories won at the center. To battle against the enemy or to battle against one's own. All is happy in a certain sense in the first category, and in a certain sense all is unhappy in the second. And defeat in the first category has a less bitter taste than victory in the second. As disastrous as a war against the enemy might be, it always comes under the category of a certain happiness. But the more victorious a war is against one's own, the more it also injures and offends, the more it sinks into the category of a certain unhappiness. A defeat in the first category, a defeat against the foreigner, can never go so far as to reduce to zero the consideration of a certain solemn happiness. But it is the victory itself in the second category, in the war against one's own, which increases, which carries to infinity a certain consideration of unhappiness.

The entire operation of a war against the foreigner, the entire operation of a war at the frontiers, the entire operation of a war against the enemy is in a certain sense an operation of a certain happiness, even if it has been disastrous, so long as it saves honor, so long as it has been engaged and undertaken in exactitude and fullness and with all strength; by its very nature it enters, even in defeat and disaster and death, into a certain category of being happy. All is unhappy, on the contrary, in the second category. The entire operation of a civil war, the entire operation of a war at the heart and the center, the entire operation of a war against one's own enters before having been born into a certain category of disaster and of being unhappy. Even though it would be a hundred times innocent, it is never once innocent. Even though it would be a hundred times honorable, it is always against honor. And even though it is pure, all the same it is impure. The most unhappy operation of a war against the foreigner, provided that it really does save honor (and is not, as they so often make it, a false semblance and an *alibi*, and they don't say *to save honor* in order pleasantly to excuse themselves from saving victory), is a happy operation. The happiest operation of a civil war is an unhappy operation and a painful one. The dirtiest hands of a foreign war are cleaner than the cleanest hands of a civil war. In the operations to all intents and purposes the most happy of a civil war, there is a certain taste of distress, of depravity, which there is not in the most unhappy operations of a war against the foreigner. It is literally an inversion. More than a perversion.

If this is the way it is in civil war and in foreign war in regard to the territorial and political, what will it be where the spiritual is concerned? There also we have frontiers and a center. (The center is Rome.) There also we have the enemy and one's own home. So there also we will have, in this sense, two categories of war: and the foreign war where the spiritual is concerned, even though it be a disaster, enters all the same into the category of being happy. But the civil war where the spiritual is concerned, even though it be victorious, and the more it is victorious, enters into the category of pain and immense regret, and into the category of being an unhappy war.

(Jesus had both of them, superimposed, or rather conjoined, he had to deal with both together, the Jews and the Romans, with his own race and the foreign race, with Caiaphas and Pilate, with the crowd and the soldiers.)

The happier Polyeucte had only to deal with the pagan world, and that is again one of the reasons why *Polyeucte* stands entirely in the category of happiness, which is the same as the category of grace. Like Saint Louis, he battles only at the frontiers (spiritual, temporal). Like Saint

Louis, he battles only against the enemy. Like Saint Louis, his operation of spiritual warfare is only ever the operation of the crusade. Like Saint Louis, he only ever undertakes the crusade. What will we say of the one who came to Orléans persuaded that it was only the point of departure for a general reconciliation of Christianity for the sake of the crusade, for the resumption and crowning achievement of the crusade, and who found, on the contrary, that this itself was the only crusade she would never undertake? What will we say, if not that in this again she realized what I will perhaps speak of one day: the closest imitation of Jesus Christ.

The happier Polyeucte had only to deal with Severus and the happier Corneille had only to deal with the youth of the world. I mean the youth of the Christian world, which was what I have called a youth of grace. He had only to deal with that birth of the world, which was, spiritually, like a recommencement of the first paradise. It is for this that *Polyeucte* is a work that dwells constantly in the category of happiness, in the category of being happy. And in the category of honor. And in the category of grace. And it is for this that we must place together Polyeucte and Saint Louis, Corneille and Joinville, on one side, and on the other side, Joan of Arc and Jesus. And it is for this that we must say that it is Joan of Arc who realized the most faithful and closest imitation of Jesus Christ.

There are also spiritual races and the world is large enough to hold saints of different races. I recognize two of them here, and they are most profoundly separated. The ones, Polyeucte and Saint Louis, were so showered with graces that they never suffered otherwise than in the category of being happy, never ceased to suffer in the category of being happy. And the others, Joan of Arc, Jesus, were so showered, beyond this, with another sort of grace, with a grace of dis-grace, that they also suffered, they explored suffering, in the category of unhappiness.

For all foreign war does not depart from the category of grace. But in all civil war there is a particular point of dis-grace.

And all foreign war does not depart from the category of honor. But in all civil war there is a particular point of dishonor.

And again it is one of those cases where the most innocent is never innocent. And where the cleanest hands are never clean. And where the one who is not a criminal is a criminal all the same, and drags behind a dreadful memory, a melancholy, an immense regret worse than remorse.

And one comes to ask oneself whether one wouldn't prefer true remorse.

Whatever Polyeucte suffers, his suffering is direct, if I may say so, and while it is extreme, it is simple. It goes only in one direction and this direction is the good. It does not return on itself. And on himself. It is vented; it is healthy and saintly. It is in the category of happiness, of honor, of grace. His suffering is neither monstrous, nor dreadful, nor inverted. His suffering, his sanctity, his martyrdom is not controverted.

Whatever, likewise, Saint Louis suffers, he only suffers it in relation to the infidels. He only suffers it at the frontiers. He only suffers it in relation to the enemy and from the enemy. He is not surrounded by traitors. He no more than Polyeucte is betrayed, denied. He must displace himself in order to go find suffering, war, illness, prison, death, insults, martyrdom. He does not find all that installed in the heart of France. His war is not in Orléans. His capture is not at Compiègne. His imprisonment and martyrdom are not at Rouen. His enemies, his torturers, his jailers are not Christians. His traitors and betrayers are not Christians and French. For he has no traitors. He has only enemies. And there is all the distance, there is that capital and monstrous difference.

He only battles against the adverse. He does not battle against himself and his own. He must go to Egypt, he must go to Tunis, to find what the other finds in Étampes and the Somme and the Lower Seine.[120] He must go to carry the crusade to the infidel. But what to say about her who found a monstrous crusade to fight in the heart of France. And not more than one hundred and sixty years afterwards.

Rosetta, Damietta, Memphis, and the ancient Nile, there is the location of his difficult battles. But she, the city where she fell was our Paris.

It is always the difference between the extrinsic and the intrinsic. Thus Jesus found right at hand two or three small hills or elevations in the terrain, the mount of the Beatitudes, *ascendit in montem*,[121] the Mount of Olives, the mount called Calvary. And Herod searched for him among his relations. And Judas found him among his band.

He did not have to go out to meet Herod. And out to meet Judas. And he did not have to look for Caiaphas. For he was dragged there. And

---

120. Péguy is referring to Paris, Compiègne, and Rouen.
121. "He went up the mountain" (Matthew 5:1).

he did not have to look for Pilate. For he was dragged there. And he did not have to ask where Calvary was.

Those saints of the first category, Polyeucte, Saint Louis, are so much in the category of being happy and in the category of grace that one could almost say they already no longer belong to the Church militant. They are already of the Church triumphant. Their militancy is already triumph. They are so victorious that one can say they are not in battle. They are in glory, in the proper sense of the word, in the sense it must always be given in theology. I don't believe there is any work in the world that belongs to heaven as much as *Saint Louis* or as much as *Polyeucte*. An extraordinary grace, a singular grace, a pre-eminent grace, a grace placed, set, situated beyond was given to Corneille and to Joinville. I don't believe there is any work in the world that as much as *Saint Louis*, as much as *Polyeucte*, belongs to paradise, gives us the *climate* of paradise, renders to us the very breath of heaven.

I don't believe there is in the world any work so anticipatory, so out in front, and in a certain sense so outside, so flown away.

From the earth.

The Gospels and the *Trials*, different altogether, are in the fullness of combat, in the fullness of militancy, in the fullness of the earth and, I would say, in the exactitude and fullness of the incarnation.

So Polyeucte walks with Saint Louis and Joan of Arc walks with Jesus. Nothing in Polyeucte, nothing in Saint Louis that recalls the agony of the Mount of Olives and the abandonment and what must be called the doubt and the "My Father, let this cup pass from me" and the terrible "My Father, why have you abandoned me?"[122] To the contrary entirely, in the imprisonment and agony and death of Joan of Arc there is an echo, a reflection, a reminder, in all of it a faithfulness to the judgment, the agony, the death of Jesus.

So Polyeucte walks with Joinville and it is the finest *cortège*. But here is Joan of Arc walking with Jesus. And whose heart could be still before the dolorous *cortège*?

So also the Virgin is House of Gold and Ivory Tower and Tower of David and Ark of the Covenant and Morning Star and Heaven's Door.[123] But whose heart could be still before the mother seven times dolorous?

122. Matthew 26:39; 27:46.

123. These title-metaphors are found in the Roman Catholic litanies of the Virgin, taken from the Song of Songs 7:4; Exodus 25:10–22; Revelation 22:16.

So Polyeucte walks with Saint Louis and it is a fine disposition. But Joan of Arc walks with Jesus. And whose heart could be still before this dolorous procession?

Polyeucte walks with Saint Louis and it is a prince and a king and it is a royal *cortège*. But Joan of Arc walks with Jesus and who will not salute this *cortège* of the wretched?

Polyeucte walks with Saint Louis and it is the very festival of God. But Joan of Arc walks with Jesus and it is a great procession.

Corneille walks with Joinville, the *Trials* walk with the Gospels. Polyeucte walks with Saint Louis, Joan of Arc walks with Jesus.

There are saints whom I will call saints of beatitude and, so to say, of anticipation. And there are saints of militancy, who could be called saints of misery and pain, and almost saints of bitterness and ingratitude. The first are the finest and the grandest. But Jesus is more particularly the patron and model of the latter.

In this category of classification. For there is another category of classification, where, on the contrary, it is Polyeucte who walks with Jesus and Joan of Arc with Saint Louis. And this makes for two fine *cortèges*. Crossed. In this second category of classification, Polyeucte walks with Jesus in having had no part in temporal government, and Joan of Arc walks with Saint Louis in having had partial or total part in temporal government; in having been king of France or suppliant of the king of France, lieutenant of the king of France at those one hundred and fifty years removed. Polyeucte walks with Jesus in not having participated at all in the things of Caesar. Joan of Arc walks with Saint Louis as having participated in the things of Caesar, as having been heir to Caesar and the frightful responsibilities of Caesar.

Polyeucte walks with Jesus as being satisfied to *render* to Caesar.[124] Joan of Arc walks with Saint Louis in not having been able to be satisfied with less than being Caesar themselves. And so it is *Polyeucte* who walks with the Gospels and the *Trials* that walk with *Saint Louis*.

Such would be this second category of classification, which I would call the category of the temporal, or of Caesar. (Our first category being the category of beatitude.) In this second category of classification, it is Corneille who walks with Matthew, Mark, Luke.

---

124. Matthew 22:21.

And in the first category of classification it was some ecclesiastical notary of the diocese and officialdom of Rouen who, without knowing it, ignorant, ignored, known, unknown, was walking with Matthew, Mark, and Luke. It was that miserable poor man, a clerk, very serious, very learned, a very good notary (the *Trials* are the proof), witnessing unawares the greatest sanctity in the world, *doctus, peritus, cæcus*,[125] who was taking up, but in reverse, from the other side, the role of Matthew, of Mark, and of Luke. It was this miserable poor man who was the evangelist, a blind evangelist, and an evangelist in reverse. It is as though we had the Gospel of Jesus Christ by the scribe of Caiaphas and by the *notarius*, the man who took notes at the audiences of Pontius Pilate.

And in this immense cathedral of souls there will be yet other categories of classification. They will be innumerable and they will cross over each other, interconnect, and support one another, like the ribbed arches of this immense nave. For sanctity is a vast cathedral. And there is more soaring in the nave, but more shadow in the lower sides and something like a silence in the light itself. When the light itself holds silence, that too is shadow. And there are those who crowd together in the choir (sanctities, fidelities). But even the gatekeeper is perhaps a yet more eminent figure. And there are saints who are in the alignments of several arches because they are keystones of the ogival vaulting. And they order so many vaults or portions of vaults. And there are several axes, parallel and perpendicular. And there are several planes. There are even very many planes. But there is only one center. And one sole keystone that is central. And one sole altar that is at the center.

Matthew, Mark, Luke were the notaries of Jesus. Joinville was the notary of Saint Louis. Corneille made himself the notary of Polyeucte. And the notary of Joan of Arc was that miserable poor clerk, the same notary of her accusers.

She was so perfectly impoverished that she was forced to make use of the notary of her judges and accusers.

She was so perfectly abandoned that she could only be recorded by the notary of her judges and accusers.

I see a third category of classification, which is classification according to practice. Many saints, and maybe the majority, a great number of saints gave themselves much trouble for the sake of practice. The others

---

125. "learned, experienced, blind."

(they are mine) didn't even think about it (didn't even have to think about it), being sufficiently practiced upon by God. In this third category of classification Polyeucte is a saint of little practice and even no practice, Joan of Arc is a saint of no practice, Jesus is a saint of little practice and perhaps no practice.

(By practice I mean here one's own practice, in the sense of *amour propre*, practice through one's self, to distinguish it from practice through God. Practice that comes from oneself, to distinguish it from practice that comes from God.)

In this sense Polyeucte is a saint of little practice and even no practice. The practice he intends immediately is death. Or rather, the sole practice he intends is immediately death. And he does not even intend it. It is a grace he receives, and an instantaneous crowning of grace:

> *Du premier coup de vent il me conduit au port*
> *Et sortant du baptême il m'envoie à la mort.*[126]

He leads me, he sends me, it's not only out of deference that he transfers to God his entire *practice*. It is because it really is thus. Such is the event for him. And it is an immediate event. It is a grace that comes to him. And comes to him instantaneously. He has martyrdom right at hand.

In this same sense Joan of Arc is also a saint of little practice, and we must say of no practice, and perhaps one day I'll be able to explain myself at a little greater length on this point. Her long vocation, her long practice is from God, comes to her entirely complete and entirely pure from God, is entirely given to her, entirely laid out by God. She doesn't introduce into it even the shadow of the invention of her own practice. She has something else to do; she has enough pain to *bear*, to cope with the practice that comes from God. Her effort, on the contrary, her high method, her special mystical task, her science and her government, is to keep her strength intact as much as she is able in order to respond to the exigencies, the expense of that long commandment. She will not have too much. She will never have enough. It's really (not) a matter of convent practices. What she has to do is a matter of war, victory, coronation, defeat, capture,

---

126. "From the first burst of wind he leads me to harbor / And on going out from baptism he sends me to death" (*Polyeucte*, Act IV, scene 3).

prison, judgment, death, and the governing and the salvation of an entire people.

It is always war and grand maneuvers. One can struggle hard in grand maneuvers, and suffer terribly, and perish, and die in a ditch from exposure. It is always death. And yet not the same thing as falling one day on the heights of Morsbronn.[127]

So in regard to the sanctity of Joan of Arc, it is necessary to sweep away one's own practice, those wretched human inventions, as she swept the front of her door: in order to allow entry to the practice that comes from God.

She would have been a bad domestic manager, she would have been an unfaithful steward, if she had dispersed what there was of her strength for the poor inventions of an individual practice. It is something to make grand maneuvers. And it is even necessary to make them very well. But what to say about someone who would want absolutely to make up their twenty-one days by counting them from the day war is declared? And who, having arrived at Coulommiers would want absolutely to climb up every morning for twenty-one days to Montanglaust (where one can very well die for that matter), instead of embarking on the third day for Nancy and beyond?[128]

She would have been an unfaithful servant if she had not kept her poor life intact and had not guarded with exactness the meager resources of a creature, as if keeping intact material for the thumb of God to model.[129]

In this third category of classification we can say that Jesus is a saint of little practice, and perhaps no practice. For it is not necessary to

127. A reference to a battle of August 6, 1870 during the Franco-Prussian war, in which there was a heroic and glorious, though doomed, cavalry charge on the part of the French cuirassiers.

128. Coulommiers, with its adjacent castle of Montanglaust, was an exercise ground for an infantry regiment (the 276th) to which Péguy, a reservist, was posted. The twenty-one days probably refers to the period allowed in wartime for training (including, presumably, a daily hill climb to the Montanglaust castle) prior to embarkation for the real front (as it would have been anticipated in 1914) farther to the east of Paris, near Nancy. According to the analogy, Joan was one who chose to embark for the real front on the third day, rather than waste her energy in twenty-one days of climbing up to Montanglaust.

129. For this image, see Exodus 8:15; Luke 11:20.

consider Jesus as a *summum* of *summa* and as a *maximum* of *maxima* in all the categories of classification, in all the categories of sanctity. He did not enter into all the classifications. He did not enter into all the categories. So the center of the central nave is not aligned with the axes of the lower sides.

Jesus is the greatest saint, and the prince and the first of the saints. But he is not the greatest saint as a mathematical or even physical *maximum*. He is not the greatest saint through a physical summation, through an accumulation of *maxima*, by effect of a mathematical summation. He is a living person, a strongly characterized figure, of which the Gospels give us the precise portrait.

He is one unique person, in two natures: he is man, and he is God. If one takes him beginning with the head, then descending according to the order of metaphysical deduction, and also according to the order of the event within history; if, in a word, one takes him according to the order of reality, it must be said: He is God, and he is man. (And even he became man. He was made human. *Et homo factus est*.) But if one takes him according to the order of knowledge, if one takes him according to the order of our access, of access for us beginning from us (that is, in sum, if one takes him according to the order of the Gospels), it must be said: He is man; and he is God.

But when we say that God is holy and when we say that the man (even in Jesus Christ) is holy, we mean this word, and I will say these two words,[130] in two quite different senses. When we say of God that he is holy, or three times holy,[131] we mean by this that he is, without any reservation and without any limitation, the seat of all the perfections that belong to God. That is, all the metaphysical perfections, all the absolute perfections. In this sense, God is truly an absolute, an absolute being, a *summum*, a *maximum*, and a metaphysical *optimum*.

But when we say, so long as we say, that a man is holy, even be this man Jesus Christ, we do not mean by this that he is without any reservation and without any limitation the seat of all the perfections (if one can thus call them), the seat of all the virtues that belong to humanity itself. For reservation and limitation belong to the human itself. Particularly

---

130. The "two words" would be "holy" as applied to God and "holy" as applied to man. In French, as in English, they are the same word (*saint*).

131. Apparently a reference to the *Trisagion* ("Thrice Holy") hymn within the Christian liturgy.

the limitation of time and place. And the limitation in the categories of classification.

It must always be considered (we have already said it) that Jesus took on the incarnation in its exactitude and its fullness. Without any limitation or reservation. Without any caution or fraudulent precaution. He became a man among men. He was made a saint among the saints. He particularly assumed the reservation and the limitation that belong to the human. Particularly the limitation of time and place. And the limitation in the categories of classification.

As man and consequently as holy, he is thus not a *summum*, a physical and mathematical *maximum*, but is organic, a man, a saint, a very distinct person, a figure of which the Gospels have left us the admirable portrait.

He is a man like others among others (the first). He is a saint like others among others (the first).

If Jesus, as human and holy, had been a *summum*, a mathematical and so to say physical *maximum* of the human virtues, we would not have needed the Gospels. For we would not have needed a portrait. And we would not have needed a history. A *summum*, a *maximum* does not portray itself, does not tell the story of itself. It does not represent itself. It calculates itself. It fixes itself at a point of absolute perfection. *Non evenit neque devenit. Cæli enarrant GLORIAM Dei.*[132] But they do not *narrate* God himself.

Jesus is a man among others, who allows the others to be human in their own way. He is a saint among others, who allows the others to be saints in their own way.

He was particular, personal, a person. He was not everybody at once. He was honestly and fully *a* man and *a* saint. He was not in all times nor in all places at once. Thus he did not occupy, did not invade, all the categories of classification.

He gets into line with human beings, he gets into line with the saints. He gets into line as the first, but he gets into line.

We rank him as the first, but the first of us among us.

He is the first star in the sky of sanctity. But the first star is the one that shines the most, that shines the first, not one that absorbs the brilliance and the content and so to say the person and being of all the others.

---

132. "He neither arrives nor becomes. The heavens are telling the glory of God." The second sentence refers to Psalm 19.

The first star is the one that shines the first with the same brilliance, a brilliance of the same order. It shines with a same first brilliance. But it allows the others to shine.

So the king is the first among and at the head of his barons, among and at the head of the ordinary people. He is of his barons and he is the first of them. He is of his people and he is the first of them. He is not everybody at once. He does not absorb everybody. He allows the others to be.

So Jesus is not everybody at once. He does not absorb everybody. He allows the others to be.

He gave it to Saint Louis to show what a king of France is and a great saint upon the throne, and he gave it to Joan of Arc to show what a great saint is at the head of armies.

It may be said that the history and the figure of Jesus the man and saint were metaphysically incalculable, like all that belongs to the human. For the freedom of human beings, which is the greatest invention of God, came into play also for him as man; I will say came into play for him most of all, for him eminently. It would be strange indeed if that freedom, which is at the very heart of the human and the finest creation of God in the human, and the most irrevocable, and the most necessary, since it alone articulates itself exactly with the gratuity of grace, had been chained in the case of one human being alone, and that being Jesus.

It is through a full play of his freedom and will, it is through a full play of his free will that he became human, was made man: *et homo factus est*. It is through a full play of his freedom that he assumed humanity, and so it is through a full play of his infinite freedom as God that he assumed human freedom. It is through a full play of his freedom as Creator that he assumed created freedom. The entire event of his life and his martyrdom and his death was free, consented to, voluntary, and willed. Up to the last moment he was free not to die for the salvation of the world. All his life and up to the last moment *he was free not to fulfill the prophecies.*

It is for this that the Gospels were necessary for us. Here again Jesus didn't want to be an extraordinary saint. He was an ordinary saint, the first in the order, but in the order. He needed his notaries and chroniclers. He needed the Gospel writers, just as Polyeucte needed Corneille, as Saint Louis needed Joinville, as Joan of Arc needed that miserable poor clerk who recorded the questions and responses. (And when I say that miserable poor clerk I am placing myself at our point of view, for he was certainly an extremely good clerk, highly regarded, with status; very well paid.)

In this also, Jesus wished to be an ordinary saint, a man, a saint like others among others. He wished to be in need of his witnesses, his martyrs, his notaries, his recorders. He didn't wish to be attested, remembered, by means of a constant miracle, a permanent miracle. He didn't wish to appeal to any other means than human means and the history and memory of human beings. *Scriptures* were necessary to him. He wished, like the saints, to be in need of scribes and court clerks, and the whole judicial and historical apparatus. He wished to offer material for the whole judicial and historical apparatus. He wished to be the material and the object of a trial, and even of two, a civil trial and a religious trial. A Church trial and a State trial. He wished to be the material and the object of the exegete and historian, the material, the object, the victim of historical critique. He wished to offer material to the exegete, to the historian, to the critic. He has delivered himself to the exegete, to the historian, to the critic, as he delivered himself to the soldiers, to other judges, to other crowds. He has delivered himself to those who carry schoolmaster's rods, as he delivered himself to those who carried sticks and whips. It is the same tradition. It is the same handing over. He has delivered himself to controversies, as he delivered himself to other insults. And the historians go on scolding at him, dead and living, as the scribes and the court clerks scolded him, present and silent. If he had concealed himself from critique and controversy, if he had shielded himself from the exegete, the critic, the historian, if his history had been shielded from the historian, if his memory had not entered into the general conditions, into the organic conditions of human memory, he would not have been a man like others. And the incarnation would not have been integral and honest. And we must always return to this.

In order that the incarnation be complete and entire, in order that it be honest, in order that it be neither limited nor fraudulent, his history had to be a human history, subject to the historian, and his memory had to be a human memory, humanly, defectively conserved. In a word, his very history and memory had to be made incarnate.

His memory and his history had to be quarreled over. Had to be delivered to the same vulgar herd. It is the same exposure of the same victim to the same executioners.

The incarnation would not have been complete, would have been holding back, if through the whole continuation of the centuries, through

DESCARTES AND THE CARTESIAN PHILOSOPHY 167

the whole of temporal eternity, he had not been delivered, in his history and memory, to the same interrogation.

It was necessary that, within time, for and before the same category of men, he be always the same man, fully man, exactly man, pursued, exposed, more than questioned, hunted down.

Such is one aspect of the mystery of the incarnation.

So that Jesus could be a man, it was necessary that his very memory and his history be the material and object not of a miracle but of a permanent process.

It was necessary that he live on as he had lived. And it was necessary that he live on as he had died. And it was necessary that he be temporally eternal as he had lived and as he had died.

In a word, it was necessary that the life of Jesus be a saint's life. And that he be exposed to our old comrade Babut, like a simple Saint Martin.[133]

The first of the saints' lives. Or the life of the first of saints. A saint's life at the head of the others, but a saint's life all the same, like the others among the others.

The Gospels are an inspired book; and a sacred book. That is, if I may say, their divine nature. But in their human nature, they come at the head, and they are of the same order of witness and inscription, of commemoration and writing, as the *Trials, Polyeucte,* or Joinville.

The Gospels are in large part the *Trials* of Jesus Christ.

If the *life* of Jesus[134] had been only the automatic realization, the mechanical accomplishment, and the methodical crowning of the prophecies, we would not have needed the Gospels and Jesus himself would not have needed them.

The Gospels are the prince among the *Trials, Polyeucte,* and Joinville.

As Jesus is the prince among Joan of Arc, Polyeucte, and Saint Louis.

---

133. Ernest-Charles Babut wrote an account of Saint Martin's life, *Saint Martin de Tours*.

134. The italics likely signal an allusion to Ernst Renan's *Vie de Jésus*, one of the most prominent of a number of nineteenth-century attempts to reconstruct a life of the historical Jesus. See also footnote 159.

The Gospels are for Jesus what the *Trials* are for Joan of Arc, *Polyeucte* for Polyeucte, *Joinville* for Saint Louis.

Matthew, Mark, Luke were for Jesus what the notary was for Joan of Arc, Corneille for Polyeucte, Joinville for Saint Louis.

If Jesus had accomplished the prophecies by way of an automatic deduction, a mechanical deduction, a purely and strictly determinative deduction; that is, if Jesus had been determinist and determined, if he had acted within the framework and the system of modern determinism, we would not have needed the Gospels. And he would not have needed the Gospels. The prophecies would have been sufficient for him. And they would have been sufficient for us also.

But he did not realize them as an automaton and automatically, he did not carry them out as a machine and mechanically, he did not unfold and develop them as a modern determinist; he accomplished them freely and as a human being. He doubtless accomplished them uniquely and eminently, but uniquely and eminently within the ordinary realm of gratuitous grace and gratuitous freedom.

In a word, the passage from the prophecies to the Gospels is in the order of the human and of the event, not in the order of the logical, mathematical, physical, supposedly scientific deduction, not in the order of modern determinism.

In a word, *the Gospels are not the prophecies put into the past tense*, transferred just as they are, transferred in whole, transferred in bulk from the future into the past through the ministration of the present. It was not only necessary, it was not enough that Jesus made them pass, transferred them, in time, made them past. It was also necessary that he realized them, that he accomplished them.

The Gospels (or the material, the subject, of the Gospels) are not only the prophecies having become; they are the prophecies having been realized.

They are not only the prophecies put into the past; they are the prophecies accomplished, that is as though made full.

It does not all come down to a change of tense. It is not merely a matter of shifting tenses. It is not merely a matter of putting the future into the future anterior. The prophecies are not merely a future and the Gospels not merely a future anterior, a future put into the past. The prophecies are an announcement (and the annunciation can be considered precisely as the last of the prophecies), and the Gospels are the consecration of this announcement.

And not merely a recording. Not merely the recording of what has been announced.

The prophecies are a prolonged promise. The Gospels are not the recording of this promise. They are the consecration of the outcome of this promise. And one could say at most the recording of the outcome of this promise.

The Gospels are an accomplishment, a making full, a putting into plenitude of the prophecies. And not merely an effectuation.

And this singular connection of the promise to the *keeping* of the promise is precisely the connection of Jesus to the prophets and the Gospels to the prophecies. This is not merely a connection of time. Take hold of all the prophecies in the future where they are and put them in the past tense. Turn them into a story, a narrative, a report, a history, a memoir, you will still not obtain the Gospels. There is infinitely more in the future anterior than in the simple future. Put the prophecies into the anterior, into the preterite tense, you will still not obtain the Gospels.

The Gospels are a bringing into fullness.

And not only is the connection of the promise to the keeping of the promise not merely a connection of time, but again not merely a causal connection. Not only is the connection not entirely exhausted by the intervention of the date, but again it is not entirely exhausted after by the intervention of determinant or determinative causation.

The keeping is not merely what is ulterior and, moreover, not merely what is caused.

The keeping is not merely what comes after and the promise is not merely what comes before. The keeping is not merely a succedaneum. The promise is not merely a cause and the keeping an effect. The announcement is the announcement, the promise is the promise, and the keeping is the keeping.

These are properties,[135] specifics.

Thus the connection of the promise to the keeping is not at all merely a chronological connection, and moreover, not merely a causal connection, but a specific, proper connection.

---

135. An example of Péguy's periodic employment of Aristotelian terms; in Aristotle's logic, a property is a necessary, but specific, determination of an object.

Now it is this same connection that is the connection of the Gospels to the prophecies, of Jesus to the prophets.

The annunciation can be considered as the last of the prophecies and as prophecy at the limit (and at the final term of the final point at the very beginning of the realization). And it is not only the most imminent prophecy. It is permissible to say it is also the highest and the chief. As Jesus is the last and the highest of the prophets, so and within the same movement, the annunciation is the last and the highest of the prophecies. It comes directly from God, through an angel, who is no more than an envoy and a herald. No longer through a prophet who is a man. And it is truly in the sequence the marvelous point where on the promise the keeping of the promise comes to be articulated.

Thus the annunciation is a unique moment in mystical and spiritual history. It is a culminating moment, a unique moment, and as a momentary instant, a singular moment. It is the complete end of a world and the beginning of another. The complete end of the first mystical world and the beginning of the other. And in one of those long beautiful days of June where there is no more night, no more gloomy darkness, where the day goes hand in hand with the day, it is the final instant of the evening and at the same time the first instant of the dawn.

It is the final instant of the promise and at the same time the first instant of the keeping of the promise.

It is the final instant of yesterday and at the same time the first instant of tomorrow.

It is the final instant of the past and at the same time, in the same present, the first instant of a tremendous future.

In the order of prophecy, in the set of what is past, in the category of the promise and the announcement, it is indeed the final and the highest and the culminating. It is as if immediate. And in effect, of all the ways of making an announcement, the salutation is the one that is more than tangential, more than immediate. For one is already there. And in the order of the keeping of the promise, in the set of the closed-off past, in the category of the Gospels, in the set of the past-become-present-and-future, it is the first instant of dawn and the first instant of presence. And moreover still, in this very future, at the center and as if in the empty hollow of this future, it is the departing point for so many *Ave Marias*, the point of the first prow of the first vessel of that innumerable fleet, and of all those that Saint Louis was going to say and all those that Joan of Arc was going to say.

In Latin, in French.

(And through a noble similitude, the departing point besides of innumerable *Salve Reginas*.)

And just as a point and a peak and a summit is narrow and fine and doesn't possess all the largeness of its base, so that large promise commencing with a whole world, then reduced to a whole people, found its end, in secret and shadow, in a humble girl-child, flower and crown of a whole race, flower and crown of the whole world. That prophecy, which had been enthroned with David and Solomon, which had been public for a whole people, published for everyone, proclaimed for a whole race, it found its end in a secret summit, in a flower, in a crowning of silence and shadow. It found its end in a confidential salutation addressed to a single, humble girl, and through the agency of a single angel. A whole people had awaited the Christ in the time when he did not come. But no one was waiting for him anymore when he was about to come.

This salutation that was going to fill the world was brought to the world reduced to the point of a confidence and a secret.

In all the royal houses births are waited on by an entire race, expected by an entire people. In this royal house alone the annunciation of the king was reduced to the point of a salutation, a secret and confidential communication.

Through a phenomenon of spiritual generation comparable to the phenomenon of carnal generation and figured by the phenomenon of carnal generation, in the way that a carnal being can only yield another carnal being by passing through a certain point of being, through the center of its race, through a point of germination, so that mystical and spiritual being that was the people of Moses could only yield that mystical and spiritual being that would be the people of Jesus by passing through a certain secret, a certain confidence, a point of mystical and spiritual germination.

The most tremendous cedar tree can only yield another cedar, a cedar still more tremendous, can only yield this tremendous heir by passing through a certain point of being and of race, which is not even the fruit of the cedar but the seed that is in the fruit.

The most public cedar tree can only yield another cedar, a cedar still more public, can only yield this public heir by passing through a certain point of secrecy and confidence, which is not even the secret of the fruit but the secret of the seed that is in the fruit.

The tremendous mystique of Israel had covered a whole people, and the tremendous and universal mystique of Jesus was going to cover the world. But the one could yield the other only by passing through a certain point of being and of spiritual generation.

Through a certain point of being and of mystical generation.

The tremendous and public race of Israel could only yield the tremendous and public and universal Christian race by passing through a certain point of mystical secrecy, of spiritual confidence.

Thus two tremendous worlds could only enter into communion through their summits, inverted one upon the other.

It is the theorem of angles opposed through their summit.

A tremendous past could only yield a more tremendous and universal future by passing through a certain point of fecundity, through a certain point of generation in the present.

A public of the past could only yield a more public and universal future by passing through a certain point of secrecy in the present.

The being of Moses could only yield the being of Jesus by passing through a certain point of being.

The people of Moses could only yield the people of Jesus by passing through a certain point of peoplehood.

The tremendous prophecies could only yield the tremendous and universal Gospels by passing through a certain point, which was at the same time the highest prophecy and the dawn of the Gospel. This point was precisely the point of that announcement made to Mary.

For in such a matter, in the matter of the event and the promise, it is not enough that day succeeds day and the effect the cause and the event the announcement and the keeping the promise. It is necessary still that one proceeds from the other and is born from the other.

The ministry of the present is not merely a ministry of date. It is not merely a chronological ministry.

The present is a certain point with its proper nature. It is a point of nature and a point of thought.

The ministry of the present is not merely one of observing a passing-by. It makes pass by.

The ministry of the present is not merely one of observing a growing-old. It makes grow old.

It is not merely the spectator, who watches the time pass by. It is the center and the agent itself and the point of the passing of time.

The point of passage is already at the same time the point of the passing.

The present is not inert. It is not merely spectator and witness. It is a point with its proper nature, and everything passes through this point, and even Jesus, being human and temporal, passed through it, and the happening, the event, the arising of Jesus after Moses, the new law after the old law, the Christian world after the antique world, grace after nature, the Gospels after the prophecies, is fully measurable and fully graspable, if not fully intelligible, only for one who has thought about the strange happening, the event, the arising of the future from the past through the ministry of the present. What there is of particular and free in this happening, this arising, is in the seed of what is unique and particular in the event of what was only an announcement, in the keeping of what was only the promise.

But I ask now which is the philosophy that for the first time in the history of the world has drawn our attention to the very being and articulation of the present? Which philosophy if not the Bergsonian philosophy? Which thought, for the first time in the history of thought, if not Bergsonian thought? Which philosophy, which thought, was not only the first to pay attention but the first to go the furthest? Who else saw that right there was the secret of the problem, that the undoing of the mechanism was there, the undoing of determinism was there, the undoing of materialism was there? Who else saw that in this point lay the secret of the whole battle? And that so long as one thought of the present as a simple date, like others, among the others, after others, before others, so long as one thought of the present as the past of today, as the instantaneous past, as the instantaneously past, as the limit on this side of the past, as the past at its limit on this side, as the most recent and instantaneously and at-the-limit recorded, one remained tied up oneself in the rigid ligatures of determinism, materialism, mechanism. For one came at the present the wrong way round. One came at this point of the present from the other side. For one took it as the final line inscribed, the final point achieved, the final point of inscription. Instead of it being the first point not yet engaged, not yet arrested, the point still in the course of achievement, of inscription, the line one is in the course of writing and inscribing. It is the point at which one's shoulders are not yet fixed in the mummification of the past.

Instead of thinking the present itself, instead of thinking the present present, one in reality thought a present past, a present frozen, and fixed, a present arrested, inscribed, a present rendered determinate.

An historical present.

Instead of thinking that secret point, which is the present, one was already thinking a history of the present, a memory of the present, that is, one was thinking the representation the present made as soon as it would have become the past. One was thinking the inscription as soon as it would have become inscribed. And one found that it was arrested, was inscribed. One was thinking life at the moment it would have become death. And one found that it was dead. One was thinking the present, one was thinking freedom at the moment it would have been bound, would have become bound. And one found that it was bound.

But one did not say it was bound because one had bound it. One said it had come into the world like that. Since one found it like that. One said that it had come into the world bound.

One did not say that the inscription was inscribed because one had inscribed it. One said that it came into the world like that. Since one found it like that. One said that it had come into the world inscribed.

One did not say that life was dead because one had killed it. One said that it had come into the world like that. Since one found it like that. One said that life had come into the world dead. One did not say that freedom appeared bound because oneself had passed by, had placed oneself on the other side of the binding and so was seeing it from across the binding. One said that it *was* bound.

One did not say that the inscription appeared inscribed because oneself had passed to the far side of the inscription and so was seeing it from across the inscription. One said that it *was* inscribed.

One did not say that life was dead because oneself had passed to the other side of death and so was seeing it, life, from across death. One said, without knowing it, without knowing what one was saying, that it *was* dead. For, continuing to call it life, one was always speaking as if about something dead, always seeing it like a dead thing.

Instead of thinking freedom, life, the present an instant before it enters into the eternal prison of the past, one thought it instantly afterwards, instantaneously after it had just signed the prison register. And one said that is was a serf, a prisoner, was imprisoned.

One believed that by going quickly, thanks to going quickly, one could with impunity take for the present the only recently passed; and speak as if about the present the only recently passed; that no one would notice; that it would come to the same thing; that thanks to going quickly it would not be noticed. That with much hurrying, one would arrive at the same time one had left. That the interval would not exist. That the freedom of the final moment in the street and the prisoner of the first moment in the prison, the freedom advancing under the doorway and the prisoner having just signed the prison register—these were so to say the same being, and consequently and by a slide in meaning, obviously and absolutely the same being.

It is only being and reality that found these were not the same being.

It is always the same intellectual temptation, the same temptation offered to the same tendency to slide, to the same profound intellectual laziness. As it is the past that retains, and even only the past that retains, and as one believes that to retain is to know better, and believes absolutely that to retain is to hold (better) and to retain is to know, it is the past to which one always addresses oneself.[136]

One believes that by taking it in all its great thickness, one actually has the past, while by thinning it down enough at the boundary where it touches the future, one makes it into the present. One obtains the present.

That is: one believes that by taking memory in all its thickness, one obtains history, but by thinning it out enough from the side where it arises, has just arisen, one obtains the present and consciousness of the present.

That is: one believes that by taking bondage in all its thickness one in fact obtains determinism, but by thinning it out enough from the side where it arises, has just arisen, one obtains freedom.

In this way, one ends up with a present that is a thin slice of the past, at the limit of the past. (At its limit, considered as present, at its limit from the side of the future.)

One ends up with a consciousness of the present that is a thin slice of history.

One ends up with a freedom that is a thin slice of bondage.

---

136. In this paragraph, we have another example of Péguy's word play, which cannot be directly conveyed in English, involving *retenir* (which I have translated as "retain" but can also mean "remember") and *tenir* ("to hold").

Rather than the present being what has not yet passed, the consciousness of the present what is not yet history, freedom, the free, what is not yet imprisoned.

The present is not what is historical of a very thin thickness. It is what is not historical at all.

The present is not what has been imprisoned for very little time and of a thin thickness (of time, of imprisonment). It is what is not imprisoned at all.

It is of another nature, of another being than the historical, of another being than the inscribed, of another being than the imprisoned.

And as for them,[137] why be surprised that they consider as past thin slices of the past, as historical thin slices of history, as imprisoned, determined, thin slices of bondage?

But maybe that is what they wanted.

It is the terrible danger, the terrible rule of the past. It alone can keep the records. And as everyone needs records, it is always to the past we address ourselves. It alone is the manufacturer of records. And it is their merchandiser. And everyone runs after it with their demands.

It is the state official for records. And as everyone believes that all science and all knowledge is a matter of records, they rush towards the recordings of history.

Here is the very center of sophism. On one hand, we can have records and history only of the past. On the other hand, they lay it down (more or less explicitly) that all science and knowledge is recording and history. After this, they talk about science and knowledge of the present.

And they understand by this the same science and the same knowledge.

This is therefore to imply that the present is a past.

How be surprised after that to find the present past?

But maybe that is, more or less obscurely, what they wanted.

For this confusion of the present with the past, this reduction of the present to the past, has been the glue that holds together determinism, materialism, and intellectualism.

And not only that. Not only are the records of the past records, they are definitive records. So all that need for rest and tranquility and not to hear anything more spoken about it, which comes from fatigue and

---

137. "Them" and "they" in this sentence refers to the historicists, intellectualists, materialists, determinists of French academic life, especially at the Sorbonne.

which is properly called laziness and notably intellectual laziness, that need of the official and controlled, the genuinely and well and duly registered, all the need of paperwork and, to the second degree, all the need of stamped paper, works on behalf of this fraudulent substitution and this confusion and this reduction.

To have peace, the great phrase of every civic and intellectual cowardice. So long as the present is present, so long as life is living, so long as freedom is free, it is a nuisance, it makes for war. It makes the news of the moment. It becomes something urgent. If only the present is past, everything calms down.

It's not in the news any more.

And at bottom, this is what everyone wants.

One has some peace.

Such is the great temptation offered to intellectual laziness, to what is called wisdom and what is called prudence. And to holy saving and holy economy. And above all to morality, which always take advantage of it.

And which is what is always pronounced.

In order to understand well what has happened, it is always necessary to think of that old rule of primary school morality, which they have made into such a marvel for us, *that you must never put off to tomorrow what you can do today*. It was the rule of wisdom itself, and prudence, and good self-government. It was the model rule. Something of the quintessence of Franklin. You recall Benjamin Franklin, the supposedly good fellow Franklin, the great hero, the great man of our primary school teachers, the greatest man in the world according to them, the only wise and knowing and moral one, and truly the guy.[138]

The only one proposed for all imitation.

In him was summed up, gathered together, all it was necessary to know, and all it was necessary to say, and all it was necessary to do, and all it was necessary to imitate.

He was the model man.

And this rule was perhaps the model rule, *that you must never put off to tomorrow what you can do today*. It was the ultimate model itself of

---

138. Benjamin Franklin (1706–90), amateur scientist and inventor, political theorist and politician, one of the "Founding Fathers" of the U.S., an embodiment of American "know-how," and apparently an important part of the modernized French primary school curriculum, which was replacing the classical humanist (Greek, Latin) curriculum.

those rules that made the model man and the model child. The same as the savings account book was the model symbol and model instrument and model book of the ultimate model of institutions.

For the savings bank was the model institution and central institution and pillar of the temple and what summed up everything. What was the most Franklin.

And this rule and this bank proceeded in reality from the same spirit, which was to put aside money or time for tomorrow, instead of employing them quietly for production today.

Well then, the same as we are perishing today as a people from our saving and our savings banks, so we were perishing intellectually from this rule, which is a rule of the intellectual savings bank.

A moral rule of the savings bank of work itself and the employment of time, an institution parallel and conjoined to the monetary savings bank. The same institution in two expressions.

Such was the great rule of our lay teachers. Such also was the great rule of our clerical teachers. For, as I said in *L'Argent*, they had the same rules.[139]

And they had a common morality. And they were the same men.

Only, if our lay teachers could not see anything, our clerical teachers would have been able to see and did not see that this marvelous rule, this famous model rule, went directly against perhaps the most profound and the most well attested of the Gospel rules, and perhaps the most serious of those given to humanity: *Let the day's own trouble be sufficient for the day, cuique diei malitia sua.*[140]

For if there is sufficient trouble for each day, why take on today the trouble of tomorrow, why take on today the work of tomorrow, why take on today the malice of tomorrow?

Thus our good teachers did not reckon, or reckoned badly, and with a secret common accord they taught this convenient rule (convenient for the teachers), which makes for sensible children and barren nations.

Neither the one nor the other reckoned that this creates infertile nations. And our clerical teachers did not reckon that it was opposed and most diametrically contrary to perhaps the most requisite and most

---

139. Péguy's essay on the subject of "money" was published in the *Cahiers* in 1913.
140. "which is the day's own trouble" (Matthew 6:34).

paternally and fondly given of the Gospel rules. Perhaps the most filled with commiseration, moistened with mercy.

And that perhaps it is not necessary to think about tomorrow.

It is this same laziness (intellectual), and this same prudence, and this same looking ahead, and this same sensibleness (and this same taste for saving), that have sealed determinism, and materialism, and intellectualism. For the saving of time is as dangerous, being also fraudulent, as the saving of money. It is as naturally and profoundly barren. It is as naturally and profoundly inexact. *To be too early*, to be too late, what inexactness. To be on time, the only exactness.

How much better I like this maxim of Mr. Benda, that *you must never put off to today what you can do tomorrow.* How exact this formula, how Christian and fresh; and how intelligently Bergsonian is our colleague here.
Is he so only here?

Bergson has been much reproached for the flux, the mobile, and for what has been called, with a word already less felicitous and less accurate, being less Bergsonian, a word already too fixed, mobility. But the question isn't to know whether this is convenient or inconvenient. The question is to know whether this is what reality is.
In reality, all this great need to arrange the mind is a need of laziness and the very expression of intellectual laziness. Before everything, they want to be tranquil. Before everything, they want to be sedentary. This same temptation of laziness, this same fatigue, this same need of a tranquil tomorrow, which makes them all functionaries, is also what makes them intellectuals. Just as they all run after university chairs, not because one teaches from it but because one is seated, so they want before all a philosophy, a system of thought, a system of knowledge where one is seated.
What they call the good organization of thought is the tranquility of the thinker.
Only, it would be necessary to know if it is the knowable that has been made for the convenience of the knower or the knower who should fit himself for the knowing of the knowable.

And more generally, if the world has been made for the convenience of human beings.

It is not a question of knowing whether it is pleasant that the present is ever-changing, it is a question of knowing whether it really is ever-changing.

When they demand arrangement, regulation, which they name good sense, which they name science, which they name knowledge and which they name method, it is the peace of the sensible, the tranquility of the scholar, the good organization of the knower's career. What they call scientific method is the method of their own establishment.

What they call the progress of science is the progress of their own careers.

What they call security, organization, establishment, is the security, organization, establishment of their own careers.

They are functionaries and quietists and sedentaries, and they have a philosophy all laid out, a philosophy of sedentaries, quietists, and functionaries.

They have a system of thought, a mental mechanism, an intellectual machinery of sedentaries, quietists, and functionaries. And all they oppose to us: that great need to consolidate the conquests of humanity, that great arranging of the human mind, that noble organization, that fine regulation—these are the reasonings of sedentaries, quietists, and functionaries, engaged in good careers like a horse pulling a cart, and asking for peace and quiet.

From one end of the line to the other, it is the same nonsense, and the same deformation, and the same *quid pro quo*, and the same fraudulent substitution, in psychology and metaphysics, in morality and economics. To think about tomorrow. Our death. In psychology and metaphysics, while being in, passing through, the present, we only consider the instant after, being after, because of our need for assurance and tranquility, and so we see, we consider the present as a recent past, as a last passed, but as a past, and we see it bound, recorded, dead. It is the death of life and freedom. We see the being of now as the being of a moment ago. In morality, we think only of the tranquility of tomorrow, instead of doing the work of today. In economics, we prepare, in order to be tranquil tomorrow, the destruction of an entire race.

In psychology, in metaphysics, we sacrifice the true present, the real present, to the instant of a moment ago, to the being of a moment ago, and in this way we reduce the true present, real being, to the past state. In morality, we sacrifice today to tomorrow. In economics, we sacrifice an entire race to our tranquility tomorrow.

It is always the system of retirement. It is always the same system of rest, of tranquility, of final, mortuary consolidation.

They think only of their retirement, that is of the pension they will get from the State, no longer for doing, but for having done (here again that same transfer of time and chronology, that same coming down a notch, that same putting the present into the past). Their ideal (if we can so call it), is an ideal of the State, an ideal of a State hospital, an immense funeral home, without troubles, without thought, bloodless.

An immense old people's home.

A retirement home.

Their whole life is for them merely a road to this retirement, a preparation for this retirement, a justification with a view to this retirement. As the Christian prepares for death, the modern prepares for this retirement. But with a view to enjoying it, so they say.

They also want to prepare the world for this. All their thought is to put the human spirit into the state of taking its retirement and enjoying its retirement. Or, so they say again, of *earning* its retirement.

It is the general mentality, it is the mentality of patients and of pensioners. The entire question, unfortunately, is to know whether the human spirit is a patient, a sedentary, a functionary, a professor, and whether it belongs to the hospital and the State.

And whether the world is destined to become an immense old people's home.

To think about retirement is the limit and the maximum of thinking about tomorrow. To sacrifice everything to retirement is the limit and the maximum of sacrificing today to tomorrow, in its supreme and most acute form. It is its very form, and since it is a matter of its establishment, it is so to say the definitive form. It is the very maxim of death and the formula of tranquility.

In this regard, economics is a kind of magnification of morality, and morality is a kind of codification of certain aspects of psychology and metaphysics. This monstrous need of tranquility, which manifests itself in the barrenness of an entire people, in the exhaustion of an entire race, is only a magnification on an enormous plane of that monstrously familiar need of moral tranquility, which makes us always think about tomorrow and sacrifice today to tomorrow, and this familiar moral need is itself only a codification of that monstrous need of tranquility, which in psychology and metaphysics makes us always sacrifice the present to the instant after.

What happens in psychology and metaphysics is codified in morality and magnified in economics.

What happens in psychology and metaphysics becomes apparent in morality and is magnified in economics.

Thus we see in economics what we would be able to see in morality and psychology and metaphysics if we had better eyes. But it is more apparent in economics: that this tranquility, which is the final object of the intellectuals, and to which all the hopes and prayers of moderns are directed, is essentially a principle of barrenness. It is always the race that pays. In order to have peace tomorrow, they don't have children today. But this picture of the abdication and exhaustion of a race is only the projection of the common moral, intellectual, psychological, and metaphysical picture transferred onto a larger and cruder plane, onto the economic and civic plane. In order to have peace tomorrow we pile up today the good sense, the foresight, the barrenness. In order to have the peace of the moment after, we make of the present a time of good sense, foresight, barrenness, a dead and mortuary time, a past tense.

Secondly, we see in economics, in civics, on the plane of the State, what we would be able to see in morality, in psychology, in metaphysics, on the plane of the soul and of being, if we had better eyes: that this tranquility, which is the final object of the intellectuals, and to which all the hopes and prayers of moderns are directed, is essentially a principle of servitude. It is always freedom that pays. It is always money that is master. In order to have peace tomorrow (and peace is only obtained through money), one alienates, one sells one's freedom today. In order to have an assured retirement (that is, the assurance of money when one is old), one does not say, does not write, what one thinks, what one has within to say and write, what the whole world knows, what no one dares to say or write. In order to have peace in one's old age, one is not free today. The modern world in its entirety is a world that thinks only of its old age.

Instead of thinking of these young days, which are the days of the race. And of the race to come.

Hence this universal barrenness and this universal servitude.

But this economic and civic servitude is only the enlargement, the magnification, the transfer, the projection onto the economic and civic plane, onto the plane of the people and the State, of a moral and intellectual, psychological and metaphysical servitude. Just as in our economic life we sacrifice the fecundity and freedom of our entire career for the assurance of a State-supported retirement, just as in our moral life we sacrifice the fecundity and freedom of today for the tranquility of tomorrow, so in psychology and metaphysics we sacrifice the fecundity and freedom and flux and presence and glorious insecurity of the present for the tranquility of the moment that comes immediately after.

Thus we transport ourselves arbitrarily, fraudulently to that moment after so that the present, having become a past, the most recent past, we will be tranquil as though in a past.

Such is the mechanism, such is the secret of this anticipation, this fraudulent substitution. And it is this fraud itself that is at the secret center of the whole immense modern intellectual fraud in metaphysics, in morality, in economics and civics. As one is tranquil in the past, since being past it is unassailable and definitive, it is a matter of bringing it about that the present, however in movement, however fecund, however free, be itself a past. For this, one transports oneself to the moment immediately following, the moment instantaneously following, the moment immediately after, and from there one looks at the present, where one is, as a tranquil past.

As a sterile past and a bound past.

It is always the system of the modern world to want to knock over both wickets at once,[141] to want to accumulate the most contradictory and incompatible advantages. To adopt as much as it wants and for its base needs, the most contradictory and most irreconcilable positions. It doesn't mind being in the present, and is actually compelled to be, and one cannot see how it could do otherwise. But at the same time, it wants to be in a future so that its present be past.

When it has passed, one is more tranquil.

---

141. An apparent reference to the English game of cricket.

Before everything, they want to enjoy this sterile tranquility, this servile tranquility, this dead and mortuary tranquility.

The modern intellectual world would do anything (and has done everything) in order to evade fecundity, freedom, life, in order to escape that present that is fecund, free, living. It has done everything to escape flux and the presence of the present.

Therefore, when the Bergsonian revolution installed itself in the secret heart of the present, through this and in this it installed itself in the secret heart of the mechanism serving the baseness, barrenness, servitude, and death of an entire world. It installed itself in the secret heart of morality, economics, civics, and metaphysics in the same movement with which it was installing itself at the heart of psychology.

In dismantling that mechanism of anticipation of the present, it dismantled all mechanism and materialism and determinism and intellectualism.

In breaking apart, in exploding time in this point of presence, this point of the present, in safeguarding, so to speak, and keeping intact the presence of the present, it broke apart all that time that served as the rod of mechanism, materialism, determinism, and intellectualism.

The immense straight rod of our servitude.

This is to say that the Bergsonian revolution is everywhere and everywhere present. Installed in the heart of the present, it does not command only psychology. By the same process, by a corresponding process of projection and magnification, it commands fecundity, freedom, life, *presence* in morality and in economics and in civic life and in metaphysics.

This is to say that it is the Bergsonian revolution that, along the entire line of battle, has put an end to modern barrenness, servitude, and intellectual death. *Per totam aciem*,[142] along the entire line of battle and with one unique and instantaneous movement, it has put an end to the whole of materialism, determinism, mechanism, intellectualism.

This is to say that it is present everywhere. It alone has broken apart the seals and it has broken apart all the seals. It alone has freed us; and it has freed us from all our servitudes. Everywhere it has rediscovered the present. Everywhere it has reinstituted, reinstated the presence of the present. Everywhere it has reestablished the place of presence of the present. A single dismantling has permitted this immense, this universal

---

142. "Along the whole line."

liberation. Because a single point of mechanism had established, had assured that immense universal servitude.

Everywhere it has re-taught us to put off to tomorrow. This is wisdom itself and life. This is freedom, health, measure, and this is fecundity. This is a being according to its measure, and this is a soul in good form. Putting off to tomorrow the cares of tomorrow. Putting off to tomorrow the tranquility of tomorrow. Not wishing to be tranquil in advance. Not anticipating tomorrow.

Putting off to old age the cares of old age. Putting off to old age the tranquility of old age. Not sacrificing today and the freedom and fecundity of today to the tranquility of tomorrow. Not sacrificing a whole life and the freedom and fecundity of a whole life to the tranquility of old age. Not sacrificing a whole world to an old age of the world, which is artificial, anticipated, fraudulent.

Not making today grow old: it always grows old enough on its own. Not making life grow old: it always grows old enough on its own. Not making a whole world grow old: it always grows old enough on its own.

There you have morality, economics, and civics. Not alienating today to the advantage of tomorrow. Not alienating a whole life to the advantage of old age. Not alienating a whole world to the advantage of old age.

The one who *economizes,* who saves money for his old age, is strictly speaking the one who is prodigal, and a bad prodigal. For he binds, he alienates his freedom, his fecundity, which are the true goods. He sells them, and what he puts aside is precisely the price of this sale.

In this way a whole people can bind its freedom, alienate its fecundity, sell its race, in order to buy State annuities. But when there is no longer a people and a race, where will the State be?

And in psychology and metaphysics, not binding, not alienating the present, which is the place of being, and the place of freedom, and the place of life, and the place of fecundity. Not making of it an anticipated past, a premature tranquility, a rest-place in a time of struggle, a leisure-place in a time of work, a retirement-place in a time of activity, a stopping-place in a time of movement, peace in a time of war, death in a time of life. Not selling the present, the flux, freedom, fecundity of the present in order to put aside the price you will have drawn from it for the moment after. Not saving, economizing on the present.

They are always saying economize, save. It would be necessary to know, save what? We must appeal here to the theory of money, and the mathematicians will understand me before I've begun to speak. Since money is in the operation of the purchase the counterpart for what it serves to buy, the whole operation of money is counter-indicated and counter-indicative, the whole operation of money is counter-posed, the whole operation of money is a counter-operation, an operation the contrary of, contrary to, the corresponding operation of the object. The one who saves money is the squanderer of what he has sold to have this money. The miser is prodigal. He is even the only prodigal, the true prodigal. The hoarder of money is prodigal with what he has sold to have money. He is the squanderer and prodigal of his soul, which he has sold for nothing, for money.

And on the contrary, it is the charitable one who is the true miser and who heaps up goods; I've said this enough in the language of poetics. And it is the miser who is a spendthrift. And it is the spendthrift who is miserly.

This is the most profound teaching of the Gospels, the most everywhere present in the Gospels, and certainly the one that Jesus evidently most honored.

We are so under the rule of money, it is so much the Antichrist and the master everywhere present in the modern world that its name is implied (familiarly, ordinarily) in our words, in our expressions. When we don't name it, we know it's what we are talking about. When we don't warn about it, we know it's there. When we say nothing, that's it.

When we don't name, it's that we are naming. When we don't present, it's that we are presenting.

When we don't think, it's that we are thinking.

We say: Save, economize, put aside, absolutely. It's a ready-made expression and it doesn't mean save, economize, put aside anything at all. It means save, economize, put aside some money, that is some counter-object, some counter-value.

If we only said it all, if we completed the expression, if we said save money, economize money, put aside money, we would be at least a little warned, we would know at least something of what we are saying. And of what we are speaking. Now this is what must be avoided above all, knowing something of what we are saying. So we employ these neutral verbs, what "they say." Being neutral, they have the air of being virtuous. And in this way they give a pass to the most sordid avarice.

The one who saves, absolutely, and who has a virtuous air, the one who economizes, absolutely, the one who puts aside, absolutely, the one who thus sacrifices the present to the future, and wants to put a whole world into retirement, does not amass strength for later; he amasses for later that for which he has sold his strength.

This is as opposed, as contrary, in the general accounting as *debit* and *credit* on the two pages of a ledger.

He is amassing goods, they say. No, he is amassing that for which he has sold his goods.

It is a counter-amassing, the amassing of a counter-treasure. *You will not have* treasures on earth.[143]

They speak innocently. They employ innocent and apparently virtuous verbs. And because they hide the direct complement, because they don't think about whether the implied direct complement is the object, the force, or the money, which is a counter-object and a counter-force, these apparently virtuous verbs cover up a turpitude, the most sordid avarice.

This is one of those nonsensical nothings, almost purely verbal and grammatical, almost purely a matter of vocabulary, which brings about the loss of a world.

This is one of those abuses of language, which are nothing, the mechanism of which is entirely simple, that brings about the loss of a world.

Here we must recall all that our teacher, Bergson, has written and said unceasingly about the use and abuse of language. And so we rediscover our teacher everywhere, not only in the great regions and in the deepenings of thought, but in every moment of the customary and daily round.

Thus this making-rigid through money, which commands the whole of modern society, this immense venality, this universal replacing of supple forces by rigid money has its economic, civic, moral, psychological, and metaphysical point of origin in the making-rigid of the present, in this ossification, this mummification of the present, which has brought about the whole of materialism and intellectualism and determinism and mechanism. All of it has come, all this immense and universal venality has come from saving and the savings account book. It has all come from

---

143. Matthew 6:19.

wanting to put aside the present, in the spirit of saving. And in order to be well and truly sure of putting it aside, they have placed it in the past.

The anterior appeared to be the surest lateral.

They sing the praises of these savings accounts. It is, however, a sad arsenal.

Not only do they praise them, but they offer them to us always and everywhere as example and model. It is the great pride of the moralists. And their great back-up and argument in reserve. They don't realize that, on the contrary, these savings accounts are the consecration and records of the venality of a whole people. What a whole people has laid out in the records of its savings accounts is the money for which it has sold its race.

The entire operation has its point of origin, the entire operation has consisted originally in the hardening, the making-rigid of the present. So long as it was supple, free, living, gratuitous, gracious, fecund it could not enter into an accounting. It did not lend itself to calculation. It could not enter into venality. Once made rigid, hardened, once having become a rigid point of the past, once having become an inert and bound point, a dead point, a point of servitude, an oppressive point and a point of disgrace and infecundity, it could begin to enter into accounting. Henceforth it leant itself to calculation. It became of the same order of magnitude and of the same nature as hard and rigid money. It could become a unity of the same order, itself a comparable point of unity, a point of unity that could enter as a unit into all the operations of this vast category. It could at last enter into an accounting within this vast and total venality.

So long as the present was supple, it was not monetary, comparable, sellable, venal. As soon as it was made rigid, as soon as it was fixed, it became all this. The property of a unit of measurement is to be fixed.

So long as the present was present, one could not commercialize it, it was not negotiable. As soon as it was past, I mean as soon as it was made into a past, as soon as it was a result, it became negotiable, it could be commercialized.

One can only pile up sous.[144] It became an item of magnitude of the same nature and the same order.

So when we give a bank account book to primary schoolchildren (instead of giving them the Gospels), we truly do the diametrical opposite

---

144. A basic unit in coin of the old French currency, roughly equivalent to one cent.

to what we did when we gave them the Gospels, we truly give them the diametrical opposite to what we gave them in the Gospels.[145]

It is not some books of debauchery that serve in the modern world as that secret point of resistance to what the Gospels are in the Christian world. It is not some books of debauchery that are the antipode of the Gospels, the secret point diametrically opposed to the secret point of the Gospels: what the modern world's secret point of resistance is, what in the modern world is the antipode of the Gospels, the secret point diametrically opposed to the secret point of the Gospels in the Christian world, what in the modern world is what the Gospels are in the Christian world, is not some books of debauchery (none would have the force), it is the bank account book.

Books of debauchery are never quite smart. They are never quite powerful. They belong to every time. The bank account book (in all its forms, particularly its own) is the distinctive invention of the modern world.

Books of debauchery could only ever make sinners. The bank account book makes the modern.

We are perishing from this rigidity, this prudence, and this avarice. Avarice has become, without any doubt, the central sin. It is at the center of the modern world. Money is at the center of the modern world. It is everywhere. And at the center and everywhere, it is master.

It is the bank account book, which is diametrically opposed to the Gospels. It only is strong enough. Is it not the contrary of debauchery and apparently of sin? Is it not honor and official virtue? Is it not honor and recorded virtue? Is it not the symbol and manual of the perfectly virtuous? Is it not the very foundation of the institution of the family?

No, it is the first wedge driven into the stock, the symbol and manual and first instrument of the making-rigid, the amortization, the drying up of the family and the people.

Both the dryness of the heart and the dryness of the people, which are the two great and dreadful modern inventions, the two great modern forms of the very annihilation of the world, both the spiritual dryness

---

145. Péguy likely has in mind the primary school saving banks, instituted in France in the late nineteenth century, which encouraged students to put aside money in small sums on a weekly basis, thereby teaching them frugality. The sums brought by the children were entered in a small book called the *scolaire*, which each kept; when the total exceeded one franc, the teacher would then take out, in the pupil's name, a savings account from a neighborhood bank, with accompanying bank account book.

and the temporal and carnal dryness, proceed from that same originating point, from that same point of desiccation and hardening and making-rigid, which has been for the modern world the desiccation and making-rigid of the present.

Everything has come from this. Everything has proceeded from this. For the civic and the economic and the moral are the extensions, the magnifications of the psychological and metaphysical, their projections onto a larger and cruder scale, only because they proceed from here.

Everything comes from this. Everything proceeds from this point of the present. Economics, civics, morality, metaphysics are ruled by the manner in which they treat this point of the present. Immediately from this point, they are ruled. And they themselves are determined. They will be able to thrive more or less, they will be able to flourish more or less, each in its own direction. But the direction itself is determined, and so they themselves are determined, from this point of origin.

Tell me how you treat the present and I'll tell you what philosophy you are.

The philosophies will later be able to succeed more or less, each in its own direction. But they are distinguished from this point of origin.

Right after that one can't take anything back. If you bind the present, everything is bound. If you keep the present free, only thus can the other freedoms be made possible.

Or put in place.

If you sterilize the present, everything is sterile, everything is empty. If you keep the present fecund, only then can the other fecundities be made possible. Or put in place.

From there begin all the roads, and the one who has entered onto a road can no longer exit it. He can go more or less farther on the road, but he cannot change roads. *Mutare viam.*[146] He is engaged. He can end up more or less far on the road. But it is on this road that he must end up.

If you venalize the present. If you rigidify that supple point of the present so as to make of it a rigid point, a rigid component, a component homologous with a point of rigid money, and consequently comparable, and consequently exchangeable, everything is venal, and the world, the entire world, falls immediately into commerce.

From this point of the present, from this point of rigidifying and amortization, from this point of avarice and venality has come all avarice

---

146. "Change the way."

and all venality. For avarice and venality are conjoined. They are connected. We have a tendency to believe that avarice is a constriction and venality a dissolution. This is an appearance. And a false appearance. And a fraudulent appearance. Nothing is so hard (if not rigid) and cold of heart (and cold of race) as the venal and the dissolute. And the miser, what would he amass, if he had not sold something (besides his soul), if he was not always selling something? What would he hoard, what would he amass, if he were not incessantly venal?

Otherwise where would the money come from? In order to be a miser. In order to hoard.

If he were not always a merchant of something?

And again, we see by this that the avarice and venality of the modern world on one hand, and its materialism and mechanism and determinism and intellectualism, on the other hand, are themselves connected. They are different manifestations, but not manifestations foreign to each other. And they are manifestations barely separated. They all proceed, the one and the other, they all proceed from that same point of making-rigid, which is the making-rigid of the present. The one proceeds from it in the order of the heart, the other in the order of thought. But what thought is without heart? And what heart is not illumined by the sun of thought?

Avarice is a making-rigid of the heart that proceeds from this making-rigid of the present. Venality, which appears to be a loosening and a dissolution, and which is in effect a loosening of morals and a dissolution of rules, or if you wish, a loosening of rules and a dissolution of morals, comes in reality, it also, from a certain preliminary making-rigid, a certain elementary making-rigid. It can only come into play, can only be produced, because elements that were supple, free, living, fecund, non-interchangeable, non-homogenous, non-exchangeable, non-buyable and sellable, non-countable and calculable, non-venal became, were made, rigid, servile, inert, dead, sterile, and therefore interchangeable, homogenous, comparable, exchangeable, buyable and sellable, countable and calculable, venal.

When the points of value have become rigid, then can begin the liquefaction of venality.

In the same way the liquefaction of a corpse can only begin because the living cells (the points of life) have been bound up in the rigidity of death.

As long as the cells are supple, they are free, living, fecund, non-interchangeable and non-venal, as long as they bathe in the liquid of life, they are not ready for the rigidity and consequent liquefaction of death. It is only when they have become rigid, inert, dead, infertile and, so to say, interchangeable and venal, that they have at the same time become ready for the liquefaction of death.

As long as the elements are supple and *present*, they are not ready for the liquefaction of death. It is necessary for them to have been rendered inert and rigid beforehand. It is necessary for them to have been rendered organically *passé* beforehand.

It is necessary that the rigidity of death precede the liquefaction of death, and so the liquefaction is a phenomenon of the rigidity.

Likewise it is necessary that a certain rigidity has preceded the liquefaction of venality, and the venality is a phenomenon of the rigidity.

It is necessary that a certain making-rigid has preceded the loosening of rules and the dissolution of morals.

And the loosening of rules and dissolution of morals is a phenomenon of the making-rigid.

And the liquefaction of the modern world is a phenomenon of the making-rigid.

This loosening, this dissolution, this liquefaction comes about because certain elements that are supple and therefore non-marketable, non-countable, non-calculable, non-measurable, have become elements that are rigid, habituated, countable, measurable, calculable: marketable.

All that can be bought and sold, that can be commercially exchanged, that is venal belongs to valuation. All that belongs to valuation, commercial and otherwise, is a matter of measurement. All that can be measured is stiff and rigid.

The meter rule is essentially and by definition a rigidity.[147]

When certain points of magnitude and value, when certain points of dignity (social, moral, economic, civic, psychological, metaphysical), when certain supple points of presence have become rigid, when presents have become pasts, when they have become dead, when they have become points and objects of measure, avarice and venality can conjointly begin. They have at last and together their material and their instrument. This point of measurement is their point of leverage and their starting-point.

---

147. In French, *le mètre* is both a meter and a meter rule (i.e., measuring instrument).

One can hoard and the other can squander, it's all the same.[148]

One can gather and the other dissolve. It's always the same operation.

One can cram together and the other pull apart. It's always the same business.

One can pile up and the other disseminate. It's always an operation of measurement.

One can regulate and the other deregulate, one can compel and the other appear to release. It's always the same operation of making-rigid.

It's always a negotiation, I mean a putting into trade, into commerce. The whole question is there: what is negotiable, what is non-negotiable. The whole question is to know what in a certain world is negotiable and what is non-negotiable. Any given world (the ancient world, the Christian world, the pagan world, the modern world), each world will be judged by what it considered negotiable or non-negotiable.

All the debasement of the modern world, all the cheapening of the modern world, all its lowering of price, comes from the modern world having considered negotiable values that the ancient and Christian worlds considered non-negotiable.

It is this universal negotiation that has created this universal debasement.

But this universal negotiation itself comes from the starting point of a universal making-rigid.

The present in its very essence was not negotiable. But if one did not negotiate it, one could not negotiate all the rest. It was the initial obstacle, the origin-point of obstacle. So, in order to negotiate it, one placed it in the past. And immediately after that one could negotiate all the rest.

And one allowed oneself this.

The present was the only obstacle.

In order to negotiate, it is necessary to count. In order to count, a unit is necessary. That is, a fixed magnitude, which does not vary, is necessary. That is, a point of rigidity is necessary.

The present, in essence, could not be this point of rigidity. It could not be this point of fixed magnitude, which does not vary. It was non-negotiable.

---

148. In regard to this discussion about the oneness of avarice and venality, hoarding and squandering, it is worth noting that Dante places the hoarders and squanderers in the same circle of the *Inferno* (Canto VII).

And not being negotiable, it was an obstacle to all negotiation, for it was at the point where all negotiation originates. It was the first door that had to be passed through.

For this reason it was made into the past. Instantly afterwards, all negotiation was opened up.

It is not an accident that the modern world is, on one hand, the world of avarice and venality, and on the other hand, the world of mechanism, intellectualism, determinism, materialism, and associationism.[149] These two groupings are themselves connected. The one and the other proceed, within the heart and the head, from that same point of making-the-present-rigid.

The head is not such a stranger to the heart, and it is intellectuals lacking in heart who invented the notion that the head is a stranger to the heart. This is what I've said under another form in my preceding *Note on Bergson and the Bergsonian Philosophy*. There is a pathos of thought and there is an enlightening and clarity of the heart. There is even a pathos of reason. There is a climate of pathos in thought, and there is a climate of knowledge in the heart.

Avarice and venality are an intellectualism and materialism and mechanism and determinism and associationism of the heart. Intellectualism and materialism and mechanism and determinism and associationism are an avarice and venality of thought. These two groups of attributes of the modern world (and it will not escape attention that I am taking attribute here in a somewhat Spinozist sense) are not only connected, but proceed, the one and the other, from that same point of making-the-present-rigid. In this germ of the present, in this point of the germ, there was enough space at the same time for the freedom of the heart and the freedom of thought, the fecundity of the heart and the fecundity of thought. An identical movement from an identical origin, and then in parallel (in precisely the sense that the Spinozist attributes are from the same origin, then afterwards indefinitely in parallel), an identical double movement, departing from the same point of origin, and afterwards in parallel, is effected in these two conjoined groups of the heart and the head. Avarice and venality have gone into binding, right up

---

149. This last is a mechanistic theory of psychology propounded in the nineteenth century by James Mill and John Stuart Mill, drawing from earlier English empirical philosophy (Locke and Hume), which held that complex mental activity can be accounted for by processes that combine simpler elements.

into the present, the elemental freedoms, the elemental fecundities of the heart. Intellectualism, materialism, determinism, mechanism, associationism have gone into binding, right up into the present, the elemental freedoms, the elemental fecundities of thought. In an identical initial, and so to say, punctual making-rigid, each of the two groups knew well how to choose the making-rigid that belonged to it and that it needed. The present was so much the key to the whole position and the center of combat and the point of decision for the whole battle that the binding of the present, the making-rigid of the present, was by itself sufficient to instantly permit the binding and making-rigid of all the rest. From this unique point of binding, from this unique point of making-rigid, each of the two groups extracted, so to speak, all the binding, all the making-rigid that belonged to it.

Thus went the world (I mean the modern world), some people by calculation, others, no doubt more numerous, by inadvertence. For it is a question of knowing whether human beings are more bad, or rather, more weak and foolish. And in any case, more lazy and more careless. They believed they were considering the present. And they were considering the most recently passed. And they believed they were considering the present and they were considering the recording of the present. The history of the present. The memory of the present. The habit of the present. A beginning of the past. A point of beginning of the past. A point of beginning of history. A point of beginning of memory. A point of beginning of habit. They believed they were considering the event they were writing and they were considering another, an identical, a falsely identical event, which they had written.

This could have gone on for a long time. And it could have gone on forever. Tireless reality could provide the present inexhaustibly. Tireless recording, tireless history, tireless memory, tireless habit could turn it inexhaustibly into the past.

Here one sees clearly, and still in another sense, that habit is literally a second nature. It has the same force, and so to say, the same command as nature. To the extent that reality, that nature makes the present well up, history, memory, habit have been turning it inexhaustibly into the past.

Like a fine river one has harnessed in order to feed a canal and that one forces to pass through a spillway. It has sufficed once and for all to mark out the canal and to establish the spillway. Starting from this moment all that the source produces is for the canal and for passing through that spillway. One knows it is not the canal that produces, and that the spillway only records. One knows it, but one does not think about it anymore. One has the habit. One does not see more than that canal which is full, and that spillway that spills out. And because it spills out, one obscurely believes, one commonly believes that it produces.

All the trickles of water from the source, all the trickles of water that went out freely from the source, have become, are now, only those immense and regular and horizontal and calculable waves of water, which pass inexhaustibly through the spillway. And one thinks no more of the source nor of the trickles of water from the source. One sees no more than those waves of water and that immense expanse of water and that immense spillway.

It is the spillway that looks like it is producing. And the more the source produces, the more the spillway looks like it is producing. The more the source produces for the river, the more it is the canal that is full.

Thus, once a certain mechanism of thought is established, once a certain canal is marked out and a certain barrage established, all that the present produces, all that the source of the present makes to well up, is instantaneously harnessed. And the more the present produces, the more it is this canal and this reservoir of memory, of history, of habit that is full. The more the present produces, the more it passes through this immense spillway and the more this spillway itself appears immense.

It is enough that a certain mechanism be once established, and so it is established once and for all. It is always the same mechanism of pouring out. It is a canalization. It is a placing in a reservoir. It is the great initial and central mechanism of the modern world. The modern world effects an immense, a total, pouring out of the present. An instantaneous canalization. An instantaneous placing into history, into memory, into habit. Or rather, an instantaneously anticipated placing.

It is enough that a certain mechanism be set up. Through that immense bar of making-rigid, through that immense spillway bar, the modern world effects an immense, a total, pouring out of the present.

An instantaneous pouring out.

Or rather instantaneously anticipated.

And there are now only those fine calculable waves of water, those immobile expanses of water, those horizontal aspects, those framed spaces, those rules, those quadrangular equalities.

(No more of that hodge-podge, of that turmoil, and of that poor anxiety of the source.)
(No more of that poor uncertainty.)
(And above all, no more of that uncertain poverty.)

So it doesn't matter that the present produces over and over; it doesn't matter that the present is inexhaustible. Once a certain mechanism is set up, the more it gives, the more we take from it, the more it gives, the more we record of it, the more it gives, the more we pour out of it. The more it gives, the more we harness it. We conquer it by its own fecundity. It can now exhaust itself. Or it can be inexhaustible. If it is not fecund, it dies by its own infecundity. If it is fecund, we conquer it by its very fecundity, and it dies. We harness its fecundity, we turn it back against itself. The dead waters will always be at the same level as the living waters. And the coffin will always be sized according to the corpse (according to the being it's a matter of putting inside).

Such is the initial, the capital importance of mechanisms. An eighty-centimeter lever can switch the direction of a train for thousands of kilometers. A light switch can shed expanses of light or shadow.

In the same way, a certain commutator of the modern world has been incessantly and instantaneously effecting a universal commutation. From expanses of the present, it has been instantaneously creating expanses of the past. From expanses of freedom, it has been instantaneously creating expanses of servitude. From expanses of fecundity, it has been instantaneously creating expanses of infecundity and death.

Or again, it is like an immense and universal parasitism. (And here we find again what we have noted so many times, that the modern world is, too, essentially parasitical.[150] It draws its strength, or its appearance of strength, only from the regimes it fights against, the worlds it has set about disintegrating.)

The more the being nourishes itself, the more the parasite fattens. The more the being nourishes itself, the more the parasite profits. The more the being nourishes itself, the more it is nourishing.

For the parasite.

---

150. Péguy notes this, for instance, in his essay, "De la situation faite au parti intellectuel dans le monde moderne devant les accidents de la gloire temporelle," 725.

In the same way, the more the present gives, the more recording takes from it. It is as if a peasant were to produce only for pruning; it is a certain parasitical mechanism, a certain pruning mechanism, once it has been set up.

In this way, a certain parasitical mechanism once having been set up, all that comes from the present only benefits the recording of memory, all that comes from reality only benefits the recording of history, all that comes from nature only benefits the recordings of habit.

It is not surprising given this that habit should be a second nature, and that it would appear to have the same strength and the same command as nature. It is the contrary that would be surprising. A mechanism of diversion, of pouring out, a parasitical mechanism has been set up. All that nature then gives is to the advantage of habit.

Nature is a great being without defense. Especially against this mechanism. We can even say in this sense that nature is a great innocent.

It has sufficed that a mechanism for pouring out has once been set up. And the urns of reality flow only to serve the carafes of intellectualism.

Why be surprised that the force of habit be equal to the force of nature: it is the same, diverted, poured out. Why be surprised that the command of habit be equal to the command of nature: it is the same, diverted, poured out.

A commutator has effected this miracle: that the very forces and command of life have been transformed, have become the forces (so to speak) and command of death.

And it is in this way that habit and death appear to have forces and a command.

And that the lesser appears to have more, and the negative appears to have something positive; and that nullity appears to have value.

It had to be that a certain mechanism of commutation, it was enough that a certain mechanism for the changing of signs, was set up.

But it was also enough, for the same reason it was enough, that a certain mechanism be dismantled for this whole immense apparatus to collapse. All that was necessary was one man with a screwdriver. But it was necessary to know which screw had to be unscrewed.

Only one man saw it. Only one man knew it.

On the pretext that the *date* of the present will be, will become in a certain future, a *date* of the past, on the pretext that today's date will tomorrow be yesterday's date, one believed that the present itself, the being of the present was what in a certain future will be a certain past. And that this idea exhausted the present, the being itself of the present, that it offered us a knowledge that was integral and absolute. And that consequently (since it was the same being), it was not worth giving oneself so much trouble to know the present, since one was going to know it so easily in an instant, immediately, as soon as it was past.

It's all there. There, in that putting off, and in that laziness, is the secret of it all. One realized vaguely, obscurely that the present is difficult to know. So one said to oneself: It's not worth giving oneself so much trouble. (One always says it's not worth giving oneself so much trouble.) Shortly it's going to be past. Then one will grasp it with all the pincers that history has given us for the apprehension and knowledge of the past.

It's all there. In that sliding. In that sliding that is always recommenced. In that perpetual sliding.

The historical sciences have made so much progress over a hundred years, and perhaps since always, that they have become like an enormous factory. For grinding out the past. It is even, with all due respect, a canning factory. They have their processes, their boilers, their pipes, they have stores. In short, all that is necessary.

And it is even strictly a refrigeration factory.

For they only conserve through cold.

(As soon as the heat returns, life would be capable of returning.)

In return for which, they provide a guarantee, certitude, tranquility like that not sold in the stores across the street.

(The stores across the street, it's just us: faith, theology, philosophy, metaphysics, morality, civics, economics, poetics, the fine and musical arts; reality in fact.)

Since this reality is so difficult to know, one thought more or less obscurely, since it creates so many problems for us, let's wait (and for so little a time). In an instant it's going to be a matter of record. And then we will have it all classified in the history stores.

It will even be better. It will be cleaner. There will be no more of that gangue.

Today, one thought, is a bad boy; and a badly brought up boy. And then one doesn't really know who he is. He would make trouble for us. Let's wait only one day. By tomorrow he will be yesterday. And we will find him again in the compartment of yesterdays at the Bibliothèque Nationale.

It was so tempting. One had only to wait a little bit. And one found the work all done. Today, today is being difficult. But tomorrow, yesterday will no longer be that way.

Thus, they believed they were considering the present. And they only ever considered its shadow. They believed they were speaking of the present. And they only ever spoke of its shadow.

A man came. And he saw instantly where the plateau of Pratzen was.[151] He saw instantly where the key was to this enormous position, the position of this long battle front.

He saw instantly that this immense battle front was set up around a single mechanism and that it sufficed to dismantle a certain mechanism in order to undo this immense battle front.

He understood that it was necessary to install himself instantaneously at the very heart and in the secret of the present; that there was the secret and the key. And that subsequently he must not at any price allow himself to be dislodged from it. That he must not grant anything. That he must not allow himself to give in to any laziness. That he must not allow himself to give in to that slight sliding, which seems to be nothing and which leads to everything.

One day history will say that the Bergsonian manoeuvre was precisely the Napoleonic manoeuvre. To insert oneself into the heart of the enemy, and then battle him in detail in all the directions he might present himself.

To occupy instantaneously a certain center of the combat, a certain secret, a certain key, a certain secret point of the position; and then not allow oneself to be dislodged, and not allow oneself to slide, under any pretext.

A man saw that the present was not the extreme edge of the past from the side of recentness, but the extreme edge of the future from the side of presence. A man saw that today is not the day after yesterday, but that, on the contrary, it is the day before tomorrow. A man saw that today is not the first day of interment, but, on the contrary, the latest day of an activity not yet dead.

---

151. This strategic plateau was occupied by Napoleon on the eve of the battle of Austerlitz.

And that the present is not only the successor of yesterday but its heir. And that today is the heir of yesterday and not merely its chronological successor.

He showed that we should not believe that the date of today was the whole of today, and that the date of the present was the whole being of the present.

And that one had exhausted today when one had given its date (especially the date in the past, the date according to tomorrow's date). And that one had exhausted the present when one had exhausted its date (especially the date in the past, the date according to tomorrow's date).

And [he showed] that the calendar did not exhaust the year whose date it bore. And that one had not said all there was to say about the calendar itself of this year, when one said that next year it would be the calendar of last year.

And that it was necessary to grasp the present in the present itself, and not wait a little bit, because it is exactly this little bit that makes it so one no longer has the present.

That there is a certain being proper to the present. And that waiting in order to understand it better, and to understand it in tranquility, is already to make it subject to the only alteration that counts.

It is to alter it in its very being, in that in which it is precisely the present. And in which it resembles nothing else. And notably not the embeddings of the past, be they the most recent.

And that we must not say to ourselves: Let's wait a little. Because it's just this little that is too much.

And that the plant in the herbarium is no longer the plant. And that the animal in the jar is no longer the animal.

And that to know reality is not a matter of being tranquil, but of being knowing.

And that avarice and venality, intellectualism and savings, materialism, mechanism, determinism, associationism, all this is for the calendar, but is perhaps not good for the year whose date the calendar bears.

For the year that is down below.

That the present is the present, and not only—and even in a certain sense not at all—what will shortly be past. That today is today, a certain distinctive being, and not only—and even in a certain sense not at all—what will be yesterday tomorrow.

That the present is the present. That it is not a future anterior, a middle term between the future and the past, between the ulterior and the anterior.

That the present is not a geometric median, a geometric, mechanical, physical bisector between the future and the past, but that it is the present.

That no more is it a combination of two ingredients, the future and the past. That it is not a mixture having a little of each, a little of the future, a little of the past. But that it is the present.

That it is not a future already a little passed. Nor a past already or still a little future. That it is the present, a very distinctive time, a very particular being, not at all a mixture nor a combination.

Not at all a future daubed with the past. Not at all a past slightly wiped by the future.

Not at all a rough-and-ready solution, a combination, an arrangement between the total undecidability of the future and the total burying of the past. But a certain distinctive passage.

And that it is neither on one hand a program, nor on the other hand an inventory. Neither a bisector between one and the other, nor a mixture nor a combination of one and the other.

And that to say of the present: Let's wait a little bit in order to know it, is to wish to know the same by the other.

And that to wish to know the present by what it will be when it will have passed, is to relinquish the very being it is a question of knowing, is to deliver it up in advance to the professional mourners and gravediggers.

So when one gives bank account books to primary schoolchildren, one is quite right. For one gives them the breviary itself of the modern world, the modern world's certificate of tranquility. That is, a certificate of avarice and venality in the order of the heart. And in the order of the mind, which is not so far from it, a certificate of materialism and intellectualism, a certificate of determinism and associationism and mechanism.

And in the two orders together a certificate of rigidity and money.

And we are quite right to present it with such ceremony and as a symbol, a crowning achievement, a gift-set of being and of the law. Just as the Gospels are a complete gathering-together of Christian thought, so the bank account book is the complete gathering-together of modern thought. It alone is strong enough to resist the Gospels, because it is the book of money, which is the Antichrist.

How much disorders, how much debaucheries appear innocent and vain in comparison with this false virtue, and this false rule, and this false law. In disorders that are acknowledged, there is always a sort of weakness that does not resist, that does not even confront. It has other things to do, and is satisfied to amuse itself in its vacuous *guinguettes*.[152] It is satisfied to amuse itself in its corner. There is no risk of its desiring to substitute itself for the law. It knows very well what it is good for. But modern avarice and venality, under the name of saving, and modern making-rigid and hardening, under the name of intellectualism and determinism and materialism and associationism and mechanism, are dangerous in a different way. For they are fraudulently rigid. And they are fraudulently hard. And because the laws are generally hard, one believes that what is hard is necessarily a law. Thus all the making-rigid of the modern world is, so to speak, authorized to present itself as a law. And it doesn't miss the chance. It also is a constraint. It also is a severity. It also is a difficulty. It also is a restraint. Consequently, it is perhaps a law.

Nothing is so dangerous as this making-rigid, nothing so dangerous as this rigidity. Disorders, debaucheries, agitations, weaknesses have never been serious candidates as regulations. They can only introduce irregularities. What is dangerous, what is fraudulent, is this false regulation, this false regularity, this false rule.

For it also obliges. It can thus be a candidate to establish a morality with obligation and sanction. It also seems to have merit and dignity. It appears to be of the order of law. It is thus authorized, it is as though qualified to try to substitute itself for the law. It doesn't fail to do it. It presents itself with all the apparatus.

Those who are far from order or obviously opposed to order cannot do harm to order beyond a certain point. But the one who imitates and counterfeits order can hope to substitute himself for order. (It is in this sense that it has always been said the Antichrist would present himself as a false Christ.)

The bank account book, with its apparatus of obligation and severity, in its rigidity, in its administrative bureaucracy, in its constraint and its system of restraint, in its seriousness, in its appearance even of sacrifice, in its prefectorial structure, in its apparatus of civics and governance, with its insidious and cold authority (paternal besides), in its solemn

---

152. These outdoor cafés or bistros, some quite minimal and others more elaborate, providing a variety of amusements, were ubiquitous in the semi-rural *banlieues* of Paris in the early twentieth century.

and quadrangular stiffness, has alone been strong enough to resist the Gospels.

In this way a whole people not only effects the destruction of its race, but finds that this is very good, because it takes place within a rigid structure.

Within a rigid morality.

I said in my first *Note* that a supple morality is infinitely more severe, more constraining, and more exacting than a rigid morality. One must add that rigid moralities or immoralities, when they get going, are infinitely more dangerous than supple immoralities. For, being rigid, they are taken for laws.

In this way, a whole people so prepares its tranquility of tomorrow that it destroys its very being, and, right from the present, buries it in an irrefutable past.

A whole people so prepares the tranquility of its future that it destroys its being of tomorrow in order to have right from today that peace, which can only be the peace of yesterday.

When he shatters this immense battle front, when he undoes this immense apparatus, when he dismantles this immense mechanism of burial and death, when he rescues us from the enslavements of the past, from the infecundities of a dead time, when he places us again exactly in the present, when he puts us back in place exactly in that point, not a little before, not a little after, when he reinserts himself in this way in the secret heart of the debate, when he reinstalls us in this situation, in the position of the present, Bergson, by this itself and already by this alone, reintroduces us into a situation and into a position that is Christian, into the only situation and position that is Christian; he literally makes us rediscover the point of Christianity, the point of view, the point of life and the point of being of Christianity. For he puts us back into the precarious and the transitory, and into that state of undress, which is truly the human condition.

Our young pillars of apologetics, our supports of the Church, our catechizing catechumens, our pale intellectuals of the Catholic Sorbonnes, would agree, in a pinch, that Bergson was useful in another time, in the time of Spencer,[153] with a preliminary, preparatory, and above all

---

153. Herbert Spencer (1820–1903) was an English sociologist and philosopher who defended and promoted Darwin's theory of evolution, using it to support his own doctrine of "social Darwinism."

negative usefulness. They would agree again that he served to clear away avarice and venality, on one hand, and on the other hand, materialism and intellectualism, determinism and associationism, the making-rigid and mechanism of the modern world. Purely negative exercises that had for their goal, obviously had for their object, obviously ought to have for their effect, only the clearing of the field for our young heroes.

I don't want to enter in passing into such a serious debate. I'm not well versed in civil wars. I've fought most of my life on the frontiers. On the intellectual frontiers and the spiritual frontiers. And also on the economic and civic frontiers, on the frontiers of poverty, touching on the kingdom of money. It's not my fault if I haven't yet fought on other frontiers. I'm very little attuned to the great wars that take place in the offices. I'm not at all rue Saint-Dominique, and I'm not at all rue de Vaugirard.[154] I've fought the war of siege and I've fought the war of open country. I even confess that I have a certain contempt for offices. I know it is the soldiers who fight and the offices that watch them. I know it is always the soldiers who win and the offices that lose. I'm an old soldier of the second class. All the additional promotions I've been given denature me.

I would like to write a *cahier* entitled: *Bergson and the Catholics*. It would be a very short *cahier*. But hard and supple, concise; one of those *cahiers* one publishes in italics of 10.[155] Unfortunately, I'm well aware that I wouldn't be able to write this *cahier* usefully under such a title, with such a subject, and say what I have to say, and above all say what must be said, without entering into the domain of Confessions, and perhaps into the domain of confession. And perhaps it's too early to enter into the domain of Confessions, and [my] confession perhaps doesn't concern the public.[156]

While we wait for me, the old soldier, contemptible veteran of all those wars, to speak out, let's listen to our young staff officers. Their plans must certainly be magnificent, for they have brand new stripes.

It's quite simple, they say (or think). We concede that Bergson has cleared away the modern world. We are clearing away Bergson. Now only we remain.

---

154. The former street in Paris was the location of the Ministry of War, and the latter of the Catholic Institute.

155. The publication font used by Péguy for the first *Note* on Bergson.

156. With this apparent reference to Jean-Jacques Rousseau's *Confessions*, it is possible that Péguy is hinting at his intention of publishing his own "Confessions," presumably focused on his relationship to Roman Catholicism.

One asks them for some detail. First of all, isn't this ingratitude?

We will be ungrateful, they say. God is ungrateful.

(Those very words. One of these young men already gave me the lesson six or seven years ago on this point that God is ungrateful and breaks the instruments he has once used. And as for God and them, it's rather the same thing.)

One asks them for some clarification.

Yes, they say, Bergson did clear away intellectualism and materialism, mechanism and associationism, determinism, and in sum, atheism. Anyway, he was wrong to clear away intellectualism. We are clearing away Bergson. Only we remain.

Richelieu and Mazarin were merely petty politicians compared to our young people. And to hear them, the rue de Vaugirard is capable of becoming so powerful that it will commandeer everything up to the rue Servadoni.[157] I would like to raise a word, however, and even two words, without entering into the secret domain of confession, staying with what is common knowledge, publishable, public.

My first word will be a response to what they say, and my second will be the word of my own position.

And to speak, with them, the language of the school, my first word will be on the negative of the Bergsonian revolution and my second word on the positive.

What they concede is that Bergsonian thought, the Bergsonian revolution, has served in a negative way, has served to clear away a certain space that is for them the site of the battle.

They concede that Bergsonian thought, the Bergsonian revolution, has served to deny what it was necessary to deny.

Bergson, they say (but less clearly) has served to displace the modern. We are displacing Bergson. Only we remain.

Bergson has eliminated the modern. We are eliminating Bergson. Only we remain.

We, that is the scholastics.

Their story is quite simple. Once, they say, there was the modern world. Bergson came and cleared away the modern world. We come and clear away Bergson. Only we remain.

---

157. As already noted, the Catholic Institute was located on the rue de Vaugirard, and further along the same street, almost at the rue Servadoni, was the office of the association of Protestant students.

There is no more modern world, since Bergson has cleared it away. And there is no more Bergson, since we have cleared him away.

May they permit us to say to them, this admirable mechanism is a mechanism of the laboratory, not at all a mechanism of the world. It's a mechanism for a display window in a world's fair, not at all a mechanism of work and the workshop. This conjuring trick is only a conjuring trick. This reasoning is only a reasoning, and it's all childish and only an agreeable childishness.

This photo-shutter conception of a change that is total, gained, and abrupt is a conception of cinematography and of the kaleidoscope. The shows of the real world are not so easily programmed. The material is more unwieldy, the forces more re-emergent, the times less demarcated.

May they permit us to say to them, they are not sufficiently Bergsonian and their conception is not sufficiently a Bergsonian conception. For there are Bergsonian conceptions too and Bergsonism does not consist in abstaining from the operations of thought. It consists in continually modeling them on the reality in question each time.

Their conception is not sufficiently a Bergsonian conception. They have of all this, perhaps quite sincerely, a static conception, a static conception of history and geography. They represent to themselves, quite sincerely I believe, the place of struggle for the domination of the world as a place that is purely spatial and non-reactive. In this spatial place there are spatial blocs, purely inert, which are or are not slotted in, which one brings in, which one takes away, which are displaced, which hold a certain place and do not hold another. So in this empty place there was the bloc of the modern world. And that was ticked off. Bergson came. He displaced the bloc of the modern world, which is to say: he took away the bloc of the modern world and he brought in the Bergsonian bloc. We, for our part, they think, are displacing the Bergsonian bloc, which is to say: we are taking away the Bergsonian bloc and we are bringing in the scholastic bloc.

So first of all, there is no more bloc of the modern world, since Bergson has taken it away; and secondly, there is no more Bergsonian bloc, since we have taken it away; and thirdly, there is now only our bloc, there is now only the scholastic bloc.

May they permit us to say to them: It's a conception of domino players. The modern world placed the double six. Bergson placed the six-and-blank. And they are placing the double blank. And again, it's a conception of domino players in a game of dominoes where one would remove the old ones as one places the new ones. So that there would ever be only one domino on the table.

May they permit us to say to them: It's a purely childish conception. And purely academic. These are houses of cards. And constructions of cubes, like those sold in book and stationary stores. Ready-made cubes. It belongs to the ready-made. It's a conception that is itself materialist and intellectualist and associationist and mechanist and spatial. It's also a determinist conception. This is all to say they are operating with a modern conception in regard to this double displacement, or rather the notion they have of this double displacement, this double elimination: displacement of the modern world by Bergson, displacement of Bergson by them; elimination of the modern world by Bergson, elimination of Bergson by them. Their vision is not Bergsonian, agreed, but no more is it Christian: they see as moderns. They do not think as Bergsonians, but no more do they think as Christians: they think as moderns.

They represent to themselves as moderns the threefold contest of the modern and Bergsonian and Christian. They represent to themselves as moderns their displacement of the modern and their displacement of the Bergsonian. And they represent to themselves as moderns their installation of the Bergsonian and subsequently their installation of the Christian.

The thing is, their Christian is not a Christian but a modern. And their thought is not Christian thought, but modern thought. And their scholasticism is a Christian theology immobilized in the structures of an Aristotelian reticulation, and consequently modern.

(Aristotle being perhaps the only ancient who was a modern, I mean a modern like we now see, like was going to arise after him only in the nineteenth century *after* Jesus Christ. The only ancient who was unclothed of ancient wisdom and above all ancient intelligence, and who re-clothed himself straight away with modern unintelligence. So that is the one they have gone looking for.)

When they say and, I add willingly, when they believe, that the modern world has been displaced once and for all, it is as if I said I am going to clear away my front porch once and for all, or I am going to nourish myself once and for all, or I am going to write this *cahier* once and for all, or I am going to go to mass once and for all, or I am going to take myself to the court of penitence once and for all. They are constantly confusing things. They constantly take what belongs to nourishment and life for what belongs to recording and history. They are profoundly, essentially modern.

They are not Christians, I mean not in their core. They constantly lose from view that precariousness that is for the Christian the most profound condition of human beings; they lose from view that profound wretchedness; and that one must always begin again.

They are in tranquility, in contentment: in the modern.

They too are in the savings scheme: at the heart of the modern. They place systems in the bank like others place savings, other kinds of savings. And they believe they are tranquil. And there is no more to do than wait and draw the pensions.

What they call Christian is a system of Christian thought according to the modern, a system borrowed from the Christian and transferred, recopied, immobilized within the reticulation of the modern world.

They are always taking history for the event, the map for the territory, geography for the earth.

May they permit us to say to them: All this is not so simple, nor so empty, nor so dead. All this *is there*. The immense spaces of the battlefield for the domination of the world are not empty and those immense worlds are not systems and blocs. They are prodigious drives and counter-drives, dreadful weights and counter-weights. They are prodigious antagonistic forces that press and push and weigh. A dynamism compressed is not a dynamism expired. A dynamism held back is not a dynamism abolished. And even a dynamism stuck is not a dynamism finally past.

Those prodigious masses and forces and worlds are there. Those pressures, those drives, those weights are always present, only compressed, held back, stuck. Always equipped, ready to set off again and occupy the field of combat.

Always ready to set off for the conquest and domination of the world.

It is an eternal debate and battle. And an eternal precariousness. Nothing gained is gained forever. This is the human condition itself. And the most profound condition of the Christian.

The idea of an eternal gain, the idea of a gain that is definitive and will no longer be contested, is all that is most contrary to Christian thought. The idea of a dominion that is eternal and definitive and that will no longer be disputed is all that is most contrary to the destiny of human beings, in the system of Christian thought.

Those prodigious worlds are present. And they will not be buried.

It is always necessary, and here more than elsewhere and more than ever, to guard against confusing right and fact, and, as they say, theory and practice. Pardon me for repeating these simplicities, but simplicities are what are most easily lost from view.

It is perfectly true that in philosophy there are systems that have been rendered unsupportable: therefore they will be supported, and they will even be the most supported.

Believe me: they will be supported more than the others.

They have been rendered unsupportable for reason, but they have not been rendered unsupportable for power.

They have been rendered unsupportable for the true philosopher. They will be supported by the schools, by the State (these have not yet been separated), by the Sorbonne, by the bureaucracy, by the powers that be, by the government, by the whole of the temporal. And maybe by the professors of philosophy.

They have been rendered unsupportable for Plato and for Epictetus: they will be supported by Caesar.

By the political parties. By the popular parties. By the parliamentary masses.

It is an error, and yet more, it is a delusion, and yet more, it is a stupidity to believe that it suffices for an idea to be rendered indefensible, once and for all, in order for one not to hear it spoken of any longer. On the contrary, that is when it begins to be spoken about; and begins to flourish.

This idea has been rendered indefensible: therefore it will be defended.

This position has been rendered untenable: therefore it will be upheld.

The Catholics are thus wrong to believe and to count on it being enough that Bergson has once and for all rendered materialism, intellectualism, determinism, associationism, and mechanism uninhabitable and unsupportable and indefensible and untenable. He has rendered them uninhabitable for us. But what is this "us"? He has rendered them uninhabitable for the philosopher. But what is this "philosopher"? He has not rendered them uninhabitable for the world. He has not rendered them uninhabitable for those who want to inhabit them all the same.

He has been able to render the system of thought of the modern world uninhabitable. But what difference does that make to the modern world, precisely since it despises thought? It is still no less there. It is still no less present. And it still exercises that dreadful pressure.

It is not a matter of convincing, it is a matter of defeating, and it is even a matter of not being defeated, or rather of not being crushed.

And not only of not being defeated once and for all, but not being defeated all the time.

And not only not being crushed once and for all, but not being crushed always.

This is to say that the preliminary distinction of negative and positive[158] is itself intellectual, in regard to such a subject, and maybe in regard to any subject, and that it is vain, arbitrary, and unworkable. It might hold for the convenience of language. It does not hold for the philosopher.

We have only one earth to share. We have only one earth to contest. We have only one earth to dispute. We have only one temporal and we have only one time. We have only one war and we can only deliver up, all and always, the same one. In a word, we are tightly bound. The intellectuals and theoreticians of every system, and notably the Catholic ones, always speak as though we were unbound. And as though all the places were still free. It is the opposite. There are very few free places. And perhaps there are none.

All that is won by one is lost by the other. And not only that, but it is irreversible, and we can almost say that all that is lost by one is immediately and automatically won by the other.

In a closed system and in a system of mutual compression, there is no absolute positive and there is no absolute negative. The negative is the negative of the positive and the positive is the negative of the negative.

It is not a question of tottering walls, which one would once and for all prop up and put back into place and, if need be, rebuild. It is a question of tottering walls, which one supports by hand, and that one can only support by hand (that is the rule of the game). Because in the time I support this wall with my hand, neither the wall nor my hand move, neither my wall nor my hand go up or down, neither that wall nor my hand win or lose; one cannot say this is a good position, to support a wall with a hand.

And above all, one cannot say it is a settled situation, and there is nothing more to do. And it is agreed. Not only is there always something

---

158. See 206.

to be done. But one is always doing. When I support a tottering wall with my hand or shoulder, during all this time my hand, my shoulder is working. And the wall is also working. Through its weight.

Nothing is so false, so intellectual, so arbitrary as that modern idea, and on the inside, that idea of our convinced Catholics that when one supports a tottering wall by hand one creates a state of fact, a static and stable situation, with which one need not occupy oneself further. A state that is recordable and recorded. What I am saying is that it is always necessary to be occupied with it. It is always necessary to be occupied with the wall. And it is always necessary to be occupied with the hand. If one is no longer occupied with it, the wall falls (again).

Materialism has in effect become unsupportable. But materialism supports itself very well. It is in power.

Materialism has become indefensible. But materialism defends itself very well. And it even attacks. And it even takes possession. And it even occupies. For it is in power.

Materialism has become untenable. But materialism holds itself up very well. And it even holds us. For it is in power.

That prodigious weight, that prodigious drive, that prodigious pressure and oppression of the modern world is upon us. If the hand that supports a world gets tired or loosens its grip, if it becomes inattentive or faulty, we again fall under that intellectual oppression of twenty-five or thirty years ago.[159]

This is the moment our convinced Catholics choose for making politics.

I don't want to enter in passing into this great debate of Bergson and the Catholics. It would be necessary to join to it the debate of Bergson and the radicals[160] and the debate of Bergson and the Action Française. All I can say today is that the attitude of our convinced Catholics towards Bergson is an essentially political attitude and this conjuring game whose form we have indicated is a wonderful invention of politics.

159. Péguy is referring here to the intellectual hegemony in France of the thought of the rationalist philosopher, Ernst Renan (1823–90) and the historicist critic, Hippolyte Taine (1829–93), before the publication of Bergson's *Time and Free Will*.

160. The "radicals" likely refers to critics of the progressive left. For more on the Bergsonian debates, see the Introduction.

Now, we know what a wonderful invention of politics is worth.

When a hand is supporting a tottering wall, it is not enough to make a note of it, to write down a history where one says that the hand supports the wall. (And consequently there is no more to think about it.) Being supported is not like being built. And above all, being supported is not like being written down. To speak the language of accounting, it is not a business deal *entered by* history. It is a business that is constantly in the present, that at every instant is in the instant. In reality the hand is supporting at every instant. And in reality the wall is falling at every instant. Every weakness of the hand furthers the fall.

(Here again it appears that we cannot advance one step without being fitted, without being cloaked in the Bergsonian language, without being equipped with the Bergsonian apparatus, without being armed with the Bergsonian instrument.)

Likewise in those prodigious, constant, mutual drives that share out the world, in those universal and tireless pressures, everyone at every instant pushes, everyone at every instant presses. It is the very condition of the world and of human beings. Every weakness of drive furthers a counter-drive. Every lapse in regard to a pressure furthers a counter-pressure.

So it is not enough to say that historically a drive has been forced back, a pressure has been countered, and to write down that it has been countered. It is necessary that the counter-pressure be constant, because the pressure is constant.

When we cease to force it back, the drive returns. When we cease to counter-pressure, the pressure returns.

No kind of ironwork, no kind of mechanism can intervene here.

Our convinced Catholics said to themselves: Bergson has cleared away materialism. We are clearing away Bergson. Now there is only us.

Well, no. Bergson has cleared away materialism in right, in theory; in mental and intellectual justice. In truth. In reality. He has not cleared it away in politics and he has not cleared it away from power.

He has not cleared it away from government.

And he has not cleared the modern world away from the world, particularly from the modern world.

He has only opposed to the appalling weight of the modern world a counter-weight. This counter-weight could be victorious. Under one condition: that no spiritual force give way and turn away from its part in this counter-weight.

I said it long ago. There is the modern world. This modern world has brought about conditions for humanity so entirely and absolutely new, that all that we know through history, all that we have learned of preceding human worlds, cannot be of service to us in the least, cannot advance our understanding of the world in which we live. There are no precedents. For the first time in the history of the world all the spiritual powers together have been driven back, not by the material powers but by one sole material power, which is the power of money. And in order to be exact, it must even be said: For the first time in the history of the world all the spiritual powers together, in the same movement, and all the other material powers together, in the very same movement, have been driven back by one sole material power, which is the power of money. For the first time in the history of the world all the spiritual powers together and all the other material powers together, in one and the same movement, have receded on the face of the earth. They have receded throughout as if along a vast line. For the first time in the history of the world money is the master without limit or measure.

For the first time in the history of the world money stands alone opposite spirit. (And it even stands alone opposite the other material things.)

For the first time in the history of the world money stands alone opposite God.

It has gathered into itself all that is poisonous in the temporal, and now it is done. By some kind of frightening venture, by some kind of aberration in the mechanism, a gap, a disruption, a monstrous mechanical spinning-out, what should only have served for exchange has completely consumed the value to be exchanged.

So we must not only say that in the modern world the scale of values has been turned upside down. We must say that is has been wiped out, since the apparatus of measure and exchange and evaluation has overwhelmed all the value it should have served to measure, exchange, evaluate.

The instrument has become the material and the object and the world.

It is a cataclysm as novel, an event as monstrous, a phenomenon as fraudulent as if the calendar began to be the year itself, the real year (and this is what it is somewhat getting to in history); and as if the clock began *to be* the time; and as if the ruler with its centimeters began to be the world being measured; and as if arithmetical number began to be the world being counted.

From this has come the immense prostitution of the modern world. It does not come from lust. It is not this worthy. It comes from money. It comes from this universal interchangeability.

And notably from the avarice and venality that we have seen are two particular cases (perhaps often the same) of this universal interchangeability.

The modern world is not universally prostitutional[161] through lust. It is quite incapable of that. It is universally prostitutional because it is universally interchangeable.

It did not procure baseness and turpitude for itself with its money. But because it reduced everything to money, it turned out that everything was baseness and turpitude.

To speak in a crass way, I will say: For the first time in the history of the world money is the master of the *curé* as it is the master of the philosopher. It is the master of the pastor as it is the master of the rabbi. It is the master of the poet as it is the master of the sculptor and painter.

The modern world has created a novel situation, *nova ab integro*.[162] Money is the master of the statesman as it is the master of the businessman. And it is the master of the magistrate as it is the master of the simple citizen. And it is the master of the State as it is the master of the school. And it is the master of the public as it is the master of the private.

And it is the master of justice more profoundly than it was the master of iniquity. And it is the master of virtue more profoundly than it was the master of vice.

It is the master of morality more profoundly than it was the master of immorality.

This universal venality of the modern world does not come from laxness but on the contrary from a rigidity that is the rigidity of money. In the same way we have separated hardness from the rigid, so we must separate laxness from the supple. Just as the supple moralities are more exacting and more severe and more demanding than the rigid moralities,

---

161. *prostitutionnel,* another of Péguy's neologisms in French, which I have translated with a neologism in English.

162. "novelties begun afresh."

so the rigid immoralities are more dangerous and more fraudulent and more corrupt than the lax immoralities.

In these conditions, I declare it solemnly, in this universal disaster and this unique disequilibrium, in this enormous distress and this monstrous disorder, in this breakdown such as has never yet been seen in the history of the world, I consider treacherous and damaging, criminal and merely gesticulatory, all politics that tends to divide the spirit from itself and turn it back against itself, all politics that tends to divide spiritual forces.

Because it will not be other spiritual forces that will gain. It will always be money.

All that one takes from spirit, all that one withdraws from one spirit, will not be gained by a different spirit but by money.

And one will increase proportionately that dreadful weight of the modern world, that disaster and disequilibrium, that enormous distress and disorder; and that universal breakdown.

All that one takes from a spiritual force, *whatever that force may be*, all that one removes, withdraws from one spiritual force, will not be gained by a different spiritual force but by money.

I've said it twenty times: the struggle (a mortal struggle), the debate is not between the Christian world and the ancient world. (And in the ancient world I naturally place all the worlds of the philosophers.) The struggle is between the modern world, on one hand, and on the other, all other worlds together. And in particular between the modern world, on one hand, and on the other, the ancient world and the Christian world together.

The cause of the ancient world (where I place the worlds of the philosophers) is the same as the cause of Christianity. It is the same contestation. *Their fates are connected.* Their fortunes are conjoined. The need to supplant, destroy, oppress them is the same. *It is spirituality that is hounded in both the one and the other.* And it is money that hounds both the one and the other and wants to supplant them.

The struggle is not between some world or other and the modern world. The struggle is between all the other worlds and the modern world.

All the other worlds (than the modern world) have been worlds of some kind of spirituality. The modern world alone, being the world of money, is a world of total and absolute materiality.

DESCARTES AND THE CARTESIAN PHILOSOPHY

Thus the modern world does not oppose itself only to some world or other. It opposes itself, it acts against, all other worlds together and in the same movement.

True, philosophy is the handmaid of theology. (Mary is properly the handmaid of the Lord.) But may the servant not quarrel with the mistress and the mistress not scold the servant. A stranger will come who will quickly put them into agreement.

When the creditor comes (the creditor, the universal creditor, is money), and when he has sold the house, where will the servant find again her humble kitchen, and where will the mistress find again her living room and her dining room?

Where will the servant find again her workspace, and where will the mistress find again her chapel and the cradle of her children?

Thus may the faithful servant not rise up against her mistress and may the faithful mistress not disdain her servant. A man will come, more hard than has ever been seen, who will reduce both of them to a common lowliness and servitude.

May the faithful servant not set out to win some victory over her mistress, and may the faithful mistress not set out to win some victory over her servant. A man, a conqueror, will come, more harsh and triumphant than has ever been seen, who will plunge both of them into an identical and common disaster.

May the servant not quarrel with the mistress and the mistress not take issue with the servant. A man will come, who will enforce a peace more harsh than the disaster itself.

When the man has come, when the master is there; when the stranger has sold the house; when the bailiff has posted the notices; when the auction has inflicted its burning, dispersing the table and the bed; when the grave and the cradle have been exposed; when there is only the creditor; when there is only money: where will the servant be; and where the mistress?

The suspicion with which they hound philosophy is the same as the suspicion with which they hound theology; and *vice versa*. The hatred with which they hound philosophy is the same as the hatred with which they hound theology; and *vice versa*. It is always metaphysics and thought and spirit and freedom and fecundity that are hounded.

When the furniture has been auctioned off, isn't it the same shame that will overwhelm the servant and the mistress?

Won't it be the same disaster, and the same death, and the same despair?

The struggle (an implacable struggle, a mortal struggle) is between money and all that possesses some spirituality, *whatever it may be.* The servant will be hunted down together with the mistress, in the same hunt and the same movement. Philosophy will be hunted down together with theology, with the same pursuit and the same movement. Everywhere it is the same humiliation, the same contempt, and the same derision. For we have a master like we have never seen.

Everywhere it is thought that is targeted, metaphysics, freedom, fecundity. It is the soul itself they want to reach and to reduce once and for all.

It is the spiritual in all its forms and in all being that they want to reduce.

In these conditions, I consider as insidious and criminal, fraudulent and dangerous, pernicious and treacherous, any politics that tends to break down the spiritual. For whatever gains against any form of the spiritual is always money, and it is the modern world that gains it. Whatever is taken away from any form of the spiritual is always money, and it is always the modern world that takes it away.

This is not a combat in fantasy and it is not a combat in theory. No more is it a combat where *one will have lots of time.* There is only one time, and there is only one field of combat. One must win or lose today and here. It is a temporal battle and it is a material battle. For it is fought for the temporal and material. And it is fought on one side by the temporal and material. The temporal and material are at once the terrain, the object, and one of the two parties. When the eternal enters into a battle with the temporal, this must indeed be a temporal battle. When the spiritual enters into battle with the material, this must indeed be a material battle. It is thus a closely fought battle. Not one point of time, not one point of space is lost. What is won by one is lost by the other; and *vice versa.* It is for this reason there is no point in speaking about positive and negative. Everything rebounds on everything and against everything. Everything counts. Every negative that denies a positive, that works *against* a positive, works instantaneously *for* a *contr*ary[163] positive, it instantaneously affirms a contrary positive, it is itself instantaneously a contrary positive.

There can only be positive and negative (barely, but this is not our question) in a system where there are empty spaces. In a full system every negative is in reality a contrary positive.

Consequently in a full system there is never a settled negative. Every negative is in reality a counter-positive, a contrary positive, which strikes out in this fullness, like the others, and which comes and goes in its turn, perpetually.

This is not a battle in theory, where there is ample time and space. It is a real battle. All the pressures and all the repulsions, all the drives and all the weights, are in perpetual contact and a perpetual weighing against each other. It is a closed field from all sides. And even interiorly closed. A closed space, a closed time. It is a combat that is terrestrial, earthly, and even earthy.

In these prodigious weighings everything advances or retreats. Always. The idea that an argument will have *settled* an advance or a retreat is not only a ridiculous idea. It is an idea, a scheme, of childish Machiavellianism.

As soon as the hand no longer supports it, the wall falls. As soon as a weight no longer weighs, the counter-weight advances.

The struggle is not between the hero and the just one, it is not between the sage and the saint. It is between money, by itself on one hand, and on the other hand, the hero, the just one, the sage, and the saint together. It is between money and all the spiritualities.

In these conditions both straitened and full, in these conditions of a struggle where not one atom of matter is free, where not one point of force is lost, may this not be misunderstood, for any other calculation would be illusory: anything lost by Bergsonian thought will be instantly and proportionately (re)gained by materialism and mechanism and determinism and intellectualism and associationism.

Anything lost by philosophy will not be gained by theology, but regained by money.

Anything lost by the sage will not be gained by the martyr and the saint, but regained by money.

---

163. The word is partially italicized in this way also in Péguy's original text (*contr*aire).

Anything lost by philosophy will not be gained by the just one, but regained by money.

In a struggle so fully exact, so exactly full, no vagueness, no void, no emptiness. And also no maliciousness. Antagonistic forces that fight to the full and give it their all, and that don't long reflect on it. A great brutality and a great simplicity. Masses against masses. Powers against powers. Forces against forces. Heavy artillery. And front lines that press on front lines. And lines of fire that decimate lines of fire.

Every ridge is occupied to the extent it is abandoned. All ground barely left is taken. Every position is gained at the same time it is lost. No place, no time for the tricks of our little schemers.

May our striplings not get too worked up in their imaginations. Bergson, and no other, has liberated us from that metaphysic of the modern world, which intended to present itself as a physics. Anything lost by Bergson will be retaken, and instantly, by this fraudulent and falsely physical metaphysic of the modern world, which presents itself with the innocence and the limitations and the supposed relativities of a physics, and which is in reality the actual metaphysic of materialism and determinism and mechanism and associationism and intellectualism.

In these prodigious weighings, no place for diplomatic balances. No place for the balances of pharmacists. It is the weight itself that will give its weight and will bring out its full effect. We will clearly see its weight because we will clearly see its effect. And we do not need to put it on a balance, we do not need to transport it with precaution and ceremony onto the scales of a balance in order to know it is there and what it weighs. We feel it, we are subjected to it, and this is how we know that it weighs.

May our youths not get carried away. Anything lost by Bergson will not be gained by Saint Thomas, but regained by Spencer.

And as for them, they will remain what they have been so many times in the history of the world, they will remain spectators and onlookers and the dupes of the farce, and if I may say, the excluded middle.

And through the efforts of our doctors there will be good days again for the radical government in France and for the radical domination in intellectual and governmental matters.

There will be good days again for materialism and mechanism, for determinism and intellectualism, for associationism and for Spencer.

I don't have anything in particular against Spencer. He was a true gentleman. I have nothing against Saint Thomas either. But finally we really must put the appropriate names on our directives, on our coordinates.

All that is taken away from Bergson will go to Spencer and not to Saint Thomas.

And once more Saint Thomas will have nothing. And he will have nobody. And he will be like he was and what he was twenty-five or thirty years ago, before the appearance of Bergson: a great saint of the past, a great doctor of the past, a great theologian of the past. Respected, revered, venerated. Without a hold in the present, without a way in, without that bite that is so unique a phenomenon, without that cutting into that alone counts and that we have begun to examine by making use precisely of the apparatus, the instrument of Bergson.

(A great doctor, held in regard, celebrated, consecrated; inventoried. Buried.)

Tried out and as if worn out.
"Agreed," one says to me, "but it was quite necessary to put Bergson on the *Index*.[164] It was the only way to prevent his being read in the seminaries. They had set about reading him in the seminaries. He was turning the heads of all those young men. They were reading Bergson instead of reading the Church Fathers. They were reading Bergson instead of reviewing their theology. And then you well know what the *Index* is. It's only . . . . Finally, it's only a list that, a list which, a list that one is really compelled . . . . And then you obtain permissions as you wish. And then finally it's only a list that it's quite necessary to . . . . The *Index*, finally, it's an indication."

"Excuse me, excuse me, you're coming across badly: actually I don't well know what the *Index* is. And I reiterate that I don't want to enter in passing into this great debate of Bergson and the Catholics. I have the idea that one can't enter into this debate without immediately getting into confession and the secret of the heart. Perhaps I will get into this, but I will get into it expressly. Today I don't want to say anything except what is public and open, and so to speak, related to the parish. Today and here I'm thinking more of the sermon than the judgment of penitence. Let's suppose we are in the realm of publications of marriage, of the banns.

---

164. The remainder of this *Note* takes the form of a debate between Péguy and a Roman Catholic Monsignor, concerning the *Index Librorum Prohibitorum,* the Roman Catholic Church's Index of Prohibited Books.

First, I avow it is true that I don't know well what the *Index* is. And I don't even, so to speak, know it at all. And the reason is very simple. At bottom, I only know what was in my catechism; when I was small. In my catechism there was the good God, the creation, the sacred history; the Holy Virgin, the angels, the saints; the calendar, the major holy days; prayer and the sacraments; the virtues; the Apostle's Creed; the final ends of man (which at that time seemed to me terribly far away; and I only believed it, so to speak, as something to be memorized; there would be lots of time to talk about it); and the seven capital sins. There was no *Index*. There was everything else: the walls of Jericho, the whale of Jonas, Joshua, Judith, Jesus Christ, Daniel in the lions' den (and ever since that time, whenever I see a Daniel, and think about a Daniel, my dear Delafarge, and you, young Daniel André,[165] I always see that image in my sacred history of Daniel in a den with bars. The king came to look through the bars. And he was awfully amazed, that king. As for Daniel, he was carelessly placing on the rump of these lions a friendly foot that I myself would not have dared to place on the rump of a modest Newfoundland dog. And I well know why.[166]) There was the Holy Spirit, which was a dove, and which it was necessary not to confuse with the dove of the ark. There was the good God, or God the Father, who was a triangle. There was no *Index*. Our catechism was designed for little boys and not for us grown men.

I imagined the virtues as three beautiful children of Mary and the seven capital sins as frightening old fellows who made faces, types of notaries. But I didn't imagine the *Index* at all, because it wasn't there.

And today still, I don't imagine it at all, because it wasn't there.

I knew well what the difference is between venial sin and mortal sin. But I had no idea of the *Index*, because it wasn't there.

There was Adam and Eve, but there wasn't the *Index*."

"But if one were to talk about it today, perhaps you could form an idea of it."

"I'm really not very intelligent."

"If, all the same, one were to talk to you about it . . ."

"It would be very kind of you to talk about something else."

"Maybe you would be able to imagine it."

---

165. The former was a friend and collaborator of Péguy's, the latter the son of the Péguy family doctor.

166. Péguy's fear of dogs apparently went back to his childhood.

"We imagine things until eleven, twelve years of age, you know. Past twelve years we no longer imagine anything. Past twelve years, we are no longer poets.

All that I didn't imagine the morning of my first communion, I'll never imagine."

"One could perhaps try to explain to you . . ."

"Don't trust in me. I'm old. I have a hard head. I'm from the Beauce."[167]

"One could perhaps try to acquaint you . . ."

"Don't rely on it. I've passed the age where one makes new acquaintances."

"One could perhaps try to teach you . . ."

"All that I didn't know the morning of my first communion, I'll never know."

"One could perhaps try to make you comprehend . . ."

"You know, as for me, I'm not very anxious to understand. I'm not an intellectual. I like obeying better than understanding. It's less tiring. And then it's more in my nature."

"One could perhaps try . . . to make you understand . . ."

"I like obedience better. It's like a well-kept house."

"One could perhaps . . . try . . ."

"I really like being obedient. It makes for a good solid day."

"Finally, this *Index*, it's like signposts."

"Chartres, forty-one kilometers."

"On a road, it's really necessary to have signposts."

"You've touched my weak spot. Nothing is so fine as a beautiful, flat road in the Beauce."

"Now you see."

"Yes, if you talk to me about a road, I begin to give way."

"It was about time."

"Provided it's a fine road, really straight and flat, and the trees all lined up."

"We give that to you."

"And the telegraph posts all lined up."

"Agreed."

---

167. An agricultural region between the Seine and Loire rivers; two of its important cities are Orléans, where Péguy grew up, and Chartres, with its famous cathedral, to which he made pilgrimages several times on foot from Paris in the years after his conversion.

"And the telegraph lines perfectly parallel."

"There we are."

"Perfectly balanced."

"That also."

"Not to speak of the gutters, the shoulders, the ditches. All that as if on parade."

"Squared up like a billiard table."

"And the kilometer markers."

"You're getting to it."

"And the hectometer markers."

"It's all I wanted to say."

"Those fine mathematical markers, perfection itself. The large kilometer markers and the small hectometer markers. There you have a well-marked road. The large kilometer markers are like large women that have been lined up on the roadside. The little markers, the hectometer markers are like their little girls that they have lost along the road. One thinks of the story of Tom Thumb (again, a story I had learned before passing eleven or twelve years of age).

It's as if it was the Ogre who passed by there, or Tom Thumb, and they scattered these large white boulders in order to find their road again."

"You must be confused. The Ogre, who was a giant, could have scattered enormous boulders, but he didn't scatter any, because he knew the roads well. And Tom Thumb, who didn't know the roads, and who did throw out white stones in order to mark the roads, and to recognize where he had passed, was a dwarf, and naturally could only throw out small stones. Your hypothesis is unacceptable, for it rests on a confusion."

"Thank you."

"Perhaps even on a contradiction."

"I give you thanks."

"Moreover, the text of the story of Tom Thumb isn't yet well established. The manuscripts present many variances."

"Good heavens!"

"Very different versions."

"Woe to us!"

"And a true critical edition of it hasn't yet been published."

"What will become of us?"

"It appears to be accepted, though, that Tom Thumb walked through the woods and didn't follow a road at all."

"So . . ."

"So, it's certainly not him who scattered the kilometer markers. And it's quite improbable that he would have scattered them so exactly."

"I was going to say so. Those big national roads are immense ribbons, unwound necklaces, unravelled rosaries. And spread out. Linear necklaces, itinerary rosaries. The kilometer markers are the large pearls, the hectometer markers are the small pearls. The kilometer markers are the large beads of the rosary, the hectometer markers are the small beads. And there are dozens and dozens, making an enormous rosary."

"Those are our milliary stones, my child. The Roman roads were lined with markers, statues of the gods along the route."

"Those fine great white metric markers, father, new and dazzling white, or having gradually received the damage of the years, it's all mathematics and perfection and exactitude. It's extension and number. It's calculation and measurement. It's at the same time all arithmetic and all geometry.

Geometrical in their form (cut), in their alignment, and because they measure and mark out a line. Arithmetical because they themselves are discrete units and are counted.

It's the whole problem of the human spirit that extends itself all along this route, father. For it's the whole problem of the continuous and discontinuous. Of space and the point. Of geometry and arithmetic. (And of their mysterious concordance. And of their mysterious mutual responsiveness.) Of the measured and the enumerated. Those markers punctuate the route, father, and there you have a great mystery of reason.

The continuous, the discontinuous. The old mystery to which man is always brought back. Those discontinuous markers punctuate that line, that continuous route. Everything is there. Or again, let's say those markers are atoms. And thus we enter the mystery of physics. And for twenty thousand years human thought hasn't moved from there. And again, it's the mystery of the surveyor. Ten staffs in the hand can measure an infinite route. It's sufficient that they are aligned, and planted in their place, and then again all the time. Those staffs also punctuate. Those staffs also mark and can be counted. For I don't need to say to you, before being the material or rather the instrument of a worn-out metaphor today, the staffs were originally surveying instruments. And when one said: Prepare the ground, that meant place some staffs.[168]

---

168. In French, the idiomatic "prepare the ground" is *poser des jalons*.

These are types of small metal pegs, pointed at one end, a ring at the other. They plant them with the point in the ground. They can thread them through the rings. It's extremely convenient.

When they align them, measure them, and plant them with the point in the ground, it's what they call marking off. When they have finished marking off (everybody finishes their day), they only have to thread them through the ring with a length of string, or with the surveying chain itself, and they carry them home. So they carry home the problem of the continuous and discontinuous.

They carry it away, but they don't resolve it.

In order to measure a hectometer, for example, eleven staffs are needed: two large staffs at the two ends for the hectometer and nine small staffs in between for the decameters.

Again, it's the mystery of the unit of enumeration and the unit of measurement.

And again, it's the problem of the meter and the metered.[169]

And again, it's the problem of the metered and of decimeters, centimeters, and millimeters. When the school kid says: I brought my *centimeters*, in order to say: I brought my ruler divided into centimeters and millimeters, he catches in a striking phrase a truly ancient problem.[170]

And again, it's the problem of the double unity: the metaphysical and dialectical Unity and the simple arithmetical unit. The unit, which makes up number, simply, which repeats itself (in order to make up the number), which is counted, and the other unity, the great Unity, which is. And which cannot repeat itself, because it is preeminent and unique. And one, precisely.

They say that geometry arose from surveying. It's not the only thing. For arithmetic also arose from surveying. And as it was the same territory, the same land, which was counted and measured in surveying, from this came that mysterious (false) coincidence of the continuous and discontinuous, that mysterious false mutual responsiveness and correspondence between arithmetic and geometry.[171]

When the lance corporal said to us: 'Number 1, how many steps are there between the edge of the cobblestone of the water pump and the corner of the orderly room?' he was raising a truly serious problem. It's

---

169. "metered" in the sense of measured (in order to retain some of Péguy's play on words).

170. The French for "ruler" is *double décimètre*.

171. Bergson discusses this question in *Time and Free Will*.

what they called the calibration of steps and evaluation of distances. Why calibration? It's like calibrating a meter according to the standard meter conserved in the Archives (but not the Archives of M. Langlois[172]). And you, father, I am not your lance corporal, but how many kilometer markers are there between two hectometer markers?"

"You would like to make me say there are ten, because one kilometer makes ten hectometers. But I'm as clever as you, and I well know there are nine, because one must not count the one at the other end."

"Well, you are mistaken, father, there are none at all, because it is the hectometer markers that are between the kilometer markers and not the kilometer markers that are between the hectometer markers. One sees clearly, father, that in your time the *curés*, the pastors, the rabbis, and the schoolteachers didn't, if you'll permit me, hoist a backpack; for it's a stupid joke played in all the barracks of France on all the raw recruits of all classes. And be reassured, father, it's a joke that was played at the Polytechnique on the great Poincaré, and the greatest geometer in a whole century and maybe several centuries fell into that trap like a child.

And again, it's the problem of fullness and the void, fullness and emptiness, and the world has not gained any ground here since Empedocles and Pythagoras, Thales, and Zeno (I mean the Eleatic).

This question of the continuous and discontinuous is so serious, father, that I had a friend, a serious and metaphysical soul, who used to say: It's enough to ask oneself if there aren't two worlds, one in the other, two creations superimposed or rather coinciding, one the continuous creation and the other the discontinuous creation, and two Gods (he used to say), a God of continuous creation and a God of discontinuous creation.

So there you have all that can be on a road, father.

On one of those roads where we have so often chanted that there is only one God, but there are two Testaments.[173]

There is the sort of problem that poses itself along a road. It's not so innocent, a road."

---

172. Charles-Victor Langlois (1863–1921) was professor of history at the Sorbonne, and one of the leading lights of the scientific historical school, which, in Péguy's view, believed that the great events of history—artistic, political, religious—could be explained through the compilation of index cards recording facts. See Roe, *The Passion of Charles Péguy*, chapters 3 and 4.

173. An old repetitive chanson of the Latin Quarter: *"Il y a deux Testaments, / L'Ancien et le Nouveau. / Mais il n'y a qu'un Dieu / Qui règne dans les cieux."*

"So, my child, you acknowledge that those markers, those signposts, are indispensable on a road."

"May I, if you don't mind, father? We were just about to be in agreement. Get me to say it's a fine thing, a signpost. Get me to say it's useful. Don't make me say it's indispensable. (I'm only talking about the ones on roads.)

So get me to say, rather, that it's very fine, a signpost, and it's very fine, a kilometer marker. And that a road is a certain kind of instrument where there must be signposts and kilometer markers *for the sake of beauty*, for order, for the system. That this makes up an integral part of it. That this is in the very being of the road. That a road without signposts and kilometer markers would not be articulated. It would not be marked out. Finally, it would not be a road. Tell me all that, father.

Tell me that a road is a certain development, a certain extensity. Speak to me the language of philosophy. Speak to me even the language of the school.[174] I don't fear it. Tell me that a road is a certain ensemble and that this ensemble would be spoiled, would be missing something of its distinctive character, if it didn't have signposts and kilometer markers.

Tell me, father, get me to say that a signpost is very fine, and it belongs to the ensemble and to the character. Get me even to say that it's indispensable. In that sense. This would be more sure than getting me to say that it's indispensable in the sense of utility.

Tell me, father, that signposts and kilometer markers are the very articulation of a road and its internal organization and even its essence. You see, I'm speaking the language of the school. Let's even speak those of the other schools. Get me to say this is the style of it; and the class. And as though the *raison d'être*. And let's speak Leibnizian language. Get me to say it's the sufficient reason. And that a road is nothing if it isn't a direction and a distance. Get me to say, I would be so happy to say it, that a man who would imagine a road without a signpost and kilometer markers would be a man without any idea of anything. Who would be neither a painter nor a poet. Nor a philosopher and metaphysician. Less than nothing.

And that a driver is nothing, if he is not a moving body; a mass and a speed.

And that even the very idea of conceiving a road without its spine and without its directive and without its axis, a road that wouldn't be

---

174. *de l'école*, the "school" refers to the scholastics, that is, to the neo-Thomists in particular.

articulated on the basis of its signposts and kilometer markers, is the idea of a man who doesn't know, a man who possesses neither head nor heart; neither reason nor breeding. Nor wisdom. A man badly brought up.

A man who wouldn't know what is being talked about.

(There are also the piles of stone and sand perfectly worn down into trunks of quadrangular pyramids, on the shoulders. More precisely, trunks of rectangular pyramids. Those piles of stone and sand are incontestably metric. But they are not everywhere. They are intermittent markers. A curious thing, they are only in the districts where the road must be remade. Remade, I mean re-leveled.)

So you have got me to say, Monsignor, and maybe I would have said it just as well without you, that signposts and kilometer markers are necessary, that they are necessary on a road or rather in a road, at the heart of a road, in the axis of a road.

You have got me to say they are necessary. But from there, to get me to say they are useful, there is an abyss."

"How, my child, would these metric indications not be useful?"

"And if you get me to say it, Monsignor, that will really be out of obedience. And from there, to get me to believe it, there is a second abyss. And I see clearly a second act of obedience would be necessary."

"How, my child, would these metric indications not be indispensable?"

"In the order of utility, Monsignor. One clearly sees that you've never gone on a road. I take it upon myself, when in Dourdan, I take it upon myself to manage without them.

I take it upon myself, when in Dourdan, and even when in Orsay, and even when in Lozère, and even when in Bourg-la-Reine, and even when at the rue de la Sorbonne, in Paris,[175] I take it upon myself to go to Chartres without consulting the signposts and without looking at the kilometer markers."

"Goodness! You know the road."

"One always knows it. I mean: there is always someone who knows it for you. I take it upon myself to go there the first time. As long as there are peasants in the fields and gossips on their doorsteps, who watch you passing by while seeming to be talking about something else, and examine you without looking at you, as long as in the villages there are

---

175. The first four are places in the environs of Paris where Péguy lived successively from 1899 until his death in 1914. The last is the location of his *Cahiers* publishing office in Paris.

blacksmiths shoeing a horse by the walkway, I take it upon myself, with some politeness, to go everywhere."

"It's a long way."

"You get there. 'Excuse me, sir, is this the right road to Chartres.'

'Yes sir, only, after Saint-Cyr, be careful not to turn right.'

(He is mistaken. You could turn right as much as you want. In this immense area all the roads lead to Chartres.) 'Excuse me, sir, how long is it still to Chartres?'

'You still have a good six leagues.'

They count in leagues. The league has something more supple in it than the kilometer. Something more sprightly, more peasant, more earthy. And then it's the same language we heard during our childhood. It was the unit of itinerary in our childhood. It was the unit of itinerary in old France. It is not rigid like the kilometer. Nowadays you haven't said it all when you've said that a league is worth four kilometers. Perhaps a league is equal to four kilometers. But it is worth infinitely more. For it is worth a world of memory. An unlimited antiquity. A profound and supple land.

The league too belongs to a profound morality and a supple one.

True, these fine fellows give directions that are rather supple, and sometimes pleasantly fanciful. But do you believe that rigid metrics, too, don't offer directions that are unpleasantly fanciful? Do you believe there is no vagueness in rigidity? One counts the number of times where the three categories of direction one finds on the roads agree among themselves. Or rather one doesn't count them. One never finds it. But perhaps you don't know, father, the three categories of information one finds on the road."

"I'm only surprised, my child, to hear you speak of categories."

"Father, we know very well the categories of others. We know very well the categories of rigidity. And rigidity does not know the exactitudes and the obligations of suppleness."

"My child, apparently not only do we not know the exactitudes and the obligations of suppleness, but in regard to rigidity itself we are more ignorant than you. For I confess I don't know the three categories indicating rigidity that are found on a road. I only know two of them, the signposts and the kilometer markers."

"There are three of them, father. For there are also the blue plaques you find at the entries and exits of villages, hamlets, towns, and even urban zones."

DESCARTES AND THE CARTESIAN PHILOSOPHY

"Entry and exit, it's the same thing. One has the right to enter a village and to leave it by one or the other end. You can take the road as you like, in one or the other direction."

"You mean they are reversible. Nevertheless, I assure you that it is not the same thing to go to Chartres as it is to return from it. And that the villages are not the same when you enter them by one end or the other. And that the roads are not the same when you take them in one direction or the other. But this would perhaps carry us too far. We were at those fine blue plaques you find at the entries and exits of towns, embedded in the walls of houses, in the wall of the last garden. These plaques are certainly not identity plaques, for you can never find them in agreement either with the signposts or with the kilometer markers, which themselves . . . . And all this was only to say to you, father, that there is often a lot of vagueness in rigidity. We have three categories of rigid classification, of metric classification on the same road. And if you believe them, they would have us believe that the same road is not the same road, and that there are two others. And they (these categories) would have us fall into the same and the same, and the same and the other, like the Ancients.

Believe me, father, (and here his voice took on a serious and melancholy distancing; he marked, despite himself, a distance and a depth; he marked a kind of time), I've done it, me, the road to Chartres. Allow me to say to you, what helps one get to Chartres isn't the kilometer markers and the signposts."

"Then what is it, my child?"

"Father, it's the old wooden cross that stands at the crossroads, ravaged by moss and old age. Sometimes it bears Christ; and so it forms what we call a crucifix, a Christ fixed on a cross. And sometimes it doesn't even bear that, it's so simple. Sometimes an inscription, often effaced. And sometimes not even an inscription, it's so simple.

Anyway you don't need an inscription to know what it is.

When, however, you can make one out, you don't find any metric direction. It seems this cross doesn't know that it has been stood up by this or that road rather than another. It is there, on some part of the earth. It seems to know that it is always the same earth.

And the few words it bears, generally in Latin, evoke a quite different voyage."

The priest felt the blow and showed it. He stayed silent for a long time, as if he also were pursuing melancholy and serious thoughts; and already far-away. Then he smiled, for he loved this grand, half-rebellious son, entirely docile, of an incalculable faithfulness and an unfailing solidity.

"So," he says, "so, *to consult the posts at the corners of the crossroads*?"[176]

"We are finally there, Monsignor, we are approaching our arrival point, our outcome. We are finally going to see exactly what a Catholic is."

He looked at me, surprised.

"But this requires (I continue), a certain . . . a certain delicacy."

(He made a sign showing he somewhat suspected this.)

"The more so," I continue, "as we are entering here into quite a foreign domain."

". . ."

"No, no, It's not the domain of Catholicity that is quite foreign. We are entering here," I continue, imperturbable, "into an unknown domain, into a foreign domain, which is the domain of joy. A hundred times less familiar, a hundred times more foreign, a hundred times less us than the kingdoms of sorrow. A hundred times more profound, I believe, and a hundred times more fruitful. Happy are they who one day will have some idea of it. So, when you walk on a road, it's a joy, a mysterious and profound phenomenon, to read the plaques on the signposts. You know very well where you are going. You know very well where you are passing. You know very well where you are. *Ubi, quo, unde, qua*.[177] All the same, you approach the edge of the road and look at the signpost. This is good. It's one of the joys of the road. Go ahead and explain that.

Well then, the Catholic is a person who knows very well that he is on the right spiritual road and yet still feels the need to consult the signposts.

Or rather, who feels a joy, a profound joy in consulting the signposts.

When you have your main friends, Monsignor, as I do, among the Protestants and the Jews, you soon realize, you know, that they can't imagine what a Catholic is. And the Protestants are yet more removed from this, more incapable of imagining it, than the Jews. They believe that they are familiar with it, understand it, are opposed to it, combat it. In reality, not only are they not familiar with it, but they don't understand it, they don't see it, they don't imagine it. The peculiar sort of gratuitousness there is in the Catholic. Here, for example, we touch on one of the points of distinction, one of the points that stands out, one of the points where

---

176. A line from Péguy's poem, "La Tapisserie de Notre Dame" (de Chartres).
177. "Where [are you]?" "where to?" "where from"? "where by"?

Protestants don't imagine what a Catholic is. Protestants are people who make their own signposts. And they each have their signposts. And not only do they make them, but they justify them all the time.

The Catholic, on the contrary (am I making myself understood; only Catholics will understand me), the Catholic is a fellow who arrives on the road and finds very good for him the signpost that is there for everyone. And not only this, but these signposts that are for everyone, he doesn't even consult them in order to know his route. He is well acquainted with his route, he knows it, he sees it, he does as everyone does, he follows as everyone does. He sees the route clearly. He consults the signposts in order to experience a certain joy, which is a ritual joy of the road, in order to fulfill a certain rite, which is a rite of the road.

A ritual joy that is distinctive, non-interchangeable, unknown to whoever is not Catholic, a joy of rite and of community, a joy of the parish.

Which a non-Catholic cannot imagine, cannot even think of.

A distinctive ritual joy incommunicable to others.

A pointless joy, gratuitous, superfluous.

The only joy.

And the others are only trade-offs.

There is the profound (the sole, irrevocable) non-communication between the Catholic and all the others together (maybe less so the Jew, however). The Catholic follows the world. Meanwhile the Protestants are each erecting their signposts.

The Catholic makes use of the ones there. He knows there are engineers, road crews, managers of the roads department. Manager, what an admirable word. One doesn't know whether they manage the road or simply manage their subordinates.

The Catholic only consults the signposts for the sake of consulting them. The Protestants[178]

---

178. Péguy ended what was to be his last work in mid-sentence, as he was called into active military service with the general mobilization in France on August 1, 1914. He was killed in combat at Villeroy on the eve of the Battle of the Marne, September 5, 1914.

Appendix

The Secret of The Man of Forty[1]

CHARLES PÉGUY WROTE AN immense amount about history, thousands of pages in fact, if one begins with his attack on the nineteenth-century historians Hyppolite Taine and Ernest Renan in "Zangwill" and finishes where he himself left off, with the very long essay entitled "Clio, Dialogue de l'histoire et de l'âme païenne."[2] It is this latter work, written over the last five years of his life, to which I would like to turn. One of the most complete expressions of his concerns, it is at once a polemic against modern historiography, a meditation on memory and ageing, and the embodiment of a way of doing history the way Péguy thought it should be done. The context in which all these reflections occur, as in the earlier essays on Taine and Renan, is the triumphant positivism of fin-de-siècle France, which Péguy turned every which way. His critique of positivism has, as its other side, a groping toward an image of who the human being

---

1. ©1993 Wesleyan University. Reprinted with permission. Original publication: Annette Aronowicz, "The Secret of the Man of Forty," *History and Theory* 32 (May 1993) 101–18.

2. Péguy wrote two dialogues on history. The one I am interpreting here is often referred to as Clio II among Péguy scholars, as the bulk of it was written later than the first dialogue, "Dialogue de l'histoire et de l'âme charnelle." This latter dialogue is referred to either as Clio I or Véronique. Several studies have discussed the relationship between the two manuscripts. Among the disagreements, there is a consensus that Clio II, the one we are concerned with, is by far the more finished of the two, just about ready for publication at the time of Péguy's death. For details on the history of these two dialogues, see: Péguy, "Avant-Propos," xvii-xxx; Burac, "L'histoire de Clio," 1–19; Onimus, "La Genèse de Clio."

Throughout this essay, I shall refer to the "Dialogue de l'histoire et de l'âme païenne" simply as "Clio."

is. It is this image I would like to examine here, both in itself and in its consequences for his hermeneutics and his historiography.

The Image of Humankind: The Secret of the Man of Forty

One of the most beautiful passages in "Clio" is a long meditation on the secret knowledge that Péguy claims only becomes accessible to the person of forty. At once melancholy and comical, extraordinarily repetitious, like all of Peguy's writings, it presents the reader with a complex image of the human being. I have appended the entire text at the end of the essay, and highly recommend that it be read prior to my comments as these can only hint at the passage's tone and rhythm, in themselves important keys to its meaning.

No one reading these pages can avoid noticing how insistently Péguy stresses that the knowledge of the man of forty is secret:

> But finally and above all he knows he knows. For he knows the great secret, of every creature, the secret that is most universally known but which, nonetheless, has never been leaked, the preeminent secret of State, the secret that is the most universally entrusted, little by little, from one person to another, in a lowered voice, in the course of intimate conversations, in the privacy of confessions, on chance roadways, and, yet, the secret that is most hermetically secret. The container of secrets that is the most hermetically sealed. The secret that has never been written down. The most widely revealed secret, and that from the people of forty has never passed, beyond the thirty-seventh, beyond the thirty-fifth, beyond the thirty-third year, has never descended to the people below. He knows; and he knows he knows.[3]

The words "secret" or "secrecy" occur nearly ten times in the course of these few sentences, building up to the great revelation. It is as though Péguy wanted to make sure that all would notice that something extraordinary, unlike anything else, happens to the man of forty. But since turning forty is a pretty ordinary experience and has happened from time immemorial, the insistence on the extraordinariness of this event is faintly comical. I shall return to this faint note of humor.

For the moment, I would like to ponder what makes the knowledge of the man of forty so very different from all other kinds of knowledge.

3. Péguy, "Clio," 1133.

In the first place, although it is forever being divulged—in conversations, on chance road-ways—it remains secret from those who have not yet reached the cut-off mark of thirty-three. Even that is early. Péguy tells us that even though we might get an inkling at thirty-three and then again at thirty-five, thirty-seven, these are mere inklings. But those below thirty-three do not get even an inkling. In other words, one of the extraordinary aspects of this knowledge is that, even though it is continually communicated, it remains unheard.

The secret's way of eluding those who hear it already indicates man's position in time. This most universal of all knowledges—known to all creatures—cannot be obtained through force of will, through greater sensitivity or intelligence. Only ageing, which happens whether we want it to or not, makes us receptive. We are in time's power for the appropriation of a key insight.

The knowledge of the man of forty differs from all other knowledges in yet another way. It does not stop being a secret, even to the person who knows it. This is signaled in the passage by the reference to the knowledge as a secret of the heart.[4] A person is fully committed to it, with his or her honor entirely engaged, but, we are told, the commitment bypasses all adherence, all compliance. This seems to suggest that the commitment did not occur as a result of deliberation, conscious choosing, which terms such as adherence and compliance connote. Rather, at forty, human beings become aware of a commitment that preceded their awareness of it. The intellect comes second and recognizes a truth it did not establish. This prior truth—of the heart—never becomes completely transparent to the intellect.[5] It precedes and exceeds it. In this sense, the man of forty is never in full possession of the secret, even when he knows it.

So far, I have only touched upon the formal characteristics of the man of forty's knowledge, its secret nature, but not its content. The content, after nearly two pages insisting on its great mystery, is pithily expressed: "He knows that *one* is not happy. He knows that ever since there has been man no man has ever been happy."[6]

4. Ibid., 1133.

5. Blaise Pascal's influence on Péguy makes itself felt from the very beginning of his career to its end, too frequent to be cited in one footnote. In this passage, it is difficult not to hear echoes of some of Pascal's most famous meditations on the difference between truths of the heart and truths of the mind, in *Pensées*, 58 (Pensée 110); 123–24 (Pensée 308); 154 (Pensée 423).

6. Péguy, "Clio," 1133.

The comical note is quite palpable. What? This banal sentiment is the extraordinary revelation we have to wait so long to receive? The anticlimactic effect in its own way points to the meaning of the secret: humankind's unhappiness is in large part due to the fact that expectations and reality very rarely coincide. But, despite the comical note, the basic point is unmistakably melancholy for it expresses the defeat of the human being by time. At twenty, we think the fulfillment of this or that goal will make us happy. At forty, either we reach that goal and realize it didn't make us happy, or we never managed to reach the goal, or we reach the goal, it makes us happy, but we realize that we can't cling to it, because like everything else, it will slip through our fingers. The secret of the man of forty is, in this respect, reminiscent of the famous four visions of the Buddha. The latter, upon seeing a sick man, an old man, a dead man, and a monk, realizes that all is suffering. In both cases, there is a head-on collision with our transitory estate, with the fact that time defeats us in our deepest aspirations and will continue to defeat us.

There is no denying that this is a melancholy insight and part of the beauty of these pages is the way the repetitions suggest the melancholy. Yet the comical note, slight but constant, points to a paradox: The man of forty's acknowledgment of defeat is also a moment of liberation. After all, what he discovers is that no one has ever been happy. This joins him to all human beings, freeing him from seeing his misery solely as the result of his own inadequacies. He is thus liberated to accept himself as he is, no bigger and no smaller. Péguy goes on at great length about finally knowing who he is, that somber and stupid young man from the provinces, a good Frenchman of the ordinary variety and a sinner of the common sort.[7] The acceptance of his limitations is simultaneously a defeat and a victory. The melancholy and the humor are inseparable.

That the secret is more than an acknowledgment of defeat is indicated in a very different way in the latter half of the passage, in what Péguy refers to as the man of forty's inconsistency. He has just found out that he is committed with his whole being to the truth that no one has ever been happy, and yet he turns around and with his whole being wants his son to be happy.

> Now, note the inconsistency. The same man. This man naturally has a son of fourteen. And he has but one thought, that his son should be happy. And he does not tell himself that it would be

---

7. Ibid., 1132.

> the first time; that this has yet to be seen. He tells himself nothing at all, which is the sign of the deepest thought. This man is or is not an intellectual. He is or is not a philosopher. He is or is not blasé. (Blasé from pain, the worst corruption.) He has an animal thought. Those are the best kind. Those are the only ones. He has only one thought. And it is an animal thought. He wants his son to be happy. He thinks only of this, that his son should be happy.[8]

Further, this same man, convinced with his whole being of his defeat, turns around and yearns to read victory for himself in the eyes of his son.

> He has another thought. He is preoccupied solely with the idea that his son (already) has of him; it is an idée fixe, an obsession, that is, a *siège*, a blockade, a sort of scrupulous and consuming mania. He has only one concern, the judgment that his son, in the secret of his heart, will pass on him. He wants to read the future solely in the eyes of this son. He searches the depths of his eyes. That which has never succeeded, never happened, he is convinced will happen this time. And not only that, but that it will happen as if naturally and smoothly. As a result of some sort of natural law.[9]

The passage indicates that the man's expectations will be disappointed. The son will soon be in on the universal secret himself. His judgment, even if favorable, cannot bring the father the affirmation he yearns for. But, in the very last three sentences of the passage, a strange thing happens. Nothing is more moving than this inconsistency, Péguy tells us, and nothing disarms God more.[10] We are in the presence of Hope, the capitalization indicating the theological virtue which is a condition for salvation.

These last three lines do not render man's position in time more comfortable. He remains defeated. All that he yearns for in the world will continue to elude him. But the conclusion of the passage suggests that defeat in time is not the same as defeat before God and that God's judgment softens precisely at the moment when human beings, accepting defeat for themselves, cannot accept it for their offspring, or, alternately, that God's judgment softens when, giving up justification in their time,

8. Ibid., 1134.
9. Ibid., 1134.
10. Ibid., 1134.

human beings seek one in a time beyond their time, the time of their children.

The image of the human being this meditation on the man of forty suggests is thus complex. On the one hand, humanity is defeated, always. But on the other hand, within that defeat flickers the freedom of self-knowledge and, beyond that defeat, outside time, there may be victory, but it is a victory that depends not on human beings' belief in God but on their visceral desire for the other's happiness and on their thirst for a judgment beyond that of their own times.

I mentioned at the beginning of these comments that the passage juxtaposes the extraordinary and the ordinary in a peculiar way. Péguy presents the knowledge of the man of forty as at once very different from any other knowledge and very banal. The same point could be made about the passage's juxtaposition of religious and secular. On the one hand, we are told in the last few sentences that the double experience of the man of forty—his complete acknowledgment of defeat and his complete refusal of it—is of profound religious significance. It modifies God's judgment. It has the potential to save him. But, on the other hand, what is the great saving act? It is embodied in every mother and father's relation to their children, in their hope for their happiness, in their yearning to be justified by them. How ordinary. In this strange juxtaposition, the secular gets sacralized, and the sacred gets secularized.

It is obvious from the above that Peguy's image of the human being is Christian. But it is also obvious that this Christianity, rather than pointing to an otherworldly realm, points to the deepest recesses of this world. In a very important sense, when Péguy turned to Christianity, he did not leave the secular world behind him. He stayed right where he was but insisted that his religious tradition, through its image of the human being, shed light on where that where was.

This staying put meant, for instance, that Péguy never repudiated the socialism of his youth.[11] It had been under its banner that he had ardently defended Dreyfus. It had also been under its banner that he founded his

---

11. There are many references to Peguy's socialism in the secondary literature about him. The best sources, however, are his own writings, "De la cité socialiste," "Marcel, Premier dialogue de la cité harmonieuse," and in fact all his early essays as collected in *Oeuvres en prose complètes I*. His first play, *Jeanne d'Arc*, also indicates the issues he saw at the center of a socialist vision, written at the height of his socialist involvements (1895–97). For his later evaluation of his socialist commitments, see "Notre Jeunesse."

journal, *Les Cahiers de la quinzaine*.[12] He founded it in part to free himself from the constraint the Socialist Party had instituted, forbidding its members from criticizing its leaders and policies publicly. But Péguy's differences with the Socialist Party in no way indicated a repudiation of socialism as such. In fact, he hoped to embody the socialist vision in his journal both through its economic and its editorial policies. *Les Cahiers* were to be financed strictly through the contribution of its subscribers, with no advertising or capitalist backing of any sort. They were to publish completely uncensored pieces, both political and literary, representing a community of individuals freed from the shackles of mere party lines. Although these policies were to cause Péguy acute economic difficulties and many enmities, he persisted in them until his own, and the journal's, death in [September] 1914.

Péguy's turning to Christianity seems to have occurred sometime in 1907, the first announcement of it to his friend Joseph Lotte occurring somewhat later.[13] Short of the confessions he often promised but never lived to write, one cannot trace with any certainty the paths that led him back. Yet, it seems clear enough that his own public defeats, starting with what he felt was the Dreyfusards' failure to keep the Affair from serving narrow party ends, eventually made him reflect on the human being's precarious position in time. Christianity did not seem to bring a change in his notion of justice. Rather, it made him understand what makes people pursue justice, even in defeat. He himself was often to say that his return to Christianity did not represent a break with his previous commitments but their deepening.[14] The passage on the secret of the man of forty illustrates this well. The Christian term "Hope" sheds light on an experience human beings already have. It is not a separate set of experiences.

The Hermeneutic: Chronicle and History

We need not go far in the text to see that the image of the human being revealed by the passage on the man of forty is connected to a hermeneutic.

12. Various questions regarding both the founding and the nature of the journal are discussed in Fraisse, *Charles Péguy 2*.

13. The confession made to his friend Joseph Lotte about his return to Christianity is recorded in many biographies. See, for instance, Adereth, *Commitment in Modern French Literature*, 68. The date generally given for this confession is 1908.

14. For a discussion of the continuity in Peguy's thought, see Dru, *Péguy*, 37–42.

That is, "Clio" presents us with a theory of how to interpret human events, how to "do" history.

In another section of the text, Péguy compares two approaches to the past, that of the chronicler and that of the historian. The chief characteristic of the chronicler is rather unusual: he is always a man of forty. Lest we take this too literally, Péguy goes on to say that chroniclers are very much like poets. At twenty, everyone is a poet. It is simply the nature of being twenty. But a real poet is one who remains so after the age of twenty. Similarly, at forty, everyone is a chronicler, as a matter of course. But a real chronicler is one who remains so after the age of forty.[15] In short, being forty becomes an existential orientation rather than a specific age.

The historian is characterized in the same peculiar way: he is always someone who has already turned fifty. In this case, too, this does not denote an actual age but an existential attitude. The man of fifty, unlike the man of forty, has become very cheerful.[16] He no longer remembers, with all the acuteness of the man of forty, the experience of losing his youth. As a result, instead of truly remembering his past, as the man of forty cannot help but do, he, without even being aware of it, merely mouths the ready-made generalizations about the past that have become current. His main concern, when reviewing the past, is to show to all the world that he had always been on the winning side, the side that a vague consensus has declared to be right.[17]

From this description, it is clear that Péguy favors the chronicler. He is the one who touches something of true human significance in his recounting of the past. The historian somehow manages to miss the point. Péguy insists on this in several images, poking fun gently, or not so gently, at the historian.

In one such image, the historian is shown as always walking "*alongside* the cemetery, alongside its walls, alongside its monuments."[18] In other words, the historian somehow avoids the problem of mortality (his own, for instance). Unlike the chronicler, with whom he is contrasted, he fails to place himself within the race. No voices come alive at the historian's touch as a result.

15. Ibid., 1193.
16. Ibid., 1192–93.
17. Ibid., 1188–89.
18. Ibid., 1177.

In another image, the historian appears as a sergeant-major following a slightly impotent general, who is inspecting his troops on a field of maneuvers. The chronicler, on the other hand, is the general on the field of battle, in the midst of his troops, urging them toward victory. The historian, once again having placed himself outside, in a situation without risk, brings back only the news that a suspender is missing. By contrast, the chronicler, having placed himself in the thick of the struggle, does not record. He fights.[19]

In a third image, we get the following description: "History is that long, longitudinal track that follows the whole length of the coast (but at a certain distance) and which stops at all the stations one wants. But it doesn't follow the coast itself, it does not coincide with the coast itself, for on the coast itself, on the coast, there are tides, and man and fish, and the mouths of rivers and streams, and the double life of earth and sea."[20]

Again, the historian has placed himself alongside, missing the contours of the land, where people actually live. That coastline is always in flux, not easily containable in ready-made categories or laws of development. By implication, the chronicler does not have a grid to contain it all but stays close to what cannot be so easily generalized, to what escapes the system.

In these images, the polemical intent is obvious. It is not difficult to see in these portraits of the historian who always manages to miss his mark an attack on the positivists in their heyday at the Sorbonne of Péguy's time.[21] Their remaining alongside rather than within events reflects their notion of scientific detachment, their desire to accumulate "facts," their urge to establish laws of development. Péguy was evidently not very impressed. And yet he could be surprisingly sympathetic to the historian. At one point, he says that it is no doubt one of God's greatest graces that he has turned most of us into historians. Life is already very difficult

19. Ibid., 1177–78.

20. Ibid., 1191.

21. Péguy's attack on the pretensions of modern historiography took many forms. In "Zangwill," he examines the metaphysical underpinnings of the French fathers of modern academic history, Taine and Renan, claiming these underpinnings to be those of the modern world itself. This search continues throughout his subsequent essays, as in, for instance, the much later "Victor-Marie, comte Hugo," 319–23. In other places, his attack takes on specific prominent academic personalities, such as Lanson, Lavisse, Rudler, Langlois, and so on, in "L'Argent suite," 848–996. For a history of the rise of modern historical scholarship in France, see Keylor, *Academy and Community*.

when one is very cheerful. How much more difficult is it to persist in the melancholy realization of the man of forty.[22]

Péguy is playing with the categories of historian and chronicler. The two terms cannot be taken as descriptions of historiography per se, although they have consequences for historiography. Rather, they refer to hermeneutics. That is, the chronicler and the historian represent two metaphysics that precede and inform historical writing. The chronicler represents the metaphysic revealed by the secret of the man of forty. He operates within a vision of humanity's defeat in time, and yet of freedom and hope within that defeat. Historians represent the denial of that vision. For them, there is a winning side with which they surely will be associated, if they carefully avoid their own mortality, the uncertainty of combat, and the unwieldiness of the data. Since the chronicler and the historian represent metaphysical types, an actual work of history may embody either one or alternate between both. Thus, the categories have a certain slippery character. They are guides to detecting underlying metaphysical assumptions present to some degree in all schools. The positivists are, by and large, "historians," but they can have moments of "chronicle," just as a Jules Michelet, who for Péguy is a chronicler, nonetheless shows traces of "history."[23]

We see that the secret of the man of forty becomes the basis of a way of interpreting human events. The gist of it is ethical. The man of forty's knowing that no one has ever been happy is the recognition of an indissoluble bond with all other human beings. His animal thought regarding his son is no mere idea but the sign of a relationship that cannot be severed. The word Péguy often uses to designate such bonds between human beings is "race." The chronicler, he had said at one point, remains or puts himself within the race.[24] To be of a certain race is to have characteristics in common with others that one has neither chosen nor is capable of changing at will. When the man of forty discovers that no one is happy, it is that kind of link he discovers between himself and others. It can neither be avoided or escaped.

---

22. Péguy, "Clio," 1192–93.

23. Ibid., 1176. Another example of this mixture of "chronicler" and "historian" in one work is to be found, for Péguy, in one of the contributors to the *Cahiers de la quinzaine*, Paul Milliet. Ibid., 1194.

24. Ibid., 1177.

I would now like to show how this hermeneutic functions in Péguy's reading of historical documents by turning to three such examples in "Clio." In each case, the hermeneutic shapes the historiography.

The Historiography

Victor Hugo

The first example of Péguy's historical interpretations occurs within his discussion of Victor Hugo's poetry. A great lover of Hugo's poems, many of which he knew by heart,[25] he toyed with the idea of submitting a complementary thesis for his doctorate on the references to history in Hugo's poetry.[26] This, ostensibly, was one of the original motivations for the writing of "Clio." And, in a small portion of the text Péguy does stick to this topic, citing all the index cards he has collected on the appearance of Clio or history in the poems. But quickly he digresses in several directions. It is one of these digressions within a digression that will interest us here.

At a certain point, he takes the reader on a search for the correct version of one of Hugo's poems, "Le Sacre."[27] The last couplet had ap-

---

25. For studies of Péguy's relationship to Hugo, see Fraisse, *Charles Péguy 3*. Three of the essays in this collection deal extensively with this relationship.

26. Péguy, increasingly crushed in later years by the responsibilities of administering *Les Cahiers de la quinzaine*, financed exclusively through subscriptions, toyed with the idea of submitting a doctoral thesis to the Sorbonne in order to become eligible for a teaching position at a provincial university, thus assuring his family's living. The proposed topic was to be on the role of history in the modern world. Several beginnings were made in this direction. See "De la situation faite à l'histoire et à la sociologie dans les temps modernes," "De la situation faite au parti intellectual dans le monde moderne devant les accidents de la gloire temporelle," in Péguy, *Oeuvres en prose complètes II*. The doctorate also required a shorter, complementary thesis and it is to it he refers in "Clio," 1105, 1146. Péguy never brought this project to completion, although all his later prose writings are strewn with reflections regarding history.

27. Ibid., 1085–1104. Péguy's comparison of different editions, with close attention paid to punctuation, capitalization, syntax, gives rise to a variety of reflections: on the force of habit; on the impossibility, in a certain sense, of ever finding the original version of a work of art, since the creativity of the author both precedes and follows what he has submitted to paper; on the fact that a historically significant work has little to do with original editions, and so on.

There are two completely different visions of what constitutes a fact in this presentation. On the one hand, the dates and other empirical details about various printed versions are presented as key evidence. But, on the other hand, the solidity of this evidence is continually being undermined by other "facts," which are not so easily measured, but whose power is great nonetheless: the force of habit, which can make

parently been printed in several variations of spelling and syntax. The correct edition that Péguy finally discovers happens to have a preface in which Hetzel, the editor, expresses in prose what Hugo had expressed poetically. In it, Hetzel makes an appeal to history. He states that these poems, published in exile, will testify to future generations that love of truth and honor still survived in the dark days of the Second Empire. Even though in their own time their cause has been defeated, people like himself and Hugo, who continue to oppose the injustice of Napoleon III's regime, will, Hetzel maintains, be vindicated by posterity.[28]

Péguy spends a long time on Hetzel's few sentences. He sees in this appeal to future generations an obvious secularization, a movement away from the notion of a judgment of God.[29] Here, God has been replaced by human beings who will render the judgment of history. Much of Péguy's commentary on this development is expressed in a tone of gentle mockery. Where will the authority to judge come from, if the only difference between the people of today and the people of tomorrow is that the latter live later? Why should human beings with the same weaknesses as oneself suddenly be able to dispense final judgment? Besides, future generations, if they are worth anything at all, will have their own deeds to submit to history, leaving them little attention for past generations. Those in the future who might indeed pay some attention to the likes of Hetzel or Hugo are most likely to be "historians," and thus ignore what was at stake in the first place.[30]

But things suddenly take an unexpected turn. When people refer to secularization, they either decry it or celebrate it. Péguy seems to be with those who decry secularization. It is, after all, foolishness to rely on one's descendants or on the judgment of history for the final justification of one's own deeds. But without denying that it is foolishness, Péguy sees it not as a break away from Christianity but as a detour that somehow manages to embody one of its central virtues without knowing it.[31] It is a

---

typesetters ignore an innovation in the manuscript; the creative process, which makes it nearly impossible to locate a point of origin of a work of art; the mythological function of a work, independent of its technical correctness. Péguy conducts a polemic here against empiricism at the same time as he is at his most empirical.

28. Ibid., 1117, 1134.
29. Ibid., 1114.
30. Ibid., 1113–31.
31. Ibid., 1127–31.

secularization but a secularization through and through religious, even if unknown to itself.

For Péguy, the central virtue embodied in people like Hugo and Hetzel is hope. In their defeat, they continue to act with the trust that their children will see the truth that their own contemporaries did not. They have placed their hope in the wrong objects, their own descendants, and yet their continued action on behalf of something that is not confirmed in their own time, but which they trust will be confirmed in the time of their children, is hope nonetheless.

Not only is the secularized appeal to history an embodiment of hope but, in its very unawareness of its potential for salvation, it may be more praiseworthy than a hope practiced as a religious virtue. In the latter case, Péguy says, the person appoints himself. In the former case, he may be appointed from elsewhere.[32] For Péguy, the virtue that is as if involuntary is more deeply rooted than the virtue practiced in order to be virtuous. We come back to the secret of the heart, lodging itself in a person independently of his or her will.

Péguy's discussion of Hugo's poem "Le Sacre," with its accompanying preface, has thus made him reflect on a key historical event of the nineteenth century: secularization. But it has also made him reinterpret that secularization. A movement away from Christianity, it nonetheless is in profound inner continuity with it. In fact, he claims that people like Hugo and Hetzel, in their struggle for justice in the midst of defeat, may embody Hope more than those pious churchgoers whose concern is only with their own piety. The key to Christianity lies in an embodiment that penetrates deeper than piety.

In what way does the secret of the man of forty shine through this interpretation? In the first place, it determines what constitutes a significant fact: Hetzel's preface. In its appeal to posterity, it echoes the man of forty's attempt to read his future solely in the eyes of his son or daughter. In both cases, this turning to "the children" occurs in the midst of defeat. The secret of the man of forty makes Péguy stop here as opposed to somewhere else. It determines what sticks out in a sea of details.

But the secret of the man of forty also informs Péguy's relationship to the people he is interpreting. In order to understand this, it is necessary to know that he had already returned to Christianity at the

---

32. Ibid., 1132.

time he wrote "Clio."[33] Hetzel and Hugo, as Péguy's interpretation itself makes clear, were of the camp that had moved away from Christianity. They represent one aspect of the secularization of the nineteenth century, with their appeal to the judgment of history rather than to that of God. Yet Péguy operates within a vision of the human condition that allows him to focus on expressions of defeat and hope, regardless of acknowledged religious affiliation. That is, his view of Christianity is not that of the social group that calls itself Christian but of an orientation towards defeat, towards others, that can be discovered even in the absence of any Christian reference. Placing himself within the secret of the man of forty he assumes a common plight—*no one* has ever been happy—without assuming the mode of its expression.

The Classical Greeks

The second example of Péguy at work as a historian involves the *Iliad*, although he makes reference to Greek tragedy as well. He claims that if one suspends the usual expectations one brings to a Greek classic, one will notice that in Homer the Greek gods and the Greek world are not aligned one upon the other.[34] That is, the gods do not represent the greatest qualities to which people aspire. Human beings may envy them their immortality, their eternal youth, their eternal feasting and lovemaking, but this envy bathes in a contempt all the stronger for not being acknowledged. Why is it that humans hold the gods in contempt? Their very immortality gives rise to it since, as a result, they need not confront the three experiences that human beings always face—destitution, risk, and death. Péguy simultaneously refers to these as the three miseries and the three greatnesses. That is, in Péguy's reading of the classical Greeks, it is within those limits that human beings rise to greatness. The gods, never risking destitution or death, or risk itself, can never give themselves or lose themselves, and thus, in Péguy's words, they cannot become great in the way a human being can because *"ils manquent de manquer,"* they lack lacking.[35]

In Péguy's reading, then, the greatest figure in the classical Greek world was not any of the gods, but Oedipus:

33. See footnote 13.
34. Péguy, "Clio," 1159–68.
35. Ibid., 1168.

> It is he who enacted, having undergone it, the greatest deed in the world. The greatest achievement. For, starting from the fact, which is to be King of Thebes, he brought about the greatest spiritual ascension, which is to have gone down, by the harshest of paths, to have become the most beggarly, the most miserable, the most errant of the blind.[36]

In this passage, Oedipus's greatness is tied not to his power as king but to his fall from that power into the most abject misery. This fall was certainly not something he chose, thus the irony in the opposition "he enacted, having undergone it." An action is equated to a passive state. This paradox is all the more emphasized in the description of his ascension. He brought it about. It couldn't be more active. Yet how did he bring it about? By falling, something he did not choose. Something about the transformation that occurs in human beings when they become utterly vulnerable defies the usual opposition between passive and active. The transformation brings humans a consecration that the gods do not know.

How does the secret of the man of forty shine through here? Once again it determines the evidence. A myriad of approaches to the Greek classics is possible. Péguy chooses the one that brings to light humanity's defeat and yet its greatness within that defeat. It is important to underline that Péguy's hermeneutic does not release the same evidence here as it did in the case of Hetzel and Hugo. In the Greek texts, there is no emphasis on the judgment of future generations. Rather, there is that peculiar reversal of high and low, of comic and tragic, which we saw in the man of forty's acknowledgment of who he is. In the face of defeat, Oedipus simultaneously experiences liberation. The secret of the man of forty selects evidence, in this case the greatness of the most lowly, the reversal of defeat and victory. But the evidence brings with it its own unexpected twist on the secret, which knows as many forms as there are human beings.

The secret of the man of forty also informs Péguy's relationship to the people he is interpreting. On the one hand, he presents the Greek vision of the human being as true. The three miseries really are the three greatnesses. On the other hand, he is Christian. How can he claim truth for a pagan tradition?

He does not do it by seeing an identity between the two. Never in his interpretation of Greek texts does he superimpose Christian

---

36. Ibid., 1165–66.

terminology.[37] Homer and Sophocles speak of the fulfillment of destiny, of self-knowledge. They do not speak of hope or salvation. Peguy's reading makes that clear. And yet, the different emphases between the two traditions do not preclude echoes. Surely, the reversal of high and low, of misery and greatness, is symbolized in both. Péguy understands it in the following way: "(The particular import of Christianity is not that it invented *de nihilo*, the three miseries [the three greatnesses], death, destitution, risk, but that it found their true intent, having added sickness, that other half of modern man.) And to have assigned their true greatness to these four, to have given them their true weight."[38]

Christianity here brings home the full meaning of certain key experiences, but it does not invent that meaning. It merely deepens it, points out its full gravity. Thus, the Greek texts activate, as it were, Christian symbols, which in turn illuminate the Greek texts. Which comes first? In his reading of the classics is Péguy upholding the Christian understanding of humanity or the Greek one? It is impossible to separate them so neatly. What comes out of such a reading is what Péguy called "a pagan, a Christian, a spiritual, a carnal nourishment."[39]

Thus, Péguy's claim that the Greek texts present us with a true vision of the human condition relies on a Christian vision, which in turns relies on the Greek, ad infinitum. But, it is the secret of the man of forty, with its stress on a common defeat and yet on something within or beyond that defeat, that allows one to perceive that there is a circle in the first place. In that circle, one is once again within the race, the division between pagan and Christian momentarily suspended.

Pierre Caron de Beaumarchais

The third example of Péguy's historiography is his analysis of a relatively unknown play, *L'Autre Tartuffe ou La Mère Coupable* (1792), by Pierre Caron de Beaumarchais, the great playwright of the French Revolution. As in the previous two examples, the text is used to illuminate the spirit of an entire era. As Hetzel's preface and Hugo's poems reflected

---

37. In an earlier essay, "Les Suppliants parallèles," Péguy explicitly remarks on the importance of not imposing Christian terminology upon classical texts, in *Oeuvres en prose complètes II*, 347–49.

38. Péguy, "Clio," 1164.

39. Ibid., 1152.

the secularization of the nineteenth century, as Homer and Sophocles reflected the classical Greeks' vision of humanity, so *L'Autre Tartuffe* will reflect for Péguy the French spirit in the aftermath of the Revolution.

He focuses primarily on one line, uttered by Count Almaviva, one of the play's main characters. Count Almaviva, as nearly all the characters in *L'Autre Tartuffe*, had also been a character in Beaumarchais's famous *Marriage of Figaro*, written twenty years earlier. In that first play, Péguy tells us, the characters were all the very embodiment of youth.[40] But the line, said in passing by the Count, indicates that youth is now gone. He refers to Cherubin, the flirtatious young man the audience knew from *The Marriage of Figaro* as "a certain Léon of Astorga, who was once my page and who was called Cherubin."[41]

For Péguy, this line reveals all. In its rhythm, tone, word choice, it conveys what it means to have aged. Cherubin is no longer primarily referred to by that nickname of love and war. He now has a surname, Léon. He comes from a specific place, Astorga. He is no longer the carefree spirit, flitting amorously about. Now he is tied to a family, to a particular town. He is caught by time and space, thus subject to ageing. In other parts of *L'Autre Tartuffe*, we find out that he died many years ago in battle. The passing of time, however, is signaled not merely by his death but also by the fact of having had a dummy for a son. "Nothing," says Péguy, with that humor that glimmers in the midst of melancholy, "ages a man as much as having a son who is visibly an idiot."[42]

It is not difficult to recognize in this interpretation the secret of the man of forty, in yet another of its manifestations. For Péguy, the play expresses the wistfulness of an entire generation, the generation that made the Revolution. By 1792, the aspirations of 1772 had given way to actions, bringing with them inevitable consequences and unexpected limitations. Actions have their own beauty. But no one, says Péguy, forgets the purity of beginnings, when nothing has yet been inserted into time. It is that awareness of loss, even in victory, that the play expresses.[43]

But the secret of the man of forty once again does more than select the significant document. It also determines Péguy's relationship to the people he is interpreting. Here it is necessary to recall that the secret of

40. Ibid., 1072–76.
41. Ibid., 1077.
42. Ibid., 1077.
43. Ibid., 1085.

the man of forty is indeed a secret. That is, it is lodged in the heart and, therefore, although accessible to reason, it never becomes completely transparent to it. It persists in overflowing any and all conceptual grids. In Péguy's case, this leads to certain precautionary measures. He needs to signal, in the very act of interpreting, that something in the other person's expression exceeds even his most subtle ideas.

He does this in a number of ways, his unorthodox use of quotations being one of the foremost. Contrary to accepted academic style, he often reprints huge portions of the text he is working on. The quotation, rather than discreetly tucked into an otherwise uninterrupted exposition, dominates his commentary. Such, for instance, is what he does with the title page and list of characters of *La Mère Coupable*, reproduced in its entirety in the essay. Taking over one whole page, it is the focal point of the many digressions that precede and follow it, all tied to one or another of its details. The length of the character descriptions and the frequency of the word "sensitive" become a starting point for reflections on classical and romantic influences on the play. The very title, *L'Autre Tartuffe*, with its reference to Molière, leads to musings on Beaumarchais's relationship to his audience, which in turn leads to musings on the trust established between author and readers in general. The date of publication, 1792, brings a disquisition on the special importance of premieres in the life and afterlife of plays, ending with a reflection on the impact of time on works of art in general.[44] These comments do not derive one from the other. Each goes back to that title page and list of characters, reprinted in the essay. Thus, rather than being supporting evidence for a thesis, the quotation becomes the center to which commentary turns, again and again, focusing now on this, now on that detail, even if it means that a straight exposition of one theme becomes impossible. The conceptual apparatus fails to contain the text. Péguy abandons the iron grid of the railroad track for the meandering curves of the coast itself, to refer back to one of his own images.

He makes the same point when he zeroes in on only one line, the line about Cherubin previously quoted. These few words, merely an aside from the point of view of the plot, reveal not the overt intent of the play, but a tacit meaning interwoven in the whole fabric. That meaning is the melancholy awareness of time's passing. The interpreter can point to parts of the text in which that meaning shines through. But he cannot himself

---

44. Ibid., 1063–72.

reproduce that meaning, depending as it does on a specific texture and atmosphere that no general statement about time passing could possibly convey.

The hermeneutic, then, not only assumes a common plight but also assumes that the common plight expresses itself indirectly, in the body as it were, rather than through ideological pronouncements. It invites attention to tone of voice, rhythm, context, and demands caution regarding theoretical schemes of all sorts.

In this interpretation of Beaumarchais, Péguy makes no reference to Christianity, as he did in his interpretations of Hugo and Homer. Yet it too can be placed within this framework. In another essay, Péguy refers to "Clio" as a meditation on the centrality of the incarnation.[45] By this he did not mean the revelation of Jesus Christ as such but what that revelation holds up as paradigmatic: the inextricable interwovenness of the spirit in matter, of the eternal in time. His desire to bore into the very fabric of a text, beyond mere theory, is the very embodiment of this notion of incarnation. This desire has been constant throughout "Clio." We notice it not only in his reading of Beaumarchais but also everywhere else, starting with the secret of the man of forty itself, buried in the heart, eschewing conceptual grasp. The hope of Hugo and Hetzel is another case in point, never aware of itself as Hope, hidden within their actions and expressions. The Greeks' contempt for their gods functioned similarly, too present to be captured in an explicit expression. In all these examples, people are motivated by something that seems to have lodged itself within them, without them even realizing it, although they can come to realize it in time and affirm it. These truths of the heart seem to choose people rather than to be chosen by them. The starting point of incarnation is not the

---

45. The reference to "Clio" (as well as to its variant "Véronique") appears in "L'Argent suite," 954–55. I have translated the passage in its entirety:

> My young comrade, since you are Catholic, it is a great mystery that it is not sufficient to be Catholic, and that one must still, and that one must besides, and that one must beyond this, toil all one's life, all one's earthly existence, in the temporal. My young comrade, Jesus himself, who was, I think, the prince of the spiritual, founded a Church that has not stopped being opposed, in the spiritual and in the temporal.
>
> This is the very mystery of the carnal and the temporal, my young comrade, and of the insertion of the spiritual within the carnal and of the insertion of the eternal in the temporal, and, in a word, it is the very mystery of the incarnation. . . . We will find this mystery in our "Clio," dialogue of history and the pagan soul, and in our "Véronique," dialogue of history and the carnal soul.

human will. Péguy's historiography points to precisely such unchosen, embodied secrets as the key to human affairs.

Conclusion

Péguy's meditations on history in "Clio" are all of a piece. At the center is an image of the human condition: a simultaneous defeat and victory, binding all human beings to each other in a way that forever overflows all explicit expressions of it. This image becomes a hermeneutic leading to a historiography whose main concern is to place historians within the race, to allow them to discover the universal. As the stress on embodiment indicates, this universal is always buried in a particularity that rebuts mere theory. The paradoxical part of this vision of history is that, although Christian, its main thrust is the suspension of the difference between Christian and non-Christian.

This makes us enter into a circle. That is, the particular difference of Christianity is precisely that it obliterates the difference between Christian and non-Christian, by allowing one to seize a common humanity, through the secret of the man of forty. This circularity—a difference that does away with difference—may go some way towards accounting for the way Christian vocabulary is inserted in "Clio."[46] It appears infrequently, almost furtively, as in the passage on the man of forty. Only the last three lines—in a description that takes three pages—use Christian terms: God's judgment; Hope. Most frequently, Christian vocabulary does not appear at all. For example, although Péguy himself says that "Clio" is a meditation on incarnation, the term never appears in it. There is a tension in the text between Christianity as universal human experience, requiring no distinguishing vocabulary, and Christianity as the particular revelation that allows one to recognize the universally human in the first place. Péguy translates the Christian understanding of humanity into a secular language but every once in a while there is a reminder that this secular language does translate into another and is itself a translation.

Péguy's emphases in his image of humanity and, consequently, in his hermeneutic and historiography, although Christian, are also the product of a historical context. He was reacting to what he called the "historian,"

---

46. The way in which Péguy inserts Christian vocabulary into his essay deserves further study. For the moment, I just want to signal that that vocabulary appears infrequently. In an essay over two hundred pages in length, the chief references occur in ibid., 1059, 1096–97, 1123, 1127–31, 1134, 1153–54, 1171.

the metaphysic that assumes that there are such things as winners in time and that the most important thing is to be associated with them. For Péguy, much of the humanities' and social sciences' concern for scientific objectivity, with their discovery of laws of development and their refusal to admit as fact anything not quantifiable, is merely such a concealed urge for power. It is in the process of exposing and combating that underlying motivation that he fashioned the image of the man of forty.

I would like, in conclusion, to reflect upon two things. The first is that, in a sense, Péguy's attack on the historiography of his time amounts to a defense of such qualities as compassion and respect for the people one is studying. To be within the secret of the man of forty is to place oneself within a common defeat. It is also to respect that surge of hope for those to come rising from defeat or that acceptance of limitations accompanying it. Perhaps the fact that words such as compassion and respect—in the context of a discussion of method—make most of us scholars so uncomfortable is a sure sign that the positivism Péguy was combating is not as dead and gone as the currency of the term "postmodernism" might lead us to believe.

The second conclusion derives from the first. Terms such as compassion and respect have a religious ring. Most of us in the academic world are profoundly allergic to our respective religious traditions, fearing that they can only narrow or taint our intellectual commitment. Could not Péguy's understanding of his religious tradition suggest that it is the positivism we think we have long overcome that is keeping us from noticing the very ground underneath our feet?

Appendix

The speaker in this passage, as in the rest of the essay, is Clio, the Greek muse of history. Péguy alternates between calling her Clio and calling her history. In either appellation, she is the one who addresses Péguy throughout the text.

Look, she said, at this man of forty. Maybe we know him, Péguy, our man of forty. Maybe we are beginning to know him. Maybe we are beginning to hear speak of him. He is forty, so he knows. The knowledge that no teaching can impart, the secret that no method can prematurely entrust, the knowledge that no discipline confers nor is able to confer, the teaching that no school can disseminate, he *knows*. Being forty, he has, in the most natural way in the world, to say the least, received news of the secret that is known by the most people in the world, but which is nonetheless the most hermetically kept. In the first place, he knows who he is. It could be useful. In the course of a life. He knows what Péguy is. He has even begun to know it, he had seen the first outlines of it, he received the first signs upon his thirty-third, thirty-fifth, thirty-seventh year. Most especially he knows that Péguy is that little boy of ten or twelve with whom he was so long acquainted, walking on the banks of the Loire. He knows also that Péguy is that ardent and somber and stupid young man, eighteen or twenty, with whom he was acquainted for several years, freshly landed in Paris. He knows also that immediately afterward began the period one would almost be forced to call, despite the aversion one has for this word, the period, in a certain sense, of a mask of a *Persona*, of a deformation of the theater. He knows, finally, that the Sorbonne, and the École Normale, and the political parties could rob him of his youth, but that they did not take away his heart. And that they could consume his youth but that they did not consume his heart. He knows, finally, he knows as well, that the entire interpolated period doesn't count, doesn't exist, that it is an interpolated period and a period of the mask, and he knows it is over and will not return. And that fortunately death will come sooner. For he knows that in the last several years, since he has passed, since he has reached his thirty-third, thirty-fifth, thirty-seventh year, and that he has biennially passed them, he knows he has found who he is once again and that he has found himself being who he is, a good Frenchman of the ordinary variety, and towards God a believer and a sinner of the common sort. But finally and above all he knows he knows. For he knows the great secret, of every creature, the secret that is most universally known but which, nonetheless, has never been leaked, the preeminent secret of State, the secret that is the most universally entrusted, little by little, from one person to another, in a lowered voice, in the course of intimate conversations, in the privacy of confessions, on chance roadways, and, yet, the secret that is most hermetically secret. The container of secrets that is the most hermetically sealed. The secret that has never been written down. The most widely revealed secret, and that from the people of forty has never passed, beyond the thirty-seventh, beyond the thirty-fifth, beyond the thirty-third year, has never descended to the people below. He knows; and he knows he knows. He knows that *one* is not happy. He knows that ever since there has been man no man has ever been happy. And he even knows it so deeply, and with a knowledge so deeply ingrained in the depths of his heart, that it is perhaps, that it is surely, the only belief, the only knowledge he values, in which he feels and knows his honor to be engaged, precisely the only one in which there is no understanding, no mask, no connivance. To say it outright, no adherence, no compliance, no *good will*. No obligingness. No goodness. Now, note the inconsistency. The same man. This man naturally has a son of fourteen. And he has but one thought, that his son should be happy. And he does not tell himself that it would be the first time; that this has yet to be seen. He tells himself nothing at all, which is the sign of the deepest thought. This man is or is not an intellectual. He is or is not a philosopher. He is or is not blasé. (Blasé from pain, the worst corruption.) He has an animal thought. Those are the best kind. Those are the only ones. He has only one thought. And it is an animal thought. He wants his son to be happy. He thinks only of this, that his son should be happy. He has another thought. He is preoccupied solely with the idea that his son (already) has of him; it is an idée fixe, an obsession, that is, a *siège*, a blockade, a sort of scrupulous and consuming mania. He has only one concern, the judgment that his son, in the secret of his heart, will pass on him. He wants to read the future solely in the eyes of this son. He searches the depths of his eyes. That which has never succeeded, never happened, he is convinced will happen this time. And not only that, but that it will happen as if naturally and smoothly. As a result of some sort of natural law. And history said, I say that nothing is as touching as this perpetual, this eternal, this eternally reborn inconsistency; and that nothing is as disarming before God, and we have here the common miracle of your young Hope. But, she said, suddenly stopping, here we come back to lands you have cleared forever.[47]

Bibliography

Adereth, Maxwell. *Commitment in Modern French Literature*. London: Gollancz, 1967.
Burac, Robert. "L'histoire de Clio." In *Charles Péguy 4: Les Dialogues de l'histoire*, edited by Simone Fraisse, 1–19. Paris: Minard, 1988.
Dru, Alexander. *Péguy*. London: Harvill, 1956.
Fraisse, Simone, ed. *Charles Péguy 2: Les Cahiers de la quinzaine*. Paris: Minard, 1983.
———. *Charles Péguy 3: Un Romantique malgré lui*. Paris: Minard, 1985.
Keylor, William R. *Academy and Community: The Foundation of the French Historical Profession*. Cambridge: Harvard University Press, 1975.

47. Ibid., 1132–34.

Onimus, Jean. "La Genèse de Clio." In *Feuillets de l'Amitié Charles Péguy*, no. 47. No loc: French Péguy Society, n.d.

Pascal, Blaise. *Pensées*. Translated by A. J. Krailsheimer. New York: Penguin, 1986.

Péguy, Charles. "L'Argent suite." In *Oeuvres en prose complètes III*, edited by Robert Burac, 848–996. Paris: Gallimard, 1992.

———. "Clio, Dialogue de l'histoire et de l'ame païenne." In *Oeuvres en prose complètes III*, edited by Robert Burac, 1997–1214. Paris: Gallimard, 1992.

———. "Dialogue de l'histoire et de l'âme charnelle." In *Oeuvres en prose complètes III*, edited by Robert Burac, 594–783. Paris: Gallimard, 1992.

———. "Notre Jeunesse." In *Oeuvres en prose complètes III*, edited by Robert Burac, 5–159. Paris: Gallimard, 1992.

———. "De la situation faite à l'histoire et à la sociologie dans les temps modernes." In *Oeuvres en prose complètes II*, edited by Robert Burac, 481–519. Paris: Gallimard, 1988.

———. "De la situation faite au parti intellectual dans le monde moderne devant les accidents de la gloire temporelle." In *Oeuvres en prose complètes II*, edited by Robert Burac, 677–774. Paris: Gallimard, 1988.

———. "Les Suppliants parallèles." In *Oeuvres en prose complètes II*, edited by Robert Burac, 312–76. Paris: Gallimard, 1988.

———. "Victor-Marie, comte Hugo." In *Oeuvres en prose complètes III*, edited by Robert Burac, 161–345. Paris: Gallimard, 1992.

———. "Zangwill." In *Oeuvres en prose complètes I*, edited by Robert Burac, 1396–1451. Paris: Gallimard, 1987.

Péguy, Marcel. "Avant-Propos." In *Oeuvres en prose de Charles Péguy 1909–1914*, edited by Marcel Péguy, xvii–xxx. Tours: Gallimard, 1961.

Bibliography

Bakhtin, Mikhail. *Problems of Dostoevsky's Poetics*. Translated by Caryl Emerson. Minneapolis: University of Minnesota Press, 1984.
Bergson, Henri. *Creative Evolution*. Translated by Arthur Mitchell. Mineola: Dover, 1998.
———. *An Introduction to Metaphysics*. Translated by T. E. Hulme. New York: Palgrave Macmillan, 2007.
———. *Matter and Memory*. Translated by N. M. Paul and W. S. Palmer. Zone, 1990.
———. *Time and Free Will: An Essay on the Immediate Data of Consciousness*. Translated by F. L. Pogson. Mineola: Dover, 2001.
Chantre, Benoît. "La logique enchantée: Péguy, lecteur des trois ordres de Pascal." In *Charles Péguy*, edited by Camille Riquier, 109–28. Paris: Cerf, 2014.
———. *Péguy, Point Final*. Paris: Félin, 2014.
Corneille, Pierre. *The Chief Plays of Corneille*. Translated by Lacy Lockert. Princeton: Princeton University Press, 1957.
Cunningham, Conor. *Genealogy of Nihilism: Philosophies of Nothing and the Difference of Theology*. Oxford: Taylor and Francis, 2002.
Deleuze, Gilles. *Bergsonism*. Translated by Hugh Tomlinson and Barbara Habberjam. Brooklyn: Zone, 1990.
———. *Difference and Repetition*. Translated by Paul Patton. New York: Columbia University Press, 1995.
Dru, Alexander. *Péguy*. London: Harvill, 1956.
Finkielkraut, Alain. *Le Mécontemporain: Péguy, lecteur du monde moderne*. Paris: Gallimard, 1991.
Grogin, R. C. *The Bergsonian Controversy in France, 1900–1914*. Calgary: University of Calgary Press, 1988.
Hoeullebecq, Michel. *Submission*. Translated by Lorin Stein. New York: Farrar, Straus and Giroux, 2015.
Jankélévitch, Vladimir. *Henri Bergson*. Edited by Alexandre Lefebvre and Nils F. Schott. Translated by Nils F. Schott. Durham: Duke University Press, 2015.
Le Guay, Damien. "Péguy et Maritain." In *Charles Péguy*, edited by Camille Riquier, 179–205. Paris: Cerf, 2014.
Leroy, Geraldi. *Charles Péguy*. Paris: Armand Colin, 2014.
Manent, Pierre. *La Cité de l'homme*. Paris: Flammarion, 1997.
———. "Charles Péguy between Faith and Political Faith." In *Modern Liberty and Its Discontents*, edited and translated by Daniel J. Mahoney and Paul Seaton, 81–95. Lanham: Rowman & Littlefield, 1998.

Maritain, Jacques. *Bergsonian Philosophy and Thomism*. Notre Dame: University of Notre Dame Press, 2007.

Milbank, John. *Beyond Secular Order*. Oxford: Wiley Blackwell, 2013.

———. "'There's always one day which isn't the same as the day before': Christianity and History after Charles Péguy." In *Theologies of Retrieval: An Exploration and Appraisal*, edited by Darren Sarisky, 9–36. London: T. & T. Clark, 2017.

Mullarkey, John. *Bergson and Philosophy*. Notre Dame: University of Notre Dame Press, 2000.

Nussbaum, Martha. *Upheavals of Thought: The Intelligence of Emotions*. Cambridge: Cambridge University Press, 2003.

Péguy, Charles. "L'Argent." In *Oeuvres en prose complètes III*, edited by Robert Burac, 785–847. Paris: Gallimard, 1992.

———. "L'Argent suite." In *Oeuvres en prose complètes III*, edited by Robert Burac, 848–996. Paris: Gallimard, 1992.

———. *Basic Verities: Prose and Poetry*. Translated by Anne and Julien Green. New York: Pantheon, 1943.

———. "Clio, Dialogue de l'histoire et de l'âme païenne." In *Oeuvres en prose complètes III*, edited by Robert Burac, 1997–1214. Paris: Gallimard, 1992.

———. "Ève." In *Oeuvres poétiques et dramatiques*, edited by Claire Daudin et al., 1177–1397. Paris: Gallimard, 2014.

———. *Henri Bergson, Péguy Correspondance*. Edited by Auguste Martin. Paris: L'Amitié Charles Péguy, 1970.

———. *Men and Saints: Prose and Poetry*. Translated by Anne and Julien Green. New York: Pantheon, 1944.

———. "Le Mystère des saints Innocents." In *Oeuvres poétiques et dramatiques*, edited by Claire Daudin et al., 777–931. Paris: Gallimard, 2014.

———. "Note sur M. Bergson et la philosophie bergsonienne." In *Oeuvres en prose complètes III*, edited by Robert Burac, 1246–77. Paris: Gallimard, 1992.

———. "Note conjointe sur M. Descartes et la philosophie cartésienne." In *Oeuvres en prose complètes III*, edited by Robert Burac, 1278–1477. Paris: Gallimard, 1992.

———. "Notre Jeunesse." In *Oeuvres en prose complètes III*, edited by Robert Burac, 5–159. Paris: Gallimard, 1992.

———. "Un poète l'a dit." In *Oeuvres en prose complètes II*, edited by Robert Burac, 774–933. Paris: Gallimard, 1988.

———. *The Portal of the Mystery of Hope*. Translated by David Louis Schindler Jr. Grand Rapids: Eerdmans, 1996.

———. "De la situation faite à l'histoire et à la sociologie dans les temps modernes." In *Oeuvres en prose complètes II*, edited by Robert Burac, 481–519. Paris: Gallimard, 1988.

———. "De la situation faite au parti intellectuel dans le monde moderne devant les accidents de la gloire temporelle." In *Oeuvres en prose complètes II*, edited by Robert Burac, 677–774. Paris: Gallimard, 1988.

———. "La Tapisserie de Notre Dame." In *Oeuvres poétiques et dramatiques*, edited by Claire Daudin et al., 1137–66. Paris: Gallimard, 2014.

———. *Temporal and Eternal*. Translated by Alexander Dru. Indianapolis: Liberty Fund, 2001.

———. "Victor-Marie, comte Hugo." In *Oeuvres en prose complètes III*, edited by Robert Burac, 161–345. Paris: Gallimard, 1992.

Pickstock, Catherine. *Repetition and Identity*. Oxford: Oxford University Press, 2013.
Riquier, Camille. "Péguy, 'Bergsonien,'" In *Charles Péguy*, edited by Camille Riquier, 149–78. Paris: Cerf, 2014.
Roe, Glenn H. *The Passion of Charles Péguy: Literature, Modernity, and the Crisis of Historicism*. Oxford: Oxford University Press, 2014.
Steiner, George. "Drumming on the Doors—Péguy." In *No Passion Spent: Essays 1978-1995*. New Haven: Yale University Press, 1996.
Taylor, Charles. *A Secular Age*. Cambridge: Harvard University Press, 2007.
Villiers, Marjorie. *Charles Péguy: A Study in Integrity*. New York: Harper & Row, 1965.
Vitry, Alexandre de. "De Deleuze à Péguy." In *Charles Péguy*, edited by Camille Riquier, 223–36. Paris: Cerf, 2014.

Index of Names

Adereth, Maxwell, 241n13
Alain-Fournier, xxxi, 25
Alliez, Eric, xxxii
Arc, Joan of, xvii, xxv, xxvin25,
    xxviii, 2, 19–20, 25, 123,
    127–28, 150, 151n119, 153,
    156, 158–62, 165, 167–68,
    171
Aronowicz, Annette, 42n20
Aquinas, Thomas, xxiii, xxivn24,
    xxvii, 15, 21–22, 220–21
Aristotle, xxxi, 88, 169n135, 208
Augustine, Saint, xiii, xxi, xxiii

Babut, Ernest-Charles, 167
Bacon, Francis, 33n11, 37, 52
Badiou, Alain, xxii
Baibars, 17, 149n116
Bakhtin, Mikhail, 17n23
Beaumarchais, Pierre-Augustin
    Caron de, xvi, 250–53
Bellay, Joachim du, 59n5
Benda, Julien, 6, 13, 15–17, 27n1,
    28n5, 60n7, 61n9, 73, 179
Bergson, Henri (see also *Bergsonian,
    Bergsonism*), xi–xiv, xvi–xvii,
    xix–xxii, xxiii, xxv, xxxi–
    xxxii, 5–9, 11–15, 16–26,
    28n5, 34–36, 38n14, 49, 53,
    58n3, 60n7, 61, 73, 82, 97,
    103, 103n54, 104–5, 106n57,
    112n63, 115, 145, 179, 187,
    204–8, 210, 212, 212n159,
    213, 220–21, 226n171

Bergsonian, xi–xii, xiv–xv, xx, xxii–
    xxiii, xxvi, xxxi, 12, 14–18,
    20–22, 26–27, 33-34, 36, 47,
    49, 51, 53, 61, 93–94, 96–97,
    103, 106–7, 112, 118, 145,
    173, 179, 184, 200, 206–8,
    212n160, 213, 219
Bergsonism, 27, 36, 49–52, 54, 207
Biran, Pierre Maine de xi–xii
Blanchot, Maurice, 11
Blondel, Maurice, xx
Boniface VIII, Pope, 125n93
Bouillon, Godfrey of, 145
Buchez, Pierre, xxxivn38
Burac, Robert, 5, 235n2

Caesar, xxv, 36, 136, 159, 210
Caiaphas, 155, 157, 160
Cairncross, John, xxixn32
Calvin, John, 73–74
Camus, Albert, 1
Cartesian (see also *Descartes*), xi–
    xii, 6, 8–9, 13–15, 28, 35–36,
    38–40, 42, 44, 47, 49, 51, 53,
    60n7, 112, 130
Cartesianism, 35–36, 49–51, 53
Chantre, Benoît, 2n2
Charles VII, King, 123n86
Chesterton, Gilbert Keith, xxxn36
Christ, Jesus, xvi–xviii, xxiv, xxivn24,
    xxv–xxvii, xxix, xxx, xxxiv–
    xxxv, 19, 67, 70, 86–87, 93,
    120, 121n80, 126n94, 135–
    37, 153–61, 167–73, 186,
    203, 208, 222, 231, 253

INDEX OF NAMES

Claudel, Paul, 121n82
Cohen, Leonard, 18
Columbus, Christopher, 59
Corneille, Pierre, xiin2, xxv, xxvii–xxviii, xxviiin30, xxixn32, xxixn33, 12–13, 17–18, 30n8, 87n37, 88, 90–93, 106–9, 113, 129–32, 134, 137–38, 144, 147, 156, 158–60, 165, 168
Cunningham, Conor, 3n3, 11n17

Dante, 193n148
Darwin, Charles, 204n153
David, King, 171
Deleuze, Gilles, xxii, xxxii, 2n2, 10
Derrida, Jacques, (see *Derridean*)
Derridean, xvii
Descartes, René (see also *Cartesian, Cartesianism*), xi, xxii–xxiii, xxv, xxixn32, xxxiii, 5, 7, 9, 13–14, 28n5, 36n12, 37, 38n14, 39–40, 42, 44–45, 46n25, 47–49, 51, 53, 56n1, 58, 73, 101
Desnouelles, Jean, 125n90
Dostoevsky, Fyodor, 2, 12, 16–17, 21
Dreyfus, Alfred (see also *Dreyfusard*), 24, 104n55, 240
Dreyfusard, xxx, 2–3, 16, 60n6, 241
Dru, Alexander, 3n5, 4n5, 104n55, 241n14

Empedocles, 227
Epicurus, 85n34
Epictetus, 210

Fénelon, François, xi
Ferry, Jules, 73–74
Finkielkraut, Alain, 2n2, 46n24
Fraisse, Simone, 241n12, 245n25
Franklin, Benjamin, 177–78

Goethe, Johann Wolfgang von, 63n11
Grogin, R.C., 7n9

Halévy, Daniel, 121
Headlam, Stewart, xxxivn38
Heidegger, Martin, 14
Herod Antipas, xxxiv, 157
Hetzel, Pierre-Jules, 246–49, 250, 253
Homer, 1, 30, 35, 88, 115, 248–51, 253
Houellebecq, Michel, 2
Hugo, Victor, xii, xxixn32, 31, 43, 49, 121, 131, 245–50, 253
Hume, David, xii, xiii, 194n149

Illich, Ivan, 21

Janet, Pierre, 77
Jaurès, Jean, xxxiv, 24, 103n52
Joinville, Jean de, 123, 125, 128, 149–50, 156, 158–60, 165, 167–68

Kant, Immanuel, xxvi, 28n2, 63–64
Kennedy, Ellen, xxiin20
Keylor, William R., 243n21
Kierkegaard, Søren, 2n2, 14

Langlois, Charles-Victor, 227, 243n21
Lanson, Gustave, 243n21
Lavisse, Ernest, 243n21
Lazare, Bernard, 16
Le Guay, Damien, 2n2, 23n29
Locke, John, 194n149
Lotte, Joseph, 8n10, 8n13, 25, 241
Louis Philippe, King, 86
Louis, Saint, xxv, xxixn32, 17, 123, 123n85, 125, 125n88, 126–28, 145, 149–50, 153, 155–60, 165, 167–8, 171
Louis VII, 124n87
Louis XIV, xxixn32, 138n106
Louis XVI, 127n96
Ludlow, John Malcolm, xxxivn38

Manent, Pierre, 2n2, 5

INDEX OF NAMES   265

Maritain, Jacques, xxxi, 2n2, 6, 8,
    15, 17, 21, 23n29, 25, 56n1,
    103n54
Martin, Saint, 167
Marx, Karl, xxxii
Mary, xxiv, xxxv, 19, 172, 217, 222
Maurras, Charles, xxvi, xxiixn32, 6,
    7n10, 103n53
Mazarin, Cardinal, 206
Michelet, Jules, 121, 244
Milbank, John, xvin8, xxn16, xxn18,
    xxviin26, xxxn35, 3n3,
    11n17
Mill, James, 194n149
Mill, John Stuart, 194n149
Milliet, Paul, 244n23
Mohammed, xxv, 149
Molière, Jean-Baptiste, 28, 134, 252
Monet, Claude, 10, 20
Moses, 67, 71, 171–73
Mounier, Emmanuel, xxvi

Napoleon, xxxn36, 36, 49, 88, 118,
    200n151
Napoleon III, 246
Newton, Isaac, 38
Nietszche, Friedrich, 2, 2n2, 12, 14
Noel, Conrad, xxxivn38
Nogaret, Guillaume de, 125
Nussbaum, Martha, 13n19

Onimus, Jean, 235n2

Pascal, Blaise, xvii, xxvii, 30, 67, 70,
    135, 140, 141, 237n5
Pécault, Pierre-Félix, 73
Péguy, Charles, xi–xxxv, 1–25, 27n1,
    28n3, 29n6, 30n7, 30n8,
    31n9, 32n10, 40, 40n18,
    42n20, 44n22, 46n24, 48n27,
    52n32, 54n35, 56n1, 59n5,
    60n6, 60n7, 60n8, 61n8,
    61n9, 63n10, 64n12, 68n15,
    68n16, 70n18, 72n22, 72n23,
    73n24, 73n26, 75n28, 81n32,
    91n41, 93n42, 96n45, 98n47,
    103n52, 103n54, 104n55,
    106n57, 109n58, 113n66,
    117n74, 120n78, 121n82,
    121n83, 123n85, 125n88,
    125n90, 125n92, 126n94,
    126n95, 131n99, 132n102,
    137n105, 143n109, 144n110,
    149n117, 151n119, 157n120,
    162n128, 169n135, 175n136,
    178n139, 189n145, 197n150,
    205n155, 205n156, 212n159,
    215n161, 219n163, 221n164,
    222n165, 222n166, 223n167,
    226n169, 227n172, 229n175,
    232n176, 233n178, 235–56
Philippe le Bel (Philip the Fair),
    xxixn32, 125, 125n93, 126–
    28, 128n97
Pickstock, Catherine, 3n3, 11n17
Pilate, Pontius, 155, 158, 160
Plato, xi, xxv, xxvii, xxxi, 7, 88,
    112n63, 210
Platonism, 50–51
Polyeuctus, Saint, xxv, xxviii, 87n37,
    144n111
Proust, Marcel, xvii
Pythagoras, 227

Racine, Jean, xii, xxvii, xxviin29, 31,
    131n101, 134n103, 138
Ravaisson, Félix, xx–xxi, xxxi
Renan, Ernst, 7, 167n34, 212n159,
    235, 243n21
Richelieu, Cardinal, 206
Riquier, Camille, 2n2, 10n17
Roe, Glenn H., 3n3, 8n11, 9n14,
    11n18, 61n8, 227n172
Rolland, Romain, 24, 31n9, 121n82
Rousseau, Jean-Jacques, 205n156
Rudler, Gustave, 243n21

Schindler Jr., David Louis, 3n4
Sertillanges, A.D., xix, xxi–xxxii
Shakespeare, William, xxviii,
    131n101
Solomon, King, 66, 171
Sophocles, 28, 250–51
Sorel, Georges, xxii

Spencer, Herbert, 204, 220–21
Staël, Germaine de, 63n11
Steiner, George, 3n3
Suarès, André, 24, 75n28, 121n82

Taine, Hippolyte, 7, 212n159, 235, 243n21
Taylor, Charles, 3, 5n7
Thales, 227
Thiers, Adolphe, 86
Tolstoy, Leo, 75

Vigny, Alfred de, 47n26
Virgil, xxvii, 88
Vitry, Alexandre de, 2n2

Wallace, Lewis, 116n68
Ward, Bruce, xi, xviii–xix
Weil, Simone, 1
Wilhelm II, Kaiser, 24
Woolf, Virginia, xvii

Zeno, 227

www.ingramcontent.com/pod-product-compliance
Lightning Source LLC
Chambersburg PA
CBHW021652230426
43668CB00008B/598